CALIFORNIA GOVERNMENT
In National Perspective

Seventh Edition

Edited by
Yuan Ting
Shelly Arsneault
Stephen Stambough
California State University

Cover images © Shutterstock, Inc.

Kendall Hunt
publishing company

www.kendallhunt.com
Send all inquiries to:
4050 Westmark Drive
Dubuque, IA 52004-1840

Copyright © 1984, 1989, 1998, 2001, 2005, 2009, 2011 by Kendall Hunt Publishing Company

ISBN 978-0-7575-9152-5

All rights reserved. No part of this publication may be reproduced, stored in a retrieval system, or transmitted, in any form or by any means, electronic, mechanical, photocopying, recording, or otherwise, without the prior written permission of the copyright owner.

Printed in the United States of America
10 9 8 7 6 5 4 3 2

CONTENTS

Contributors v

Chapter 1 **California's Constitution** 1
Phillip L. Gianos and Yuan Ting

Chapter 2 **California: Political Culture in the Migrant State** 11
Matthew G. Jarvis and Paul Peretz

Chapter 3 **California's Voters** 21
Phillip L. Gianos and Stephen J. Stambough

Chapter 4 **Ballot Measures: Initiatives, Referendums, and Recalls** 35
Alana Northrop and Shelly Arsneault

Chapter 5 **Political Parties in California** 45
Stephen J. Stambough and Bert C. Buzan

Chapter 6 **California Interest Groups** 57
Bert C. Buzan and Stephen J. Stambough

Chapter 7 **Executive Leadership: The Governor of California and the American President** 69
Scott Spitzer

Chapter 8 **The California Legislature** 87
Matthew G. Jarvis

Chapter 9 **The Courts of California** 101
Pamela Fiber-Ostrow

Chapter 10 **California Public Administration** 117
Yuan Ting

Chapter 11 California Local Governments   139
Yuan Ting

Chapter 12 Comparing California and Federal Policies   157
Sarah Hill and Paul Peretz

References   173
Index   179

CONTRIBUTORS

Shelly Arsneault is Associate Professor of Political Science at California State University, Fullerton. Her areas of research interest include welfare, poverty, health, and education policies. Her work has been published in journals such as *State and Local Government Review*, *American Review of Public Administration*, and *California Politics and Policy*. Her current research involves the role of not-for-profit organizations in the policy process.

Bert C. Buzan is Professor of Political Science at California State University, Fullerton. He does research in the area of constitutional law and Chicano political behavior. Articles of his have appeared in *Western Political Quarterly*, *Southeast Political Quarterly*, *Georgetown Immigration Law Review*, and *Aztlan*. His current research contrasts legitimate human genetics with pseudoscientific theories of race.

Pamela Fiber-Ostrow is Assistant Professor of Political Science at California State University, Fullerton. Her areas of research interest include gender and politics, constitutional law, and fetal personhood. Her work has been published in journals such as *Duke Journal of Gender, Law and Policy*, *Yale Journal of Health Policy, Law, and Ethics,* and *California Politics and Policy*. Her most recent publication will appear in *Journal of Women, Politics & Policy*. Her current research involves California's primary elections and gender.

Phillip L. Gianos is Professor of Political Science Emeritus and former chair of the Division of Politics, Administration, and Justice at California State University, Fullerton. His teaching deals with American politics, political behavior, and politics and film. He is the author of *Political Behavior: Metaphors and Models of Politics in America* and *Politics and Politicians in American Film* and articles and book chapters on film and politics and the politics of divided government.

Sarah Hill is Assistant Professor of Political Science at California State University, Fullerton. She received her Ph.D. from the California Institute of Technology. Her research interests are in public policy, specifically education finance reform, and she also has projects on election administration and public opinion surveys.

Matthew Jarvis is Assistant Professor of Political Science at California State University, Fullerton. He does research on public opinion, congressional elections, Congress, vetoes, voting technology, redistricting, and California. His work has appeared in books, reports, *Congress and the Presidency, Perspectives on Politics,* and *California Journal of Politics and Policy*. His current research is on the politics of veto threats.

Contributors

Alana Northrop is Professor of Political Science at California State University, Fullerton. Her previous research has been on municipal reform, bureaucratic effectiveness, quantitative methods, and government use of computers both in the U.S. and comparatively. She has published a book, authored numerous book chapters, and her articles have appeared in *American Journal of Political Science, American Politics Quarterly, Public Administration Review, Public Administration Quarterly, Journal of Criminal Justice,* and *Social Science Computer Review.* Her most recent research has been a two-year longitudinal study of U.S. city website and major use of social networking.

Paul Peretz is Professor of Political Science at California State University, Fullerton. He specializes in public finance and government, and the economy. He is the author of *The Political Economy of Inflation in the United States* and *The Politics of American Economic Policy Making.* His articles have appeared in *International Journal of Public Administration, Journal of Health, Politics, Policy and Law, Women in Criminal Justice,* and *Policy Studies Journal.* His most recent article, "Financial Regulation in the United States: Lessons from History," appeared in *Public Administration Review.*

Scott Spitzer is Assistant Professor of Political Science at California State University, Fullerton. Before joining the faculty at CSUF, Spitzer was an Assistant Professor at Seton Hall and Chapman universities. In addition to his academic positions, Spitzer has held positions in a number of nonprofit organizations, including the National Center on Addiction and Substance Abuse at Columbia University (CASA). His research is based on archival sources and focuses on the U.S. presidency, federal welfare policymaking, and racial politics. He is currently revising a manuscript for publication: *Responding to Race: Presidents Johnson, Nixon and America's Failure to Win a War on Poverty.*

Stephen Stambough is Associate Professor of Political Science at California State University Fullerton. He received his Ph.D. from UC Riverside in 1997. He has published a book about direct democracy and several articles in leading journals about congressional elections, gubernatorial elections, and gender issues in campaigns. Dr. Stambough also serves as Faculty Director for the Cal State D.C. Internship Program and as graduate advisor for the graduate program in political science.

Yuan Ting is Professor of Political Science at California State University, Fullerton. His research and teaching interests include administrative behavior, human resource management, public administration theory, and research methods. His articles have appeared in *Administrative Science Quarterly, American Review of Public Administration, Industrial and Labor Relations Review, Public Administration Review,* and *Public Personnel Management.* He was a Fulbright Scholar (China) in 2007.

Chapter 1
CALIFORNIA'S CONSTITUTION
Phillip L. Gianos and Yuan Ting[1]

Constitutions are the most fundamental political documents in American society. Constitutions establish governments. In a basic sense, constitutions govern governments. In this chapter, we examine how California's political process is governed by its constitution, with emphasis on three topics: broad similarities among all the American states with respect to their constitutions; a brief look at California's own constitutional history; and finally, our most important topic, the special features of the California constitution that help give the state its distinctive political character.

State Constitutions in the Federal System

Constitutions establish the basic institutions of government and allocate power among those institutions in two ways: by granting certain powers to one or more institutions, and also by denying certain powers to one or more institutions. Frequently, constitutions also deny specific powers to any governmental institution by granting (or "reserving") them solely to the people. Constitutions also provide for their own change through their mechanisms for amendment.

Since constitutions are the final word governmentally, they are always superior in legal and moral force to laws passed by the governments they create. But while state constitutions are superior to state laws, the federal (United States) Constitution is superior to state constitutions. The U.S. Constitution directly refers to state constitutions but once, and does so to assert the supremacy of the federal Constitution and its laws and treaties. Article VI of the U.S. Constitution states:

> This Constitution, and the Laws of the United States which shall be made in Pursuance thereof; and all Treaties made, or which shall be made, under the Authority of the United States, shall be the supreme Law of the Land; and the Judges in every State shall be bound thereby, any Thing in the Constitution or Laws of any State to the Contrary notwithstanding.

Boundaries and Limits in the U.S. Constitution

The U.S. Constitution draws various other boundaries between what the national government may do and what the state governments may do. For example, in Article I, Section 10 the states are forbidden to make treaties with other nations;

---

[1] Previous versions of this chapter were co-authored with Keith O. Boyum, to whom we extend our thanks.

only the national government of the United States may do that. Likewise, the same section of the U.S. Constitution forbids states from impairing the obligation of contracts, thereby protecting a key feature of American capitalism.

Constitutional Flexibility

Since the federal Constitution is one of delegated or granted powers, the national government may not exercise any power not given to it by the U.S. Constitution. But this is not as simple as it seems. This is mainly due to the general and sometimes imprecise language used in assigning powers to the national government. Here is the essential genius of the architects of the U.S. Constitution, for, the way in which 220-year-old language pertains to the specifics of contemporary circumstance allows flexibility to the Constitution through its interpretation, a matter that stimulates continuing debate. Pending the outcomes of these debates, the specifics of what powers the national government may exercise can change.

State governments, by contrast, are assumed to have powers unless they are denied them by either the U.S. Constitution or the states' own constitution. This creates considerable latitude within which state governments may operate. In practice, however, there are several important similarities among virtually all state constitutions, to which we now turn.

Similarities in State Constitutions

All state constitutions have preambles—an opening statement of purpose and intent. Each state constitution has a bill of rights, closely modeled on the federal Bill of Rights (Amendments 1 through 10 of the U.S. Constitution). In California, however, these rights are stated at the very beginning of the document in Article I. The California Constitution provides for freedom of the press, of speech, freedom to assemble and petition, freedom of religion, due process of law, and in general parallels the U.S. Constitution as to rights specifically secured to the people. Though state constitutions are essentially autonomous documents that do not have to rely on the federal Constitution for granting civil rights to the states' citizens, there have been attempts to limit judicial independence in interpreting the language of state constitutions (see Chapter 9).

All state constitutions reflect the U.S. Constitution's provisions for checks and balances and separation of powers by establishing separate legislative, executive, and judicial branches, and by sharing powers among them. California is no exception to this, though specific applications of this general rule in the state's constitution are an important feature of California politics and will be discussed in detail below.

Within this broad setting of similarities to other states, there are specific provisions of California's constitution that make the document, and the political system it creates, distinctive.

California's Constitutional History

One of the more interesting features of California's political history is that the state has had two constitutions. (Louisiana leads the states in this respect with eleven.) The first was adopted in 1849, just before California became a state in 1850. Hastily drafted, much of the language was taken from other state constitutions without necessarily taking into account the essentially frontier nature of the territory that became California. While the document served reasonably well for thirty years, by 1879 its deficiencies became so severe that a constitutional convention was called to draft a new document.

Delegates to the convention fashioned an extremely long and detailed document, with particular emphasis on expanding and strengthening the bill of rights and placing severe limits on the power of the state legislature. This period was also the dawn of the Progressive movement in California, a movement whose profound effects we still see in the present-day state constitution.

Progressivism was essentially a middle-class movement created in response to the political consequences of great economic power. Progressive political ideas profoundly affected the politics of many states, especially those in the West, including California. The greatest evil in the world of California Progressives was the Southern Pacific Railroad, whose power and reach made it the most powerful force in the state, dwarfing, in the views of its critics, the ability of the state government to control it. During this period legislators could be rented, if not necessarily purchased outright, by the Southern Pacific. The architects of the constitution of 1879, by limiting the power of the legislature, were indirectly trying to limit the power of the railroad.

A further set of Progressive reforms, added to the 1879 constitution via amendment, occurred between 1900 and 1913. Foremost among these were the direct democracy institutions of the initiative, referendum, and recall. These are discussed below, and also in more detail in Chapter 4. These direct democracy mechanisms are central to California's politics and to this day give the state much of its distinctive political character. It was also in this period that distinctive and politically important regional differences began to appear in California, a topic discussed more fully in Chapter 2.

Between 1879 and 1962, the state constitution, responding to the enormous growth and increasing diversity of the state and driven by the use of the direct democracy reforms, grew rapidly and unevenly. The California Constitution had become a large and unwieldy document, and while periodic attempts were made to simplify the constitution none really succeeded. In 1962 the voters approved, and the legislature appointed, a commission to revise the state constitution. Its goal was to examine the 1879 document completely, including its many amendments, and to recommend changes and a complete reorganization.

The process took years of study, and many more years of proposing amendments for voter approval in many successive elections. During this period the constitution continued to grow. By 1966, when the first "clean-up" amendments were offered to the voters, the document had been amended 344 times, and its length had grown from sixteen thousand words to seventy thousand, making it the fourth longest constitution of any government in the *world*, after those of Louisiana, Alabama, and India. By the 1974 elections most of the proposed amendments had been submitted and voted upon, and the revision was essentially complete.

The Progressive legacy and the reform period of 1962–74 largely created the document that governs California today. As this brief history suggests, California's formal written constitution is largely a creature of the state's social, economic, and political setting. Formal constitutional provisions define the rules of the political game, but these provisions also affect the informal setting of California's politics. California has two constitutions, one formal and one informal, each of which affects the other. The root word of "constitution" is "constitute," and California politics is constituted of both formal and informal rules. In the section that follows, we briefly describe some of the special features—formal and informal—that shape present-day political life in California.

California's Formal and Informal Constitutional Features

The California Constitution is Long and Complex

The length of California's constitution is remarkable. On identically sized pages, the U.S. Constitution, including amendments, occupies twenty-seven pages. The California constitution takes up 154. To compile an index for the U.S. Constitution requires seven pages. To do the same for the California Constitution one needs seventy-five pages.

One reason for this length is that all state governments create county and city governments. Accordingly, the California constitution devotes considerable attention to these topics. But that does not fully explain the great length, or the bewildering variety of specific and rather narrow topics addressed by the state's constitution. For example, the California Constitution speaks to such things as the sale of alcoholic beverages on airplanes, the alumni association of the University of California, the use of bingo games by charitable organizations, the cafeteria budgets of state agencies, the right of citizens to fish, and property tax exemptions for grape vines less than three years old.

One looks in vain for comparable topics in the U.S. Constitution. Why all the detail? One answer is the ease with which the California Constitution may be amended via direct democracy procedures. Initiative measures present an avenue for amending the constitution apart from actions that may be taken by a governor and legislature. Another part of the answer has to do with the weak political party system of the state, a topic that we will discuss in more detail below and later in Chapter 5. Weak political parties tend to go hand-in-hand with a strong interest group system; groups tend to fill the vacuum created when parties are weak.

Across the United States, states with strong interest groups and weak parties tend to have longer and more complex constitutions. Groups, as Chapter 6 describes, can be very effective in achieving their political goals through amending constitutions in addition to their usual activity of lobbying legislators and governors. This last point is significant, for it is important to remember that provisions in the California state constitution that deal with, for example, exempting grape vines less than three years of age from property taxes are part of the constitution itself, not simply ordinary laws (called statutes). Constitutional provisions are much more difficult to change or remove than are statutes.

The California Constitution Provides for "Direct Democracy"

At the heart of the Progressives' reforms was the belief that an effective way to circumvent the power of economic interests over state government, especially the legislature, was to permit the citizens to vote directly on major issues and to recall public officials from office. California's constitution provides for just that in the form of the initiative, the referendum, and the recall. The initiative permits citizens to propose, and then vote on, either statutes or constitutional amendments. The referendum permits citizens to halt enforcement of laws already passed by the legislature and signed by the governor, and then to vote on whether those laws should be continued or repealed. The recall permits citizens to remove public officials from office. This provision lay largely unused for many years until 2003, when the combination of an unpopular governor—Democrat Gray Davis, who was re-elected in 2002—combined with a well-financed recall campaign led to Davis's replacement in 2003 by Republican Arnold Schwarzenegger, an election that received worldwide attention.

These direct democracy provisions of California's constitution give extraordinary power to citizens, but also to interest groups, who have been their most frequent users. The initiative, referendum, and recall are among the most important and interesting features of California government, and they raise significant questions about democratic politics and the nature of representation. These are discussed in detail in Chapter 4.

The California Constitution Provides for Weak Political Parties

Political parties link citizens with government; they also link those inside government with each other through a system of party loyalty and mutual aid. To the extent that parties are weak these linkages are weak, and government and politics thereby change in character. To some, relatively weak parties are desirable since they encourage citizens to evaluate issues and candidates free of party constraints. To others, including many political scientists, weak parties encourage irresponsibility in governing and make it difficult for citizens to get a thoughtful grasp on complex issues and to assign credit or blame for government actions.

California's parties are weak by virtue of political tradition and constitutional design. Local political contests—those for county and city government—are officially nonpartisan. State laws that govern the activities and organization of political parties also contribute to party weakness. The most important recent example of this is the 2010 passage of Proposition 14 which created what is known as a "top two" system in which candidates for state office from all major and minor parties compete in a first round of balloting with the top two vote recipients, regardless of power, advancing to the general election.

Such provisions mean that other institutions, primarily interest groups and professional campaign management firms that use the media heavily, fill the vacuum left in the absence of strong political parties. Chapter 5 treats these important topics in detail. The weak party system also significantly affects the manner in which the state's voters behave, and this topic is addressed in Chapter 3.

The California Constitution Provides for a Strong "Plural" Executive

The governor of California—the state's chief executive—is given some powers beyond those given to the president of the United States. Chief among these is the item veto, which enables the governor to void specific items in the state's budget. Thus California governors have greater power over the state budget, and greater bargaining power with the legislature, than a president has with respect to these matters in the national arena.

Unlike U.S. presidents, however, a governor may find his or her own executive branch fragmented. California's constitution provides for what is called a plural executive branch in which the executive branch offices of governor, lieutenant governor, secretary of state, attorney general, treasurer, insurance commissioner, and controller are elected in individual races. Divided party control of the executive, with some elected Democrats and some Republicans, is always possible and often happens. In fact, the nominally nonpartisan superintendent of public instruction may be a member of the political party opposed to the governor's party, too. In the Deukmejian administration (1983–91), all the other partisan executive branch offices were held by Democrats though the governor was a Republican. From 2007-09 Republican Governor Schwarzenegger's lieutenant governor was Democrat John Garamendi. In contrast, U.S. presidents and vice presidents are elected together, and the other comparable national officers are nominated by presidents and serve in the president's cabinet.

California's governorship is thus an office with some significant differences compared to the position of U.S. presidents. Chapter 7 explores the role of the governor in comparison with the American presidency.

California's Constitution Provides for a Nonpartisan Judiciary

In accord with the political tradition of the state, the California Constitution establishes an extensive and nonpartisan judicial system. All levels of the California judiciary—municipal courts, superior courts, courts of appeal and the state supreme court—must be filled by members of the state bar—that is, licensed attorneys. As in many other states, California's judges are subject to election. Unlike some states, however, such elections in California are officially nonpartisan. In practice, most judges in California are initially appointed by the governor to fill a vacancy. All are subject to periodic election. For the higher, appellate judicial offices, incumbents are subject to what is called retention elections, in which voters determine whether an appellate court judge shall be retained in office for another term (normally 12 years). In these elections, voters do not choose between two candidates but instead vote whether to retain a single judge. Chapter 9 addresses these and other aspects of California's judiciary.

California's Constitution Established, then Abandoned, a Professional, Full-Time Legislature

One of the most celebrated aspects of California government between 1966 and 1990 was its state legislature. Unlike those in many other states, California's legislators are full-time, well-paid, professional lawmakers. Also unlike the practice of many other states, California used to provide considerable staff support for its legislators. In the 1970s, in fact, the state legislature was a model for other states for what a competent, informed legislature should be. A 1990 constitutional change adopted by initiative (Proposition 140), however, dramatically and fundamentally changed the legislature by reducing its staff and imposing term limits on its members. In the twenty-first century, California has an institutionally weakened legislature populated by short-timers. Chapter 8 analyzes the legislature in greater depth, coming in the end to pessimistic conclusions about the nature and future role of the institution.

California's Constitution Establishes an Extensive, Highly Professional Bureaucracy

The sheer size, wealth, and diversity of the state mean that California's state government engages in a number of activities: establishing and maintaining universities, protecting wildlife, aiding small businesses, and seeing to it that a myriad of state regulations are enforced. All these are the job of the state bureaucracy. The values of nonpartisanship and efficiency lie at the heart of the state bureaucracy, but as with any form of apparently neutral administration there are nonetheless important political choices made by nonelected officials, as Chapter 10 describes; that chapter also discusses recent proposals to improve the efficiency and performance of the state bureaucracy.

California's Constitution Establishes an Extensive System of Local Government

A major responsibility of any state constitution is to create local government, chiefly counties and cities. In California some of these jurisdictions are immensely large and powerful, even when considered on a national scale. The city and the county of Los Angeles, for example, dwarf many state governments in the range of their responsibilities, the size of their budgets, and the power wielded by their officials. Focusing as we frequently do on national and state government it is easy to forget that many of the things most important to citizens—the quality of their children's schools, how good the local parks are, the level of public safety—are the responsibility of city and county officials.

California provides for an extensive system of local governmental institutions that emphasize nonpartisanship and the efficient delivery of services. Underlying these apparently politically neutral ideas, however, is a complex system of political activity, as described in Chapter 11.

California's Constitution Faces Increasing Criticism and Pressures for Revision

At the heart of the California Constitution lies something of a paradox: while the basic structure of the document has not recently been changed, it has been nonetheless frequently—usually through the initiative process—amended in ways that have substantially altered state politics and policy. Fiscally, the state operates under a number of initiative-established constraints: Proposition 13 (passed in 1978), which capped property tax increases and shifted some traditional county responsibilities—especially education—to the state; Proposition 4 (1979), which established government spending limits; and more recently Proposition 98 (1988), which guaranteed a fixed proportion of state revenues to K–12 public schools; Proposition 99 (1988) and Proposition 10 (1998), which increased taxes on tobacco products and earmarked those revenues for antismoking and early childhood health programs; and Proposition 39 (2000), which made it easier to pass school bond measures. More recently, in response to severe budget problems, voters in California have passed Proposition 22 (2010) which prohibits the state from borrowing or taking funds used for transportation, redevelopment, or local government projects and services; Proposition 25 (2010), which changes legislative vote requirement to pass budget and budget-related legislation from two-thirds to a simple majority, but retains two-thirds vote requirement for taxes; and Proposition 26 (2010), which requires approval of two-thirds vote for certain state and local fees. These measures dictate where revenues come from and where they may be spent, and they do so in ways that are hard to change. Chapter 4 also describes ballot measures and how have they changed state politics and policy.

At the same time, initiatives have also been used to substantially modify California's political processes by providing for an elected insurance commissioner in 1988 and both term limits for state officials and reductions in state legislative expenditures in 1990. All this added up to fundamental changes in the fiscal and political environment of the state and to increasing criticism that the state had become ungovernable, a belief that Arnold Schwarzenegger used to his advantage in the 2003 gubernatorial recall election.

In the mid-1990s an effort to address constitutional reform arose in the form of a state Constitutional Revision Commission. A wide variety of proposals for changing the state's basic charter was brought to the commission, including reform of the budgetary process, modifications of the initiative process (the initiative was the prime suspect in the minds of many critics), and the creation of a unicameral (one-house) legislature. Other observers were more pessimistic. Their forecast was for more piecemeal, sometimes thoughtless, constitutional change promoted via the initiative process whenever an interest group could raise enough money to mount a campaign. No action was taken on these proposals, however. In late 2004, in another move to restructure state government and address the state's huge budget shortfall, a commission established by Governor Schwarzenegger forwarded a complex and controversial set of more than twelve hundred recommendations for change. With a succession of what became yearly crises, a dismal pattern was established: a budget crisis followed by a messy resolution followed by calls for reform followed by another budget crisis. Even as the budget crisis of 2009 was temporarily resolved in late February, there were new calls for a California constitutional convention to attempt, yet again, to make the state more governable. And these calls have led to the passage of Proposition 20 (2010), which redistrict congressional districts in the state and Proposition 25 (2010). These constitutional amendments represent the latest attempt by voters to change the political and budgeting processes to address the increasingly severe budget problems in California.

Conclusion: California Government in National Perspective

A discussion of California's formal and informal constitutional features inevitably involves references to how those features affect the state's politics, and how in turn California's politics affects its constitution. Constitutions, including informal constitutions, are neither pure symbol nor only a matter of historical interest. Constitutions are enormously important in understanding why California government is the way it is—sometimes rational and efficient, sometimes inefficient and frustrating, always a matter about which groups and individuals contest, normally out of the sight of the casual citizen observer, but occasionally in colorful, public, and bewildering ways.

If there is a moral of this story, it may be this: State constitutions set the tone, define the structure, and outline the limits within which laws and administrative decisions govern the lives of us all, no matter in what state we live. Our lives as citizens in a federal system are a complex and changing mix of local, state, and federal laws and rules. As a starting place for understanding California government in national perspective, a review of the California Constitution is the best place to begin. But there is more to be said. The outlines of the rest of the story follow in the next 11 chapters.

Table 1.1 Comparison between the California and United States Constitutions

	California	United States
Designation:	The Constitution of the State of California	The Constitution of the United States of America
Shape/Design: • Length • Variety of Provisions	• Extremely lengthy • Ranges from broad, essential topics to extremely specific and limited ones	• Very short • Deals only with broad essentials
Special Features:	• "Direct democracy" provisions (initiative, referendum, and recall) make amendment more frequent and open to ordinary citizens	• The Supremacy Clause provides that the U.S. Constitution prevails in instances of conflict with state constitutions
Importance:	• Restrictions on actions by government, especially regarding taxing and spending	• Rights secured by the first 8 and the 14th Amendments are enforced by all courts, federal and state

Chapter 2
CALIFORNIA: POLITICAL CULTURE IN THE MIGRANT STATE
Matthew G. Jarvis and Paul Peretz[1]

Republican ex–talk show host Bob Dornan represented two different congressional districts from 1985 to 1996. The first was in West Los Angeles, a seat Dornan lost when district boundaries were redrawn. Dornan moved to Orange County, where he ran successfully in a district centered on Garden Grove. For most of this period his ultraconservative positions resonated with his conservative Orange County constituents. Dornan adapted successfully as his district became increasingly diverse, especially with the influx of immigrants, especially those of Vietnamese descent. But over the years increasing numbers of Hispanics came to live in his district and Bob Dornan adapted less successfully to them. Democratic political unknown Loretta Sanchez looked at the changing nature of the constituency and thought that there had been enough shift in the population that a moderate Hispanic candidate would be able to mobilize sufficient support to defeat Dornan. In a hard-fought election in 1996 she won with 51% of the vote, becoming the first Democratic congressperson from Orange County. In 2008 she was reelected by a margin of 54,000 votes. In 2010 while Republicans were winning in most of the nation, she won with 57% of the vote. The moral of the story is that in politics, demographics matter.

Introduction

In a democratic society political outcomes are largely determined by the political beliefs of its citizens. *Political culture* is the term used by political scientists to describe the networks of beliefs about politics and policy that undergird political action in that community. These beliefs are in part dictated by the self-interest of individuals. In most societies, poor people and rich people, minority and majority groups, and rural and urban residents have somewhat different beliefs, and typically these follow the self-interest of the people in that group.

But self-interest does not explain everything about citizens' beliefs. People are heavily influenced by those around them. Most influential are the beliefs of one's family members, with children often voting in very similar ways to their

---

[1]Earlier versions of this chapter were authored by Phillip L. Gianos.

parents. But the views of their friends, their church, their union, their teachers, those in their ethnic group, and the media all have an effect on people's political beliefs. This can lead people to vote to support those in other groups, or to identify with the interests of the group they belong to, rather than their own personal interests. Examples are Oprah Winfrey, one of the richest people in America, campaigning for the Democrats, or rich people on the West Side of Los Angeles giving more support to programs for the poor than those living in San Bernardino, a much poorer area.

In general the political beliefs of Californians are similar to those of people in the rest of the United States. They believe in democracy, freedom, justice, a system of laws, and political (but not economic) equality. There is general support for our federal system of government and for the federal and California constitutions. But Californians' beliefs are not identical to those in the rest of the United States and within California those in different regions of the state have somewhat differing beliefs.

Migration and California

The differences between California and other states and the differences within the state are largely explained by California's migration patterns. In 1848, when California was taken from Mexico in the Mexican-American War, the population of California was 15,000 people, excluding Native Americans. The discovery of gold in 1848 led to a huge increase in population, with the number of Californians rising to 380,000 by 1860. What the newcomers found was a land with a temperate climate and abundant fertile land and water in the northern half of the state, but little water in the semi-desert south and central valley. Most early migration was therefore to the north, and it was only after the development of extensive irrigation projects in the twentieth century that growth in the southern half of the state began to outpace that of the northern half.

As we can see in Figure 2.1, California's population grew much more rapidly than that in other states. While the rate of growth was highest in the 1850 (not shown) to 1930 and 1940 to 1960 periods, in terms of sheer numbers the growth was highest in the 1970 to 2000 period when California's population rose from 20 million to 33 million. By 2010 California had a population of 37.2 million people, constituting over one-eighth of the population of the United States.

Immigration from 1850 to 1970 was primarily from the eastern half of the United States and to a lesser degree from Europe. Most migration followed the east-west roads and rail lines, with Northerners settling disproportionately in northern California, and those from the South and the border states moving to southern and inland California. More recently there has been extensive immigration from Asia and Latin America, leading to yet another adjustment in the political culture of the state.

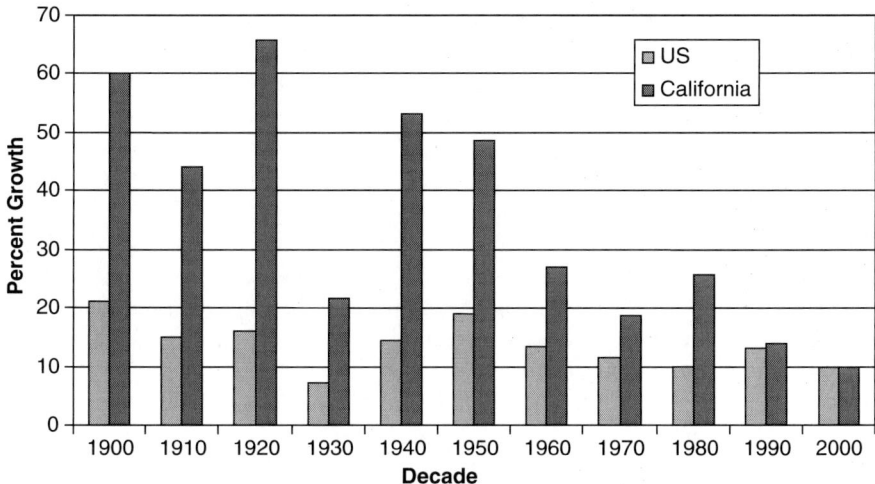

Figure 2.1 Percent Growth in Population

A Theory of Migration

Migrants are not the same as people in the areas they come from or the areas they go to. Because migration is costly, they tend to be more affluent than those where they come from. Because most people migrate to better their standard of living, they are generally less affluent than those in the areas they migrate to. They are also more willing to change, more willing to take risks, and display more drive and entrepreneurship than those in the country they move to.

Immigrants do a number of things to reduce the isolation attendant on migration. Successful first immigrants often encourage others from their family or area to join them. This second wave of migrants typically settle next to one another and recreate much of the culture of the place they come from, creating new areas that feel a lot like the places the migrants came from.

These new communities can threaten the existing inhabitants who generally feel that those coming to their community should behave as much like them as possible and should accept their guidance. When economic times are bad the old inhabitants can come to resent these readily identifiable newcomers who may be prepared to work harder than they do for less money and thereby threaten their livelihood.

The newcomers typically steer away from politics initially, concentrating their energies on making money and building up assets that will enable their children to be even more successful than they themselves have been. In some immigrant communities parallel governing structures can grow up with the community, settling many of its problems internally though quasi-governmental mechanisms.

In democratic societies existing political parties eventually come to see them as potential supporters and seek to bring those votes to their party. This partly integrates them into the existing political structures. Over time as they become more integrated, and a new generation arises that grew up in the new country, there is increasing dispersal into the wider community, the old informal quasi-governmental structures erode, and the group begins to seek a more active part in the political process.

In the areas where they have come to be a majority, the new groups will eventually run for office and take part in governing. But by the time this happens they will have become much more integrated into the preexisting culture, with their leaders being more integrated than their followers. As a result the ascent of new political leadership will cause less change than one might initially expect.

Effects of Heavy Immigration in California

As we have seen, there are few states in the Union that has been more formed by migration than California. Many think that this continual influx of entrepreneurial migrants has led California to be a leader in seeking new solutions to old problems and in creating new industries and processes. As a result California has often led the rest of the United States into new areas in fashion, media, industry, and government. Movies, television, theme parks, airplanes, and information technology are California's signature industries and most of its cultural innovations have heavily influenced other areas of the United States. California has also been innovative in politics, leading the way on direct democracy, diversity, and tolerance of homosexuals.

This willingness to experiment was shown in California's reaction to the political domination of the Southern Pacific Railroad in the late nineteenth and early twentieth centuries. Instead of simply retaking control of the legislature, Californians instituted the complex experiment with direct democracy described in Chapter 4, in an attempt to prevent any future firm from using money and influence to overturn the will of the people. And when Californians thought the local political parties had become corrupt, instead of simply reforming the parties they banned local candidates from mentioning their political party affiliation and instituted a more professional council-manager system.

But heavy immigration often leads to fear among existing inhabitants that their culture, their morality, their religion, their jobs, and their political power will be eroded by the new immigrants. This too has been a recurrent feature of the California scene, with many pushing to slow down change. Such a reaction is likely to be larger when the incoming group is more different from the existing groups and when economic hard times increase the competition for jobs.

California has seen much anti-immigrant activity. The anti-Chinese Los Angeles Massacre of 1871 led to gradually increasing anti-Chinese policy and culminated in the complete banning of Chinese immigration until the 1940s. In the 1930s there was considerable resentment against Mexican Americans who were seen as taking American jobs, and by the end of the decade one third of the Mexican American population of Los Angeles, including many citizens, had been forcibly repatriated to Mexico.

During the Second World War there was much popular support in California for the forced internment of Japanese Americans, and in more recent years every economic downturn has led to agitation aimed at illegal immigrants. This fear has sometimes gone beyond reaction to immigration itself, to a more general political movement toward more stability and law and order, especially in Southern California.

If these two things seem contradictory it is because they are. Many observers see California as shifting periodically from one of these poles to the other, with periods of reaction often following periods of innovation.

Regionalism and Political Culture in California

The basic political cultural fact is simple: the relatively small area of Southern California—traditionally defined as the seven counties south of the Tehachapi Mountains—contains roughly 53% of the state's population. The immediate political effect is that a small geographical portion of the state has the majority of the state's population, wealth, and voters. Most of the rest of California's population is split between the northern coastal region and the inland areas of California in and around the San Joaquin Valley.

Historically, many issues in California politics have been sharply and enduringly defined in terms of region: state legislative apportionment, water rights, gasoline tax revenue allocation, the location of public university campuses— indeed, any issue that involves allocating resources within the state. Candidates for statewide office are regularly described in terms of their home region, and Southern California candidates often have an advantage over northerners because of the population concentration in the south. In recent years, governors have been exclusively southerners: Jerry Brown, Arnold Schwarzenegger, Gray Davis, Pete Wilson, George Deukmejian, and Ronald Reagan were all from Southern California, while U.S. Senators Feinstein and Boxer are distinctive in not only both being female but in both being San Francisco Bay area Democrats.

Such differences are common in large, diverse states: New York and Illinois, for example, have their own versions of state regional politics, and Tennessee's present-day voting patterns were established in the Civil War. California's version of this is the existence of two historically distinct political cultures in the northern and southern parts of the state, with a more recently emerging political region in the San Joaquin Valley. The political consequences of these differences are clear. Historically Southern California and the San Joaquin valley have a more conservative voting history than northern California. The results of statewide races, including those for governor, U.S. senator, president of the United States, and statewide ballot propositions, often depended on the ratio of more liberal and Democratic northern votes to more conservative and Republican southern and central votes.

In the 1964 Republican presidential primary, for example, Barry Goldwater took all the state's southern counties by a sufficient margin to overcome the support for the more liberal Nelson Rockefeller in the rest of the state. The primary win in California was critical in Goldwater's eventual nomination for president. In 1994, Proposition 187, which dealt with illegal immigration, won in every part of the state *except* the Bay Area and was especially popular in the Riverside–San Bernardino area, where it won by 40 percent, and in Orange and San Diego counties, where it won by 34 percent. In Orange County, the headquarters of California Republicanism, Republican presidential candidates until recently had been able to count on two-to-one or even three-to-one advantages over their Democratic opponents, offsetting the rest of the state and assuring the Republicans winning all of California's electoral votes, an increasingly valuable prize as California has grown into the most populous state.

One of the most dramatic acknowledgments of regionalism in California has been the regular revival of proposals to split California into two or more separate states, including several nonbinding pro-breakup advisory measures placed on the primary ballot in some rural northern counties in 1992, where, preaching to the choir, they won considerable support. In 1993, for the first time in 130 years, the state Assembly briefly considered a proposal to split the state into three parts: north, central, and south.

But in recent years, while the San Joaquin Valley has remained steadfastly conservative, Southern California has been trending steadily to the left, narrowing the difference between the southern and northern regions. Democrats have been sent to Congress from Orange County—long considered a bastion of conservatism—and the state that gave the United States Richard Nixon and Ronald Reagan has been conceded in advance to the Democrats by more recent Republican presidential candidates such as George W. Bush and John McCain.

Table 2.1 shows the current division between the three main regions in terms of two recent votes. Proposition 8, which banned gay marriage in California, is a good indicator of cultural conservatism. The support for Republican John McCain in 2008 shows the degree to which the regions support the more liberal Democratic Party or the more conservative Republican Party. As can be seen the north remains more liberal than the south, but the voters in the south are now much less conservative than those in the San Joaquin Valley.

Table 2.1 Regional Differences in Political Conservatism

	Opposition to Gay Marriage (2008)	**Vote for McCain (2008)**
North	39%	26%
South	52%	38%
Central Valley	64%	49%
California (total)	52%	38%

California's Regions: Some Explanations

How did these differences come about? The reader will not be surprised to find that we think that both the difference between the north and south and the recent leftward trend in the south can primarily be explained by patterns of migration. The bulk of post-Depression immigrants to Southern California came from the Midwest and the states bordering the South, following the east-west roads and railway lines. Few came from Europe. A total of 6.5% of the 1940 population of the Los Angeles area came from Italy, Ireland, Sweden, England, Germany, France, or Russia. The comparable proportion of Bay Area residents was double that for Southern California.

The most telling figure is this: between 1920 and 1940, 400,000 people moved to Los Angeles. Less than one-tenth that number moved to San Francisco (Wilson 1966, 40–41). The primary reasons for this disparity of numbers were the attractiveness of Southern California as an economic alternative to the Dust Bowl states, its climate, its inexpensive housing, and, as World War II approached, military employment.

Besides the differences in region of birth and in the sheer numbers of immigrants that differentiated northern from southern California, cultural and religious differences existed as well. Los Angeles emerged, relative to the Bay Area, as a predominantly Protestant area with a strong fundamentalist flavor. Catholics were not only more numerous in San Francisco but what Catholics there were in the south were disproportionately of Latino descent compared to Bay Area Catholics, and were relatively powerless.

Religion also appears to have been a more central part of life in the south than in the north: during the 1920–1940 period, per capita church membership in Los Angeles was the highest in the nation. Southern California was thus settled by people whose regional and religious characteristics predisposed them toward a more moralistic and conservative social, economic, and political orientation.

Two important consequences followed from this immigration pattern. First, these relatively conservative new arrivals in the south shaped the Southern California political culture in their own image. Second, the affinity ties discussed earlier led people to move to areas where they felt more comfortable, strengthening the regional difference.

But the conservative character of the south gradually eroded as new migration patterns led to a gradual change in the character of the voters. Some of this new migration dates back to the Second World War when the extensive war production in the south (Los Angeles contributed 17 percent of all war production) and its status as an embarkation center for the Pacific theatre brought African Americans and Hispanics to the Southland. While we do not have reliable figures for Hispanic growth, the number of African Americans quadrupled between 1940 and 1950.

But the key event was a major change in American immigration laws. Prior to the 1960s overseas immigration had come primarily from Europe, tied to immigration quotas for European countries, and the impact was primarily on the East Coast of the United States. But in 1965 an amendment to the 1951 Immigration Act made a crucial alteration. The amendment made family reunification rather than skills or national origin the primary basis for immigration into the United States. This was intended to put a kinder face on continued European immigration into the United States, by allowing in family members of previous European immigrants.

However, it turned out that the families of European immigrants were enjoying the new prosperity in Europe and were disinclined to migrate. But the large impoverished families of previous Latino and Asian migrants were only too eager to migrate. This tendency was further increased by the admission of refugees from Asia and the legalization of illegal immigrants from Mexico. This opened the floodgates to migrants from Asia, Mexico, and Latin America who gained much more from migrating than those in prosperous Europe. Asian immigration rose from about 150,000 to 1.7 million and Mexican and Latin American immigration tripled. A disproportionate number of these new immigrants settled in California, leading to a slow transformation of the political culture of the state (DeLaet 2000, 79–83).

At first, as theory would predict, the new migrants were relatively apolitical with much lower voting rates than the rest of the population. But as the migrants became more settled and had children educated in the United States, they began to take more interest in politics. A key event was Proposition 187, Governor Wilson's attempt in 1994 to deny benefits to illegal aliens, which was perceived by Mexican immigrants as being discriminatory. This led to increased voting and increased political mobilization.

African Americans were the first minority group to gain political power in California, and their political achievements remain the most notable, though Latinos have recently increased their representation. The first African American was elected to the state legislature in 1918; in 1948, his successor was joined by a second African American in Sacramento. In the 2009-2010 session, there were six African American assemblypersons and two state senators. The first African American member of Congress from California was elected in 1962; there have been four African American seats in Congress for much of the time since the 1970s. Willie Brown, generally considered the most powerful Assembly speaker in the last 40 years is African American, as is the last Speaker, Karen Bass. However the political power of African Americans in California has peaked, and we expect that many of the positions that they currently hold will be taken by Hispanics as Hispanics become the majority in formerly African American areas such as Watts and Compton.

Latinos have only recently begun to flex their political muscle in California. Starting with the election of Ed Roybal to the Los Angeles City Council in 1949 there were a gradually increasing number of elected local government officials. By 1973 there were 231 elected officials and by 1989 this had increased to 580. In 1962 the first Hispanics were elected to the California Assembly and Ed Roybal was elected to Congress. By 1990, there were four Hispanic assemblypersons and three Hispanic state senators. Redistricting and the rapid increase in Latino voter participation during the 1990s have yielded as many as 29 members of the state legislature and 10 seats in Congress. Latinos have also recently been elected to important political positions such as Mayor of Los Angeles, and Lieutenant Governor. Four of the last seven Speakers of the Assembly (generally seen as California's second most powerful post) have been Hispanic including John Perez, the current Speaker.

The increasing political power of African Americans and Hispanics has shifted the balance of power between the two parties in California. The California Assembly has had a Democratic majority for all but two of the last forty years. In 2010 when there was a big national surge towards the Republicans, California Democrats maintained control of both the state Assembly and the state Senate won the governorship, and all the other statewide races, won the U.S. Senate race and won 34 of the 53 House seats. The voting in the Governor's race shows why. Exit polls showed Republican Meg Whitman as receiving 50 percent of white votes to 45 percent for Democrat Jerry Brown. But 64 percent of Hispanics and 77 percent of African Americans voted for Jerry Brown, giving him a solid majority in the race.

The Future Political Culture of California

What does the future hold? Part of that future is already here: the 2000 census confirmed that California is a "majority-minority" state, meaning that whites are not a majority in California, though whites are still the largest single racial group in California. By 2016, it is estimated that Latinos will outnumber whites in California, and by 2044, Latinos will likely comprise a majority of Californians.

Figure 2.2 shows the current and projected balance of ethnic groups in California. The elephant in the room is the increasing percentage of Californians

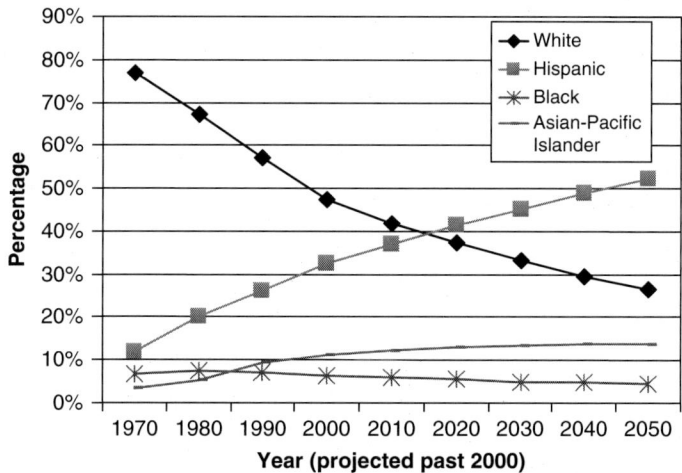

Figure 2.2 Racial Breakdown of Californians 1970–2050 (projected)

of Hispanic origin. This is largely driven not by continued immigration from Mexico (though that plays a part) but by the relatively high birthrates of the Hispanic population. In the last 20 years we have also seen periods of white out-migration, often driven by the desire to find cheaper housing.

What this means for the political culture of California remains to be seen. One likely result is the continued dominance of the Democratic Party in California politics, as lower income Hispanics become a steadily larger part of the electorate. But over time Hispanics, like Asian Americans, should become more integrated into the general culture and their income and status may well rise over time, making them more receptive to the Republican Party.

Finally, it seems worth pointing out that the future political culture of California is hard to predict. Lower house prices could bring whites back to California. Lower Hispanic birthrates would slow down the rise in the number of Hispanics. Future wars might lead to new floods of refugees. But absent these shocks it seems likely that current trends toward a more diverse and inclusive political culture will continue.

Chapter 3
CALIFORNIA'S VOTERS
By Phillip L. Gianos and Stephen J. Stambough

A voter in Fullerton, Orange County, California, was able to cast more than twenty separate votes in the 2008 general election: one for a presidential and vice-presidential ticket; one for the U.S. Senate; one for the U.S. House; one each for State Senate and Assembly; several for high school district board; local school district board; city council; numerous other local offices; and sixteen on statewide propositions.

That's a lot of voting. In fact much is asked of California voters every election. Much, also, is asked of U.S. voters in general. By putting so many things up for a vote—including, in California, everything from amending the state constitution via initiative to electing city clerks—Americans cast votes in numbers that lead the world (Dalton 1996, p. 46).

The National Setting

Candidates, while they must always deal with local issues, also act in an environment in which national parties and candidates set the tone of the electoral debate. Voters use national issues to help them assess local and statewide candidates. Asking a candidate his or her position on domestic spending preferences or foreign policy issues is a convenient way of establishing a candidate's broad philosophical position.

The sheer size, diversity, and political importance of California make it impossible for the state's voters to be insulated from national partisan politics. Members of every social, economic, ethnic, and religious group in America—in the world, for that matter—live in California, usually in numbers that cannot be safely ignored. No issue arises at the national level that does not affect California, and nothing happens politically in California that is ignored nationally.

The California Setting

But within this context of similarity between the California and national electorates, there are several distinctive features of the California electoral landscape.

Weak Parties

The American national party system is weak compared to many of those in the rest of the world (Dalton 1996, ch. 7). Voters' commitments to their party, formal party organization, and the independence of state organizations from national parties all play a role in this. California parties are even weaker than those of many other states (Mayhew 1986), leaving the voter less likely to seek party cues or display party loyalty in voting. Voters even pass reforms through our system of direct democracy that are designed to further weaken political parties such as our new nomination system (see Chapter 6).

New Issues

It has long been said that things happen first in California, and in some political instances that is true. Proposition 187 in 1994 and Proposition 209 in 1996 emphasized immigration and affirmative action policies, both of which became part of the 1996 presidential campaign of Republican nominee Bob Dole. Dole was advised by then-Governor Pete Wilson to use these issues in his presidential campaign because they worked for Wilson in his reelection campaign two years prior. These issues were nationalized by first being submitted to the California electorate, and their failure in California in the 1998 statewide elections was a signal to the national Republican Party that they had outlived their usefulness. In 2000, California voters passed an initiative designed to prevent same-sex marriage, an issue that later rose to national prominence in the presidential election of 2004, as did the issue of stem-cell research, which was the subject on a statewide initiative measure also on the 2004 ballot and the highly controversial Proposition 8 in 2008. As a result, national politicians and journalists watch California's voters carefully.

Comparing the California and National Electorates: Some History

To look at the electorate is to look primarily at its two main elements, Republicans and Democrats. The present structure of the California Republican and Democratic parties was established during the New Deal era. The benchmark election for the New Deal was the defeat in 1932 of Republican Herbert Hoover by Democrat Franklin Roosevelt. In its response to the New Deal, the California electorate demonstrated both its responsiveness to and independence from national trends.

In 1930, California voters sent only one Democrat to the U.S. House of Representatives; in the national Roosevelt sweep of 1932, ten California Democrats went to Washington. From 1932 until 1948, Democratic presidential candidates won California's large crop of electoral votes; and from 1932 to 1946, the Democrats controlled the state's Congressional delegation. In these respects, California was typical of the nation.

But there was a big exception to this pattern of Democratic ascendancy: while in many states the national Democratic sweep helped establish the Democratic party as the dominant party in *state* as well as national politics, California voters remained steadfastly Republican when voting for statewide offices. In 1932, the year of Roosevelt's huge win over Hoover, the Democratic Party was unable even to field candidates in 17 of 80 contests, and it was not until 1938 that the Democrats were able to elect a governor.

Why this pattern? The Democrats, even by California standards, were a weak and poorly organized party and were not able to capitalize effectively on the national Democratic trend. The state's press, led by the *Los Angeles Times*, was intensely Republican. Finally, the Democrats ran a number of candidates who attempted to capitalize on the Depression by supporting radical economic programs that frightened more voters than they attracted.

The election to the governorship in 1942 of Earl Warren continued Republican domination at the state level, even while Democratic candidates did well in elections for Congress and the presidency. In 1953, Warren resigned the governorship to become Chief Justice of the United States. In the aftermath of Warren's departure, the state Republican Party suffered a series of internal struggles for control, as the Democrats had during the Depression era. With the end of the Eisenhower era in national politics (1953–61) came the end of Republican dominance of state offices. Since that time, the broad contours of the California electorate have been similar to those of the nation, due in part to a simple fact: over the years, with population growth, California has constituted an increasing fraction of the national population.

Comparing the California and National Electorates: Partisanship

The most basic political orientation most of us have is partisanship—the sense that we are Republicans, Democrats, or identify with a third party, such as the Libertarians or the Greens. While this sense of partisanship is weaker than it was several generations ago (Wattenberg 1996), it is still the single most important fact of political life for most people. Partisanship is the primary—and for many people the sole—way they relate themselves to the political world.

When we compare survey responses from both California and the entire U.S. on partisanship three things are especially noteworthy. First, the advantage Democrats had in the 1950s and 60s both nationally and in California was reduced by the end of the twentieth century, though not enough to reduce the Democrats to second place. Second, partisanship in California closely follows partisanship in the U.S. In 1972, for example, the California and national electorates were essentially identical in their partisan preferences, and since then differences are slight. Third, the electorate overall has become less committed to either the Republicans or the Democrats; the fastest growing part of the electorate in California is comprised of those who decline to state an affiliation with any political party, large or small.

At present neither major party can claim a majority of voters in California, and third parties, though small, command a greater total share of the electorate than they did a generation ago, as does the number of those who decline to state a party affiliation when they register to vote. Many Californians, formerly Republicans or Democrats, are now registered with the American Independent, Green, Libertarian, Peace and Freedom, Natural Law, or Reform parties, among others.

According to the California Secretary of State's Office, over the past decade party registration has been stable among Democrats in California. In 2003, 44.4 percent of registered voters identified as Democrats. By 2011 that number was nearly identical at 44.0 percent. The story is different among Republicans in California. Over the past decade, Republican identification declined from 35.2 percent of the registered voters in California to 30.9 percent. The Republican decline was accompanied by a subsequent increase in voters who declined to declare any partisan affiliation.

Voters, Non-voters, and Turnout

Turnout is critical in elections; since both major parties have the potential to win statewide contests, mobilizing supporters to reach that potential is vital. Mobilization means two things: getting people registered, and then getting them to turn out on election day.

Comparing voters and non-voters in the U.S. and California reveals some similarities and some differences. While sex and regional differences between voters and non-voters are insignificant, the young and the less well-educated are heavily *under*-represented in the electorate and the older, better educated, and more well off are substantially *over*-represented. Republicans and conservatives are slightly more likely to turn out to vote than Democrats and liberals. In these respects the California voter is like his or her national counterpart. Voters live in different social and economic circumstances than non-voters, and they carry these characteristics with them into the voting booth. The result is that voters are slightly more conservative, more Republican, older, and better educated, and have higher incomes, than those who do not vote.

Examining turnout shows some additional similarities between California and the U.S., but some differences as well. Between the arrival of the New Deal in 1932 and 1972, Californians turned out at higher rates in presidential election years—sometimes substantially higher rates—than the U.S. as a whole. Since 1976, turnout in California kept up with or occasionally lagged behind that for the country as a whole, at a time when the national turnout rate in presidential elections was declining to around fifty percent.

Part of this turnout decline in the United States and in California is due to the expansion of the electorate, via the 26th amendment to the federal Constitution in 1971, to include those 18 to 20 years of age. This age group, then and now, is noteworthy for its low turnout rate. But the even steeper decline in California's turnout relative to the rest of the country has also to do with another demographic change: a greater proportion of California's population is now comprised of just those groups who have tended to historically vote at lower rates, most especially Latinos.

The big story of California politics over the last ten years is this growing Latino electorate. Ten percent of the state's registered voters in 1990 were Latino; by the turn of the 21st century that proportion had nearly doubled. These newly registered Latino voters generally were younger, less well-educated, had lower incomes than their predecessors, and were much more likely to be Democrats. Despite their Democratic registration, however, these new Latino registered voters were very similar ideologically to the rest of California's voters. This means there are many young Latino voters whom both parties are working to attract and retain.

Two more aspects of turnout deserve attention. The first is the advent in 1994 of federal "motor voter" legislation designed to increase registration and turnout by making it more convenient to register at such places as state motor vehicle offices. Approximately 800,000 Californians registered to vote under motor voter, and while it is difficult accurately to assess its effects, the statewide turnout rate since motor voter suggests that while registration may have increased registration it did not increase turnout, primarily because motor voter was designed to encourage people to register who are also the least likely to vote.

A second aspect of turnout is the significant increase in recent decades in Californians' voting via absentee ballot. Originally designed as a convenience for people who were going to be away from home on election day, absentee ballots have now become a regular part of campaigns' GOTV (get-out-the-vote) efforts. Absentee ballots allow campaigns to target their strongest supporters and virtually assure that they will vote.

Both parties now use absentee ballots vigorously, which explains the significant upsurge in their use. In 1966 just 3.3 percent of all votes cast in California were via absentee ballots; by 1986 the percentage had almost tripled to nine percent; by 1990 it was 14.1 percent. In the elections of 2000 and 2004 roughly thirty percent of all votes cast were absentee—a figure matched in the United States as a whole, as increased absentee voting became a national phenomenon. In the days when absentee ballots were rarely used, a large majority of absentee voters favored Republican candidates and issues. This is much less the case now that absentee ballot campaigns are employed by both major parties and the number of Democrats and Republicans voting absentee is quite similar.

The tendency for the California electorate to be Democratic might appear to predict a state electorate consistently though not overwhelmingly Democratic in its voting, but turnout tends to equalize the parties' chances. In recent decades the state has elected four Republican governors (Reagan, Deukmejian, Wilson, and Schwarzenegger) and four Democrats (Edmund G. "Pat" Brown, his son Jerry Brown, Gray Davis, and Jerry Brown again for non-consecutive terms), supported Nixon, Reagan and Bush for president with its electoral votes, elected Republican Wilson to the U.S. Senate, and passed conservative initiatives supported by Republicans and opposed by Democrats.

But California has also elected Democrats to the U.S. Senate (Cranston, and currently Feinstein and Boxer), voted twice for Bill Clinton, divided its state legislature between a Democratic Senate and a Republican Assembly, divided its 52 seats in the U.S. House down the middle in 1994-1996 with each major party holding 26 seats, and elected a Democratic governor and legislature in 1998. Heading into the 2004 elections, the House delegation was comprised of 33 Democrats and 20 Republicans.

The pattern of divided control has weakened, however. In the 2000 elections, California voted for the Democratic candidate Al Gore, re-elected Democratic U.S. Senator Dianne Feinstein to rejoin another Democratic U.S. Senator, Barbara Boxer, and sent to the House of Representatives a delegation that was nearly two-thirds Democratic. The voters in 2000 also sent to Sacramento a State Assembly that was nearly two-thirds Democratic and a State Senate that was also nearly two-thirds Democratic. The shift towards the Democratic Party in California reached a new high with the elections of 2010. Even though Republicans nationwide were the big winners of the 2010 elections, California went the other direction, every statewide elected office in California was won by the Democrats.

California Voters and Presidential Elections

How California votes is important for another reason: the state's 54 electoral votes comprise twenty percent of the minimum 270 electoral votes needed to elect presidents. Under the Electoral College, winning the California popular vote by a single individual's vote delivers to the winner one-fifth of what is needed for victory. In any presidential election in which the winner's national popular vote margin is narrow but includes winning California, the state becomes particularly important. In the fourteen presidential elections since 1948, Californians have been on the presidential ticket eight times as nominee for president or vice president. Remarkably, all these California national candidates were Republicans. In fact, no Republican had won the presidency without carrying California since 1880, when James Garfield was elected, until the election of 2000.

Over time California's share of all electoral votes has increased as the state's population and therefore its electoral vote has grown while the total number of electoral votes has remained constant at 538. In two cases in recent decades—Kennedy in 1960 and Carter in 1976—the national winner lost California. In all other cases, California voted for the winner. In the election of 2000, California supported the popular vote winner Al Gore, but not the electoral vote winner, George W. Bush.

In several presidential elections California's electoral votes were an especially important fraction of the winner's electoral vote total. For Harry Truman in 1948, for Richard Nixon in 1968 (but not in Nixon's 1972 landslide reelection), and for Bill Clinton in 1992 and 1996, California's electoral votes were especially important. In Clinton's, case, this was made clear by the record number of trips he made to California in his first term (more even than Ronald Reagan, who had a home in the state) as well as during the 1996 campaign. As far as the popular vote percentage is concerned, Californians have voted in presidential elections in much the same way as the rest of the country but has been trending more Democratic since Clinton's victory in 1992.

California's voters have not been especially hospitable to third-party presidential candidates. California supported Ross Perot's 1992 and 1996 candidacies to almost exactly the same extent as the rest of the country, Ralph Nader's Green Party candidacy of 2000 captured 3.9 percent of California's votes, which closely matched his national popular share. In the 2004 presidential election, Nader did not qualify for the California ballot. This close match between California and the rest of the nation was also the case with respect to moderate Republican John Anderson's run as an independent in the 1980 presidential election. However, Strom Thurmond's segregationist Dixiecrat candidacy of 1948 played less well in the California popular vote than it did nationally, and George Wallace's 1968 right-wing populist candidacy also did less well in California than nationally.

Party Coalitions in California: Social Composition and Ideology

American political parties are loose coalitions of many groups rather than well-organized, integrated institutions. California party coalitions differ along social, economic, and ideological lines in ways similar to those of national parties.

The Republican coalition is evenly divided between males and females; the Democratic coalition, however, is skewed in the direction of female identifiers. Republican partisans are overwhelmingly white, the Democrats much less so. This is especially true with respect to blacks, who comprised in recent years 16 percent of Democratic identifiers but less than one percent of the Republicans'. Asians are roughly divided between the two parties, and Latinos are Democratic in tendency.

Simply put, the Democratic coalition in California is more diverse and representative of the state's population than its Republican counterpart. This is also true among Republicans and Democrats nationally, and helps partially to explain why the Democrats, while they have historically held an edge in identification over Republicans, have also had a turnout problem. The more diverse Democratic coalition includes proportionately more individuals whose social characteristics—especially lower levels of education—are associated with lower levels of political activity.

Policy preferences between each of the major parties' identifiers differ in predictable ways. For example, while both Republicans and Democrats support abortion rights in the first three months of a woman's pregnancy, Democrats' support is considerably greater. On this and many other issues, California's Democrats differ from its Republicans in predictable ways, and both parties' identifiers in California are similar to their national counterparts.

The Three Electorates

One final aspect of the California voter deserves attention because it focuses on some distinctive aspects of voting in California: the three different settings in which the California voter may act.

The California Voter in General Elections

In a *general election* the most visible races are usually for control of political office: the winner in the race for governor or U.S. senator in a general election wins the office outright. This is a crucial distinction between general elections and primary elections, for the winner of a primary (held in March) wins only the right to run in the general election (held in November) as the official candidate of his or her party for the office. General elections also, however, almost always involve on initiative measures as well.

In the general election, races are contested between highly visible candidates of the major parties. The candidates are usually well-known, they get substantial media attention, and the voter is more likely to use partisanship as a cue in guiding the voting choice. Such elections are termed *high stimulus* elections, and because of this, turnout tends to be relatively high as well.

This means that marginal voters—those who are unlikely to vote when the stimulus value is low—are more likely to vote in a general election than in other types of elections, especially primaries. Marginal voters add an element of volatility to the electorate because they are more easily swayed by considerations other than partisanship. Media campaigns, candidate personality, and a strong concern with a single issue—of the kind that can be generated by an initiative campaign, for example—may be more important for such voters than they are for the committed partisan voter. These tendencies hold for California as well as for the nation.

The California Voter in Primary Elections

The second electoral setting is the *primary election*, and here there is no direct national comparison. A primary is essentially several parallel elections, one for each party, in which party nominations for office are at stake, though primary ballots also include initiative measures. Primaries are elections *within* parties, not between them—or they were until voters approved a blanket primary via initiative in 1996, discussed at the end of this section.

Since primaries involve several candidates from the same party—i.e., Democrats versus other Democrats, Republicans versus other Republicans—several important consequences follow. First, because partisan lines are not drawn, and because the candidates are often philosophically closer to each other, turnout tends to be lower in primary races than in the general election. The electorate shrinks, but it also changes in composition, not just size. The Democratic primary election electorate is not only smaller but also more liberal than the Democratic general election electorate. Likewise, the Republican primary electorate is not only smaller than its general election counterpart but also more conservative. The primary electorate for both major parties is therefore smaller, more ideologically aware, and less centrist

Candidates facing such an electorate face a different strategic problem than general election candidates. Candidates must appeal to people who are more politically involved, more politically informed, and more intensely ideological in their beliefs. This means that primary electorates are more likely to nominate "extreme" candidates who appeal to the party faithful but who may not be as palatable to the larger, more diverse, and more moderate general electorate. Even if the more moderate candidate wins the primary the primary race itself may be divisive for the party in the general election.

California primary elections were changed radically, however, with the March 1996 passage of Proposition 198, which created a blanket primary—one in which voters are not limited to voting only for the candidates of the party with which they are registered. Under Prop 198, any registered voter could vote for any candidate in primary elections regardless of the candidate's party affiliation. The March 2000 primary was the first to be held under these rules, with a single primary ballot on which the names of all candidates for a given office appeared. This procedure, similar to those in several other states including Alaska, Louisiana and Washington, permitted crossover voting—i.e., a Republican could cast a vote for a Democratic primary candidate, and a Democrat could likewise cast a vote for a Republican candidate for a given office, and then vote for a candidate of his or her own party for another office on the same ballot.

This raised the possibility that parties would be even further weakened and that one party could raid the other's ranks in primary elections, hoping to damage the party by nominating a weak opposition candidate who would be easier to defeat in the general election. Supporters of the blanket primary argued the precise opposite, claiming it would promote more moderate nominees in both parties by encouraging candidates with bipartisan support.

There was indeed crossover voting in the March 2000 primary: seven-and-one-half percent of Republicans voted in the Democratic primary, three-quarters of them for Al Gore. Twenty-two and one-half percent of Democrats voted in the Republican primary, with just under two-thirds of them supporting Arizona Sen. John McCain. There was little evidence that either Republicans or Democrats made any effort to do mischief to the other party but instead voted sincerely, not strategically. Still, there were a few close state races in which one could argue, as the losing candidates did, that mischievous crossovers might have made affected the outcome.

Both major parties, joined by the Libertarian and Peace and Freedom parties, challenged Proposition 198 in the courts and in June 2000, the U.S. Supreme Court held on a 7-2 decision that the measure was an unconstitutional violation of the first amendment, saying it "forces political parties to associate with—to have their nominees, and hence their positions, determined by—those who, at best, have refused to affiliate with the party and, worst, have expressly affiliated with a rival."

In response to this decision, two competing measures were placed on the November 2004 state ballot. Proposition 62 required primary elections in which voters could vote for any state or national candidates (with the exception of the presidency) regardless of the candidate's or the voter's party affiliation, with the two highest vote-getters being listed on the general election ballot, even if both candidates were members of the same party. The measure was designed to revive the open primary in a way that would survive review by the courts. Propositions

60 was intended specifically to counter Proposition 62 by requiring that the general election ballot include the candidate who received the most votes from among the candidates running in each party's primary election the previous March. In the November election, voters reaffirmed the closed party primary by supporting Proposition 60 and defeating Proposition 62. Reformers kept trying and were successful with the passage of Proposition 14 in 2010 (see Chapter 6 for more detail). This proposition altered the primary process for future elections. It will be interesting to see how parties and voters respond to the new structures.

The California Voter and Initiatives

The third electoral setting is one that occurs in both primary and general elections and involves voting on initiative measures (see Chapter 4). In this situation the citizen votes directly for or against a proposed law or constitutional amendment. These issues are frequently highly controversial, involve extensive and costly media campaigns, and arouse intense emotions. Because of the controversy and intensity of such campaigns, the party organizations and their candidates frequently avoid taking positions. One of the first laws of campaigning is to avoid taking a position unless it is absolutely necessary; another law is that if one must take a position it should be as ambiguous as possible.

Because parties frequently take no position on an initiative, or offer a deliberately fuzzy one, the voter has virtually no party cues. This third electorate is therefore largely cast adrift from party ties. How does this electorate decide?

Separated from the usual party and candidate guidance, members of this third electorate are much more sensitive to media campaigns, which means that voters' decisions are more sensitive to the use of money. Cutting voters loose from their usual partisan bases makes them vulnerable to such campaigns.

The main factors reducing the likelihood of voters being completely at the mercy of money and media are time and, ironically, money. Often, a well-financed campaign is countered by a more-or-less equally well-financed campaign and the increased media attention that such campaigns attract. Highly visible campaigns encourage voters to become aware of an issue and to think it through. Here, time is the voter's ally. Voters over the course of the long campaigns that are typical in the U.S. and in California have time to sort out conflicting claims, acquire additional information, and to make a reasonable judgment (see Popkin 1994, ch. 10; Page and Shapiro 1994). Visible campaigns, media attention, money and time can all create a crude kind of public dialogue that permits voters to sort out their positions, even without party cues.

Choosing One's Own Electorate

The most common way the California voter deals with the number and variety of voting choices on the ballot, however, is through "roll-off." Roll-off refers to the tendency for voters to cast some, but not necessarily all, of the votes available to them. The voter mentioned in the first paragraph of this chapter, eligible to cast up to twenty-four votes, might well decide that he or she is not sufficiently informed or interested to cast all the votes available and might instead cast, say, only ten. Roll-off effectively enables voters to choose which electorate they will be part of. Shall I be part of the electorate for governor *and* state controller *and* Proposition 123 *and* city clerk, or shall I just vote for governor and go home?

In the general election of 2004, for example, if we define casting a ballot for president as the high-water mark of 100 percent voting, roll-off on the sixteen propositions ranged from a 96 percent rate of participation (for a measure on stem cell research) to 86 percent (on a measure dealing with state authority over local government finances).

Voters who opt out of voting for some candidates and measures tend to vote for the high-profile items at the top of the ballot—president, governor, U.S. Senator, a heavily debated proposition—but forego voting for what are termed down-ballot items. All voters immediately subdivide themselves into what become multiple electorates for specific offices and measures. Much of this complexity gets lost in election reporting, where exit polls tell us what the governor's supporters were like or what kinds of people voted for or against Proposition X, but very little about the kinds of support for other candidates and measures on the ballot.

After Florida: A Note on Voting Procedures in California

Much of the drama and complexity involving Florida's role in the 2000 presidential election occurred because most election procedures in the U.S. are creatures of state—not federal—law. Most elections in the United States are conducted under a combination of state and county rules. Since states create counties, the amount of latitude counties have in running elections depends on how much latitude they are given by the states.

Florida provides relatively little guidance in these areas, and this latitude complicated matters in Florida considerably when different county-based canvassing boards debated over such matters as whether to count hanging chad ballots in which tiny rectangles of cardboard on voting cards were not completely removed, or dimpled chad ballots in which only an indentation was present on a ballot. Individual Florida counties also varied considerably in how they secured the integrity of ballots, especially absentee ballots, before they were counted. There was also concern about important decisions in Florida being made by local and state officials who were active, partisan participants in the campaign, most prominently Florida's Secretary of State, who was co-chair of George Bush's Florida's campaign and who was also the chief election officer of the state.

California law provides more guidance on these matters than does Florida law. While the Secretary of State of California is, as in Florida, an elected official who runs as a member of a political party and is also the chief election officer of the state, most county election officials in California (and unlike Florida) are not themselves elected but are rather appointed, on an officially nonpartisan basis, by county boards of supervisors. Some other comparisons with the Florida case: the confusing butterfly ballots, of the kind used in Florida's Palm Beach County, are not used in California. There is a statewide standard for counting chads: if they dangle from two corners, they count. Any other pattern, including dimpled chads, does not. In Florida, overseas absentee ballots were allowed additional time, under Florida law, to arrive for counting. In California, such ballots must arrive by election day. And under California law, officials have 28 days in which to count ballots and certify the results; Florida law provides for a period of seven days. After that 28-day period, *any* candidate in California can ask for and get a recount, provided the candidate pays for its costs.

Conclusion

The California voter is a closely watched political animal. In many respects—partisanship, presidential voting, turnout, and issue positions—voters in California look a lot like U.S. voters in general. But there are differences. Operating in a huge and diverse state with weak parties, and able to vote regularly on everything from obscure local offices to amending the state constitution, voters in California have enormous latitude and great power.

California's reputation as a political bellwether derives not from some magical quality granted its citizens but from the realities of the state's demography and its politics. Size and diversity mean that any interest or issue will likely be found in California; weak parties mean voters have considerable latitude; and the tradition of direct democracy via initiative means voters' wishes on virtually everything are often decisive. All this means that California's voters make a difference, not just within the state, but in the nation as well.

Table 3.1 The California and the National Electorates

	California	**The United States**
Designation:	• The California electorate, composed of sane adults registered to vote in California elections	• The American electorate, composed of sane adults registered to vote in one of the 50 states, or in the District of Columbia (or other U.S. possession)
Shape/Design:	• Smaller than the American electorate, of course; but broadly representative of the mix of persons and groups found in the American electorate	• Encompassing all voters in the United States, the American electorate is enormously varied ethnically, regionally, and in political points of view
Special Features:	• 3 distinct settings define essentially 3 different electorates: a general election electorate that roughly mirrors the American electorate; a primary election electorate that is more ideologically extreme (Democrats are more liberal; Republicans are more conservative) than the general election electorate; and a third electorate that votes on ballot measures and is especially vulnerable to advertising campaigns (and thus to the influence of money)	• Nothing exactly comparable to the three California electorates
Importance:	• Ballot measures give the California electorate frequent and important power to make policy directly	• Choices for president of the United States, in both primary and general elections, can amount to important policy impact

Chapter 4
BALLOT MEASURES: INITIATIVES, REFERENDUMS, AND RECALLS
By Alana Northrop and Shelly Arsneault

Initiatives and referendums allow citizens to participate directly in making state law by voting on what are termed propositions. *Initiatives* may be used to change a state constitution or to make an ordinary law (a statute, of the kind that state legislatures make). *Referendums* allow citizens a chance to overturn or to affirm laws that a state legislature has already adopted. *Recall* elections determine whether an elected official presently in office will continue in that office. In other words, voters through a recall election may remove an elected officeholder before the legally defined expiration of his or her term. Californians did this in 2003 when they voted out Governor Davis and voted in Governor Schwarzenegger.

California, like 23 other states and the District of Columbia, provides for these important ballot measures. But 26 other states and the national government do not allow initiatives, referendums and recalls. The nearly even division among the states on whether to have these provisions shows disagreement about whether these kinds of direct citizen participation are wise. This disagreement is fundamentally a debate between the idea of direct democracy, which includes initiatives, referendums and recalls, and the idea of representative democracy which excludes them. The issue is whether representative bodies, like Congress, fulfill the ideals of democratic government better than direct citizen voting. Before we address this issue we briefly consider why initiatives, referendums and recalls were adopted in California, and how they work.

Ballot Measures: An Overview
Historical Roots
The initiative and referendum were first proposed as part of the Progressive movement, which strongly influenced American politics between 1896 and 1932. Progressives viewed the political and economic systems as corrupt and in need of reform. Underlying Progressive reforms was a belief that party politics stood in the way of practical, politically neutral solutions to public problems. Thus on the local level, reforms such as the city manager form of government, the use of city planning departments, and nonpartisan elections were urged and often adopted (see Chapter 11).

The major aims of the Progressive movement were to protect and empower the average citizen and to weaken political institutions, especially parties. Thus recall elections were provided for, as were initiatives and referendums. And on the national level Progressives successfully pushed for the direct election of U.S. Senators as a way to return control of the corrupt (in their view) political world to the citizenry. Progressives also stood for anti-trust laws, product standardization and safety, and laws prohibiting child labor, among others; their ideas had substantial impacts on a wide range of governmental features. (See the discussions of the Progressive movement in Chapters 1 and 5.)

In 1911 Governor Hiram Johnson, a leading Republican Progressive, sponsored a series of constitutional amendments establishing the initiative, referendum, and recall in California. Johnson and his many allies wanted to free California politics from the powerful hands of the so-called robber barons who owned the powerful Southern Pacific Railroad. There is no good evidence, though, that providing for initiatives, referendums and recalls was successful in controlling the power of these economic interests.

Constitutional Amendment Initiatives

Amendments to the California Constitution are the most common initiative type. Any person or group can submit a draft of a proposed constitutional amendment to the Attorney General of California. The attorney general's office then prepares a statement known as a *circulation title*, which must appear on each petition. The next step is to collect signatures that total at least eight percent of the vote cast in the last governor's race (about 807,614). After the Secretary of State officially determines that the requisite number of registered voters' signatures have been collected within 150 days (usually 20 to 25 percent of the signatures are invalid), the amendment appears on the next general or primary election ballot. If approved by a majority of those voting on the measure, an amendment to the California Constitution remains in force unless ruled by the courts to be in conflict with the U.S. Constitution or repealed by a later constitutional initiative. The key advantage of a state constitutional initiative is that the courts cannot rule it unconstitutional unless it violates the U.S. Constitution.

Statutory Initiatives

The procedure to get a statutory initiative on the ballot is the same as for a constitutional amendment, except that the required signatures must total only five percent of the vote cast in the last governor's race (about 504,760). Thus it is easier to qualify a statutory initiative than a constitutional initiative. However, the courts can invalidate a statutory initiative if it is ruled in conflict with *either* the California *or* the U.S. Constitution.

Referendums

Referendums are distinct from initiatives because referendums pertain to laws already passed by the state legislature. Opponents of the law first make a formal filing with the state attorney general's office, delaying the enforcement of the law until the electorate can vote on it. Sponsors of a referendum must still collect registered voters' signatures which amount to five percent of the last gubernatorial total vote within 90 days in order to delay the law's enforcement until the next general election. The referendum is rare compared to the initiative process. Since 1912 there have been fifty attempted referendums; thirty-nine qualified for the ballot, and only twenty-five have been approved.

One reason for this lack of use may be the difficulty of collecting some 504,760 valid signatures within 90 days. Initiative campaigns have 60 more days to collect the same number of signatures, and thus the groups prefer initiatives when the effect would be the same. A second reason is that the need for referendums has diminished since the state legislature began to meet almost continuously, instead of every other year, as was the pre-1966 pattern. (Major constitutional changes in 1966 professionalized the legislature: see Chapters 1 and 8.) With the legislature in continuous session, groups have more opportunities to seek amendments to statutes within the regular legislative process rather than pursue a more costly and time-consuming referendum strategy. Thirdly, one cannot use a referendum to delay statutes that are deemed "urgent"—those adopted by a two-thirds vote of the legislature as necessary for the "immediate preservation of the public peace, health or safety." The California legislature frequently designates statutes urgent, thereby reducing the opportunities to start a referendum drive.

Other Ballot Propositions

For convenience, initiatives and referendums alike are termed propositions when placed on the election ballot. Some are constitutional amendments and statutory initiatives put on the ballot by petition, and some are measures put on the ballot by the state legislature. In fact, many propositions on a typical election ballot originate in the legislature as it seeks to do one of three things: place the state in debt, usually through bond issues for major projects (like building new prisons); change the state constitution (often in incidental ways, but any constitutional change requires approval by the voters); or alter or amend the provisions of laws initially adopted as ballot measures.

Recalls

Recalls are elections held to decide whether to remove a local or state elected official from office. In order to do so, a citizen notifies the county clerk or the Secretary of State of his/her intention and must give a reason—any will do—for the recall effort. Then the recall backer must collect signatures of registered voters supporting the request for a recall election. How many signatures must be collected and in how many days depends upon the size of the jurisdiction represented by the target of the recall. For example, to recall a mayor in a city with 10,000 to 50,000 registered voters, one needs to collect the signatures of 20 percent of the registered voters within 120 days. To recall a state legislator, one needs to collect the signatures of 20 percent of the total vote for the office in the last election within 160 days, and to recall a governor, the signatures of 12 percent of the total vote in the last election (nearly one million) must be collected within 160 days. If enough signatures are collected within the time limit, an election is held in which voters cast "yes" or "no" votes on whether the official should be removed. Los Angeles became the first government in the U.S. to adopt the recall in 1903. The state of California followed in 1911.

At the state level, the recall only gained importance recently. First, in 1994, Republican Paul Horcher, a Southern California legislator, declared himself an independent and voted with the Democrats. The division between the two parties at the time was so narrow that Horcher's decision permitted Democratic Speaker Willie Brown to remain in office by a single vote. Republicans organized a successful recall of Horcher in December of 1994, setting up what was expected to be Republican control of the Speakership. The party, however, was unable to elect its own Speaker the next year because another Southern California Republican, Doris Allen, was elected Speaker with the support of the Democrats and one other Republican. Allen's siding with Democrats led to another successful recall in the fall of 1995. With a closely divided legislature, and politicians willing to make deals with the other party, the recall can become an important political tool—in these two cases, a powerful tool to enforce party discipline.

It can also be used as a political tool in another way. In 2002, Republicans narrowly lost California's race for governor. Instead of waiting four years for the next election, one man with a cool $2 million and a desire to be governor, financed a recall of the newly reelected Democratic Governor Davis.

Voters had much to be angry with Davis about including a failing economy, the electricity crisis of 2001 and Davis' tripling of automobile registration fees. Many also argued that Davis only won the 2002 election because his opponent, Bill Simon, was too conservative for the average California voter.

The recall effort, initially financed by wealthy Republican Assemblyman, Darrell Issa, quickly picked up steam. In the end, 135 people qualified for the recall ballot including current and former television personalities, students, and an adult film actress. The winner of the race was moderate Republican Arnold Schwarzenegger, whose movie stardom made his a household name. If Davis had not been successfully recalled, the state would have had to reimburse him for expenses he made in fighting the recall effort.

The Use, and Cost, of Initiative Drives

The use of the initiative is experiencing a resurgence. Many more initiatives are being proposed in our era than in other times although a lower proportion of them are qualifying for the ballot than in the past.

Who Uses the Initiative?

Generally the same groups who lobby the state legislature—interest groups with something to gain or something to defend, as described in Chapter 6—will turn to the initiative process when it suits them. Users of the initiative process have included realtors (who some years ago supported anti-open housing measures), bankers (who have supported the elimination of interest rate ceilings on loans), teachers, and Native American tribes. Grassroots organizations also sponsor initiatives. Such groups have sponsored measures regulating the use of California's coastline, nuclear safety, cigarette smoking, services to illegal immigrants, same-sex marriages, and genetically engineered crops. In recent years elected officials, especially governors, have used the initiative to advance their policies. For example, in 2011, Governor Brown proposed ballot initiatives to balance the state's budget (see Chapter 12).

Interest groups see the initiative as an alternative to the usual legislative process in Sacramento. They may turn to the initiative after failing to get what they want from the legislature. A successful constitutional initiative changes the state constitution—and that means that the legislature and the governor may be prevented from tinkering with or watering-down the policy. If a group wants to protect its interests for the long term, a constitutional initiative is particularly appealing. On the other hand, high costs make any group think twice before beginning an initiative drive.

Direct Democracy is an Expensive Undertaking

The initial cost is the amount required to get an initiative or recall on the ballot. It can easily require over $1 million just to qualify for ballot inclusion. It is common to hire a professional organization to run the drive for signatures, and such organizations usually hire paid petition circulators, many of whom may attempt to gather signatures for more than one measure. Initiative campaigns—both gathering signatures and mounting expensive statewide media campaigns—are expensive, but the firms who run such campaigns essentially guarantee that, with enough money, they can qualify virtually any measure.

Once an initiative qualifies for the ballot, money must be spent to encourage its passage or defeat. In 2010 all sides spent some 235 million dollars on campaigns involving the nine statewide measures on the ballot (www.followthemoney.org). A single initiative can be very expensive if it is controversial. For example in 2008 campaign spending on Proposition 8 (Same-sex Marriage Ban) was over $75 million. Interestingly, large amounts of money spent on an initiative have not guaranteed success at the polls although when one side significantly outspends the other the big spender's side usually wins. There are no limits on initiative spending. While attempts have been made to limit such spending, the California Supreme Court has ruled them unconstitutional because they violate the freedom of speech guaranteed in the First Amendment to the U.S. Constitution.

The 2003 gubernatorial recall was a very expensive undertaking for candidates and government alike. In addition to the initial $2 million invested by Assemblyman Issa to begin the recall, the campaign cost the 135 candidates nearly $27 million. Citizens, however, were the biggest spenders during the recall as California's 58 counties spent between $42 and $55 million on running the special election, while state government spent another $11 million to provide voters with state voter election guides.

Tension Between Representative Democracy and Direct Democracy

How Ballot Measures Can Work Against Majority Rule, Minority Rights, and Political Equality

Almost a century ago Progressives supported initiatives and referendums as a way to return politics to the people. Yet paradoxically initiatives, referendums and recall may work against the very democratic principles they were meant to implement.

Every citizen is theoretically represented when laws and constitutional amendments are adopted by a vote in the legislature. State Senators and members of the California Assembly join in a deliberative process knowing that they represent the people who live in their districts, and they must in turn deal with other legislators and with a popularly elected governor.

But the use of direct democracy means that only those who vote have a hand in the decision-making process. That can be a small number. For example, an exceptionally popular initiative might win the approval of more than two-thirds of the voters, an apparently overwhelming majority. Yet taking into account the failure of half or more of citizens to vote; a third or less of eligible Californians would actually have voted for such a popular initiative. It may be hard to call that majority rule. Even Schwarzenegger got less than 50 percent of the vote and less than 30 percent of the eligible electorate voted for him.

If you don't vote, many might ask why anyone should worry about your opinion. But that does not entirely address the representation problem; and the problem grows when we notice that one's likelihood of voting is shaped by one's status within society. Anglo whites as a group and people from economically comfortable families are usually taught to believe that they should vote and that voting can make a difference. The same groups are usually better educated, and educated people participate in politics more than people without much formal schooling. Still further, educated, well-off white males may see that maintaining the system (which, after all, favored them) is in their interest—and thus they participate in politics.

Ethnic minorities, people with less education, and less income are at a disadvantage in all of this. Lacking knowledge and resources, they can feel helpless and alienated from politics. Failing to participate, their interests may go unrepresented in instances where policy is made through direct voting, as with initiatives and referendums.

In addition, the time and money required to place initiatives and recalls on the ballot mean people with few resources are disadvantaged not just in the voting but also in putting forward proposals and campaigning for or against them. Moreover, these high costs lead both sides to target likely voters rather than the public at large during their campaigns. Again, this campaign strategy targets those with power, money and high levels of education leaving those at the lower ends of the socioeconomic ladder alienated from the system.

And finally there is the problem of complexity and sheer number of ballot choices. Many ballot measures are so complicated that only well-educated people (at times, so educated that they would seem to need a Ph.D. or law degree) can judge whether a proposal is in citizens' best interests. People with little education are disadvantaged. How then should the average citizen handle the number and complexity of initiatives and the sometimes-confusing media campaign associated with them?

One way is to examine the brief description of the measure provided by the Secretary of State's office in the material sent to all registered voters. But even a fairly simple measure described in simplified form can be quite difficult to understand. Another way is to take a cue from political elites. Do you support the people and groups spending money for or against an initiative? A final way is to avoid the uncertainty of what effect an initiative might have by voting "no" because a "no" vote is a vote for keeping things the way they are.

It can be argued, then, that initiatives qualifying for a ballot usually are for the benefit of those already well off, and it is the well-off who are more likely to vote. Given that majority rule and political equality are principles of democracy, ballot measures in practice fall short of these principles of democratic government. They also fall short of the principle of minority rights. Frequently the California Supreme Court has called an initiative unconstitutional because it violated a minority's rights. An example comes from Proposition 22, a ban on gay marriage, passed by 61 percent of voters in 2000. Prop 22, a statutory initiative stating that, "Only marriage between a man and a woman is valid or recognized in California," was struck down as unconstitutional by the California Supreme Court in May 2008. As a result however, Proposition 8, similar to Proposition 22, made the November 2008 ballot and the ban on gay marriage was passed. The key difference is that the 2008 initiative was a *constitutional amendment*, unlike the statutory initiative of 2000. While Prop 8 has been challenged in court, its status as a constitutional amendment has made Proposition 8 difficult to overturn.

How Ballot Measures Can Work Against Representative Democracy

There are other issues involved in the controversy over initiatives, referendums and recalls. One is whether propositions weaken the institutions of representative democracy, especially the legislature (see Chapter 8). For example, with the option of the initiative available, legislators have the option of doing nothing when difficult issues arise. Where there is no initiative process, the legislators may in the end be forced to decide; but in the states that maintain the initiative option, legislators can pass the buck. Why get involved in considering controversial legislation and risk re-election when you can let the voters have only themselves to blame through the initiative? No one can hold initiative sponsors accountable if their initiatives cause economic or social havoc. Yet the theory behind representative democracy is precisely that if legislators do not pass sound legislation, citizens may vote them out.

Policy may also be poorly drawn in initiative processes. A deliberative legislative process features a give-and-take in which problems are debated and flaws in proposals are solved through amendments. Various interests, not just one or a few, can be taken into account. That is almost entirely absent in the initiative process. Moreover, a proposition that sounds good can come with serious flaws, both anticipated and unanticipated.

This has been considered one of the key reasons for the failure of Prop 19, the legalization of marijuana, in 2010 (see Figure 4.1). While the proposition title indicates that it allowed for local governments to regulate and tax the production, distribution and sale of marijuana, as the campaign season went on it became increasingly clear to voters that the hodge-podge of regulations and taxes that would be created across the state would lead to great confusion and possible unintended consequences. For example, opponents worried that not all cities would impose adequate regulations over marijuana use. They also argued that there was no good way to determine how much revenue could be raised through taxation under this law, and both sides argued about the effects that legalization would have on violence from Mexican drug cartels. Further, with marijuana still illegal at the federal level, Federal Attorney General Eric Holder came out strongly against California's Prop 19 saying that the federal government would "vigorously enforce" existing federal laws in California. Many feared that the federal government would withhold federal funds to California—particularly highway funds—if the state legalized pot. Finally, just a month before election-day, Governor Schwarzenegger approved legislation downgrading the penalty for possession of up to an ounce of marijuana from a misdemeanor to an infraction; the penalty is equivalent to a parking ticket and does not appear on a person's criminal record. With all of this uncertainty and decreased penalties for marijuana, it is little wonder that the majority of California voters said no to legalization. As is common with

---

LEGALIZES MARIJUANA UNDER CALIFORNIA BUT NOT FEDERAL LAW. PERMITS LOCAL GOVERNMENTS TO REGULATE AND TAX COMMERCIAL PRODUCTION, DISTRIBUTION, AND SALE OF MARIJUANA. INITIATIVE STATUTE.

SUMMARY

- Allows people 21 years old or older to possess, cultivate, or transport marijuana for personal use.
- Permits local governments to regulate and tax commercial production, distribution, and sale of marijuana to people 21 years old or older.
- Prohibits people from possessing marijuana on school grounds, using in public, or smoking it while minors are present.
- Maintains prohibitions against driving while impaired.
- Limits employers' ability to address marijuana use to situations where job performance is actually impaired.

Figure 4.1 Official Title and Summary of Proposition 19 Prepared by the Attorney General Proposition 19

the initiative process, proponents of legalization have vowed to return the issue to the ballot in 2012.

Further, initiatives can obligate the state to spend millions without a source of revenue to pay for them or without consideration of whether the state has money to carry out the initiative without cutting more basic or important services. While the state's budget woes of the early 21st century are not likely a direct result of citizen initiatives, the state's financial obligations to fund propositions may become a bigger issue over time. Then there is the cost of just running elections that focus exclusively on initiatives and recalls. The state and, therefore, the taxpayer, pay for these elections even if the views of the small number of initiative or recall signers do not reflect those of the majority of Californians.

In sum, badly crafted policy that fails to consider various interests, a failure to uphold crucial principles of democracy, and a weakening of the representative democratic legislative process, is a sorry record in the view of many critics of direct democracy.

In the end there is a tension not so much between the initiative and democracy, but between two different models of democracy. Initiatives and referendums are features of *direct democracy*, in which citizens make policy directly through the ballot. The model with which the initiative conflicts most apparently is exactly that which has been the foundation of a stable, popular government respecting of citizen's rights in the United States: *representative democracy*. Observer Henry Fairlie (1978) made the point well:

> The point of representative democracy as distinct from direct democracy—of voting in an election and not a referendum—is that it forces one to relate one's own interest to those of others. This is one of the main functions of the representative, to adjust the needs of his own constituents to the needs of the constituents of other representatives, and this is what all the haggling in a representative body is all about.

The future does not appear to offer a reconsideration of the initiative process. The public continues to believe that statewide ballot propositions are a good thing, according to the California Poll's periodic surveys, though reforms proposals (e.g., having the courts review the language of proposed initiative to see if they are constitutional) appear regularly. In November 2010, there were nine initiatives on the ballot. In fact, with increasing mistrust of government, initiatives are continually proposed.

The tension between California's version of direct democracy via initiative on the one hand and representative democracy on the other will remain a mainstay of California politics, and we as citizens will continue to live with its consequences, good and bad.

Table 4.1 Ballot Measures

	Constitutional Initiatives	**Statutory Initiatives**	**Referendums**
Designation:	Means by which changes to the state constitution are proposed	Means by which laws are proposed	Means by which laws passed by the state legislature are subject to a yes/no vote of the electorate
Shape/ Design:	Signatures of 8% of the voters in last election for governor collected within 150 days	Signatures of 5% of the voters in last election for governor collected within 150 days	Signatures of 5% of the voters in last election for governor collected within 90 days
Special Features:	• Puts the measure beyond the reach of legislative or judicial alteration in California • Vulnerable to a judicial finding of unconstitutionality if it conflicts with part of the U.S. Constitution	• Vulnerable to a judicial finding of unconstitutionality if it conflicts with either parts of the California or U.S. Constitution	• Used rarely since the establishment of a full-time legislature in 1966
Importance:	• Tension with deliberative features found in representative democratic institutions • Open to what some would regard as misuse through simplistic appeals to the mass electorate on what in fact are complex issues • Tension with majority rule and minority rights principles in a democracy • Financial impacts without revenue to pay for the initiative or trade-off in service costs		

Note: There is no parallel to these processes in the national government. California is one of 24 states (plus the District of Columbia) in which initiatives and referendums are allowed.

Chapter 5
POLITICAL PARTIES IN CALIFORNIA
By Stephen J. Stambough and Bert C. Buzan

Political parties in California are similar to political parties nationally in many ways. Like the entire United States, California is dominated by the two major political parties accompanied by a number of minor parties that exert little influence over politics or policies. Additionally, California's political parties have adjusted to a new era of party resurgence by evolving into service organizations and as tools to bring together a number of like-minded organizations. There are some differences between California's political parties and both our national parties and parties in other states. By its sheer size, the California political party organization structure is likely to be different as are their functions, bases of support, and strategies.

In this chapter, we explore California's political parties in several ways. First, we discuss the Progressive legacy in California that still impacts (and weakens) California's political parties. Second, we look at the state of the two-party system in California by exploring levels of party competition in California and trends in partisan support. Third, we examine the cohesiveness of California's political parties from the perspective of the voters and legislators. Finally, we comment upon changes in party structure and tactics in contemporary California.

The Progressive Legacy of Party Restrictions

California's parties have been structurally weak throughout much of the last hundred years because of laws passed by the state legislature and the voters in initiative measures, laws that provide for direct primaries, civil service reforms, legal prohibitions on endorsements and financing, non-partisan elections, and a shortage of party conventions and offices. Most of these laws were passed during the Progressive Era, a time shortly after the turn of the century when middle-class reformers in America rallied against corrupt political machines and business monopolies.

The progressive leader in California was Governor (later U.S. Senator) Hiram Johnson. He rode to office on a campaign against the power of the Southern Pacific railroad and "political bosses" in both parties. Like most progressive leaders, Johnson found the "political machine" a more vulnerable target than the railroads and other corporations. Therefore, the main thrust of progressivism in California was not effective regulation of business, but the destruction of the traditional party organization (McConnell, 1970). The direct primary, civil service, the initiative, referendum and recall, non-partisan local elections, the detailed restrictions on the ability of party leaders to endorse or fund candidates and the weak, formal party structure survive in contemporary California politics as a legacy of progressive power in the state.

Progressive Republican domination of the state's politics continued into the 1950s, more than thirty years after progressivism's decline as a national force. The progressive emphasis on nonpartisanship, administrative efficiency and political individualism thwarted the development of a strong Democratic party in California long after the economic crisis of the 1930s had given the Democrats a clear edge in voter registration (Burke 1953). Progressive Republicans such as Governor Earl Warren (1943–1954, later Chief Justice of the U.S. Supreme Court) could attract widespread support by promising to administer national Democratic social welfare programs efficiently without creating a Democratic "machine" or disrupting the partisan status quo.

California's partisan politics became more competitive and more ideologically polarized in the 1950s. As progressives such as Warren passed from the scene, conservatives became unbeatable in most Republican primaries, thereby improving the liberal Democrats' chances for victory before the progressive California general election electorate, at least until recently. But this belated ebbing of the progressive tide came too late to change the habits of California's mid-twentieth century political activists.

California voters choose party nominees in direct primaries open to any voter registering as a "member" of that party thirty days before the election. As a result of this flexibility, party leaders and organizations can do little to affect the composition of the primary electorate. Even though a U.S. Supreme Court decision freed state parties from legislation dictating the composition of the primary electorate (*Tashjian v. Republican Party of Connecticut*, 1986), there has been no effort on the part of California party leaders to seize the initiative in this area. Indeed, in 1996, the voters of the state endorsed Proposition 198, which instituted a blanket primary. In a blanket primary, voters of either party can vote for a candidate seeking the Republican **or** Democratic nomination (but not for both) for any office on the ballot. This scheme, opposed by the leaders of both parties, destroys the entire notion of a primary election as gathering, however impersonally, the party faithful. Proposition 198 was later invalidated by the courts.

Supporters of reform came back with another attempt in the form of Proposition 14 passed in 2010 that created what is known as a "top two" system. In this system, parties do not nominate candidates through the traditional primary system for offices other than president and a few party organizational offices such as Party Central Committee members. For all other offices, all potential candidates from all major and minor parties will compete in the first round of balloting. The top two vote recipients—regardless of party—advance to the general election. Reformers hope that this will create situations for more moderate officeholders. Opponents are expected to challenge the new law in court as well.

Likewise, state law for many years expressly forbade state party leaders and organizations from endorsing candidates in primaries or contributing money to their campaigns. These strictures deprived California political parties of several of their major functions: the recruitment of new candidates, the management of campaigns and the balancing of a party ticket along class, ethnic, factional and regional lines. In 1988, the U.S. Supreme Court struck down California's prohibition against party endorsements (*Eu v. SF Demo. Comm.*). The Democratic Party has exercised its option to endorse candidates. But the Republican leadership, as a study of Orange County Republican officials many years ago had predicted (Berg 1980), preferred to continue operating as small, informal cliques of influential private individuals. The classic progressive tradition dies hard in contemporary California.

Other legal restrictions deny party leaders in California access to political patronage, those government jobs and other perquisites that often are necessary to the maintenance of strong political organizations. Civil service is extensive, and the vast bulk of state employees have little personal financial stake in the outcome of elections. A 1990 U.S. Supreme Court decision (*Rutan v. Republican Party of Illinois*) apparently has nationalized California's progressive outlook on patronage, a practice that appeared already to have been headed for extinction (Katz 1991).

Indeed, large numbers of elected offices stand completely outside the partisan arena. All local elected officials in California are chosen on a non-partisan basis. A mere handful of states go as far as California in carrying out the traditional American ideal of "taking party politics (or, at least, party labels) out of government." The U.S. 9th Circuit Court of Appeals struck down California's prohibition against partisan endorsements of local candidates in *Renne v. Geary*, but the U.S. Supreme Court reversed that decision on procedural grounds (*Los Angeles Times* June 18, 1991).

Finally, the organizational structure required by law in California dooms the party to ineffectiveness. Precinct "captains" and conventions, even county conventions, simply do not exist in California, as they do in many other states. As a result, extra-party clubs, campaign management firms, and interest groups perform many of the linkage functions that might be fulfilled by the party, in California and, increasingly throughout the nation.

Traditional Partisanship versus Post-Partisanship

There has been much talk recently in California about a *post-partisan* era. Former Governor Schwarzenegger who won election under unusual circumstances during the 2003 Recall election tried to position himself as a politician that rejects traditional labeling of political parties and governs from the middle. In his second Inaugural Address, Governor Schwarzenegger presented his vision of a post-partisan California when he said, "At one time, the greatest public policy innovations came from the liberals, such as during the New Deal. Then the most innovative ideas came from the conservatives such as Ronald Reagan. It is time that we combined the best of both ideologies into a new creative center" (Office of the Governor 2007). The Governor went on to present an image of California politics that was essentially centrist and argued for California government to forward such a centrist policy agenda. Furthermore, the Governor argued for an approach to governing that brought the two parties together with a focus on California in its entirety instead of the more ideological parts of each party.

There were many assumptions and hopes built into the Governor's vision of a post-partisan era for California. First, it is assumed that California is a centrist state. In terms of self-identified ideological positioning, it is perhaps more accurate to say that there is no one dominant ideology. According to a survey by the Public Policy Institute of California conducted in December of 2007, the percentage of Californians who identified themselves as middle-of-the-road, liberal, or conservative were all within a few percentage points of each other (Baldassare 2007). Thirty-six percent of those surveyed identified as conservative or very conservative, 32 percent identified as middle-of-the-road, and 28 percent identified as liberal or very liberal.

In looking at these numbers, it is easy to see the strategy Governor Schwarzenegger was trying to employ. Since it is not possible for one ideological approach to obtain stable majority support, the post-partisan vision is one in which the direction of California politics is driven by the center in a way acceptable to the ideologues on each side. The alternative, as Schwarzenegger sees it, is a politics defined by whichever more ideological group makes a coalition with the center forcing the losing side into a defensive mode of obstructionism. Because of the structural barriers to majority rule in California discussed in other chapters (such as the two-thirds rule in the legislature), if a minority party can stay united in their desire to stop certain governmental actions it is next to impossible to overrule the will of the minority. The three-way stalemate between the self-described post-partisan governor, liberal legislative majority, and conservative legislative minority over the California budget is a perfect example.

Political Party Cohesion in California

Voters

Another problem in implementing a post-partisan vision is that neither California voters nor California's legislative branch truly fits with the post-partisan idea of centrist politicians. In fact, the 2010 elections suggest a different reality for parties in California. While most of the country turned to the Republican Party following two consecutive wave elections that favored the Democrats, in California Democrats swept the elections. The Democratic nominee won every statewide Constitutional office and Democrats maintained their sizable majorities in the State Legislature and with the U.S. House delegation. While it is true that the voters who do not identify with either political party can sway elections one way or another it has become very difficult for Republicans to win major elections in California. In addition, the partisan identifiers themselves reflect a highly polarized electorate (Baldassare 2007) and, thus, demonstrate a high amount of partisan cohesion among both Democrats and Republicans.

Political scientist Leon Epstein (1986) defines political parties as *"Any group, however, loosely organized, seeking to elect governmental officeholders under a given label."* There are several dimensions to this definition. First, there must be an identifiable group that generally must have some common goals for public policy. Second, this group can be viewed as a group of citizens voting for office, a group of candidates seeking office, or even a group of successful candidates making policy and preparing for their reelection. Third, there is reference to at least some basic level of organizational structure with the purpose of contesting and winning public offices.

In this section, we examine the first two of these components by looking at the cohesiveness of California political parties. Does knowing an individual's partisan affiliation tell us something substantive about the political positions of the individual? Individual people may be Democrats, Republicans, Greens, or a member of any number of even smaller parties for a variety of reasons. Few individuals agree with every policy any one political party promotes and instead base their party affiliation on whatever issue they believe is most important or even nonissue related concerns like family tradition (to some degree partisanship is inherited), influence of peers, or even the appeal of charismatic leaders.

Even with some variation of beliefs within the political parties, in California Republican and Democratic identifiers are comprised of groups that differ demographically, geographically, and ideologically. Demographically, California Republicans and Democrats follow similar patterns to the composition of the national party coalitions. According to research by the Public Policy Institute of California, Californians follow the same pattern as the national parties in that women are more likely to identify as Democrats while men are more likely to identify as Republicans (Baldassare 2007). Furthermore, ethnic minorities make up a larger percentage of Democratic Party identifiers then are found among Republican Party identifiers.

These demographic differences are reflected in policy preferences. The same report found that Democrats were much more likely to be in favor of more taxes versus cuts in social programs, in favor of gay marriage, and to believe that immigration is a net benefit instead of a net burden for Californians. Fundamental differences on social and economic policy issues by Democrats and Republicans create a difficult hurdle for those who advocate a post-partisan California. Even if the "typical" California voter is more centrist, the options they are presented with tend to be chosen from the ranks of the partisans who participate in primaries. Therefore, the real policy differences between Republicans and Democrats are often difficult to overcome by moderates since their role in the system is often relegated to that of a referee who may determine which side happens to win a given political struggle. Political scientist Morris Fiorina describes this as a centrist public appearing to be polarized because they are forced to choose between two polarized options (2006). As we see the impacts of Proposition 14 reforms, we will see if the role for centrist voters remains marginalized.

Legislators

In our understanding of political parties however, the goal of a political party is to elect officeholders who will enact policy. Therefore, a more comprehensive

50 Political Parties in California

examination of the cohesiveness of contemporary parties should include what political scientist V.O. Key called *party in government*. In other words, how cohesive are the political parties in their legislative voting patterns on the issues faced by these officeholders. Political scientist Keith Poole collected data that allows us to examine this question by computing a score for members of Congress based upon their voting records for every two-year period. These scores range from −1 (most liberal) to +1 (most conservative). Using these scores we show partisan cohesion from 1991–2007 in Figure 1. This figure shows the distribution of ideological placement

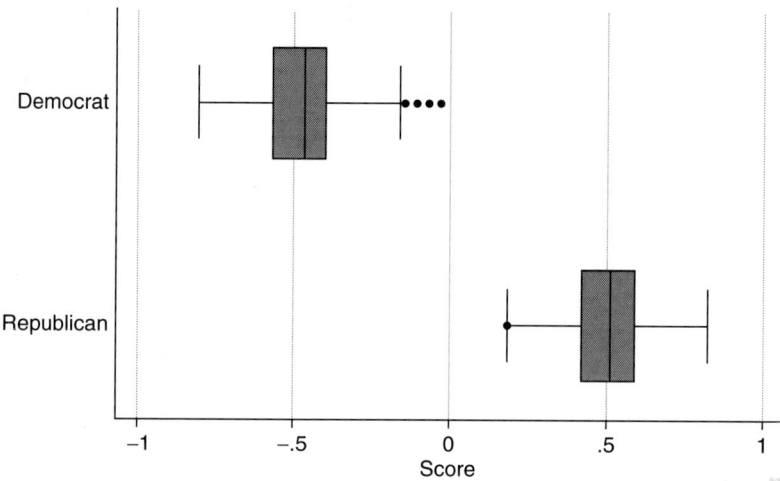

Figure 5.1A Ideological Cohesion among California's U.S. Congressional Delegation, 1991–2007

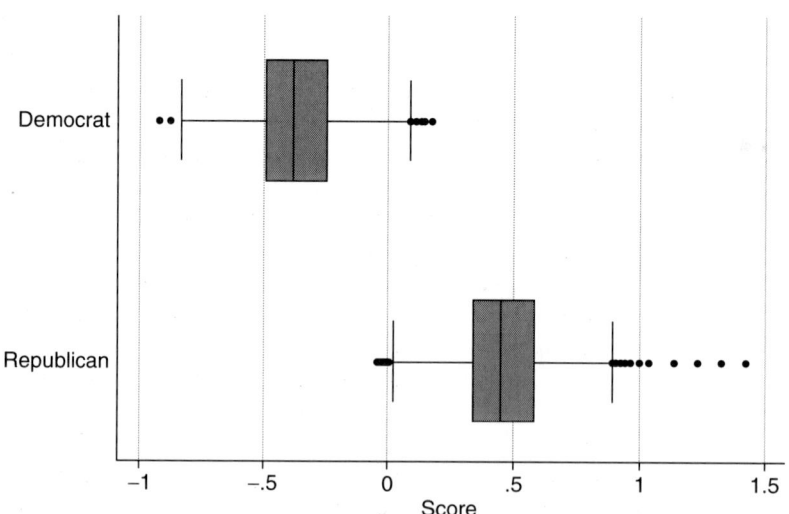

Figure 5.1B Ideological Cohesion among Non-Californian U.S. Congressional Delegation, 1991–2007

for every member of each party during that period. The top part of the figure shows this distribution for only the California congressional delegations during that time. The bottom figure shows the distribution for the other 49 states combined.

A quick examination of the figure suggests that although both parties are fairly cohesive with the Democrats staking out positions to the left of the Republicans, there are some differences between the California delegations and the rest of the country. California's delegations are a little more distinct with no overlap by the parties. Throughout the decade there is not a single Democrat or Republican from California who is further to right than any Republican. That is not true at the national level where there is some overlap among the conservative Democrats and liberal Republicans although greater polarization has been developing at the national level as well. What this suggests is that the California congressional delegation is more polarized than the rest of the country as a whole. This level of party cohesiveness is advantageous in that the parties do offer the voters distinct, consistent alternatives in public policy. However, it can be disadvantageous since the Congressional delegation does not seem to have anyone representing the ideologically moderate positions favored by many voters. Therefore, if California is ever to reach the post-partisan vision that Governor Schwarzenegger envisioned, we have a long way to go.

Trends in Party Structure and Tactics

As mentioned earlier in the chapter, California's political parties developed in a decidedly anti-party political environment. Dating back to the Progressive era, many reforms have been passed to try to weaken the power of political parties in California. As seen in the previous section, the end result for California's congressional delegation is still a polarized and cohesive party. Therefore, somewhere along the process parties must have some strength to forward an agenda. That strength cannot be found, however, in the classic understanding of organization. In fact, party organization in California is so weak that one of the classic distinctions in political party analysis, the division between temporary institutions (e.g., conventions) and permanent organizations (e.g., central committees) is insignificant.

By state law, the state party conventions are the only "temporary" party structures in the entire state. There are no precinct or county conventions to form the classic "pyramid of participation" in which local activists gather at their voting precincts, pass resolutions and elect delegates to the county convention who, in turn, pass resolutions and select delegates to the state convention. No one votes for the California parties' state convention "delegates" as such: all party nominees for state executive offices, state legislature and Congress (plus a few other party officials at the Republican convention) constitute the state convention.

These *ex officio* delegates, delegates by virtue of holding some other office, write a meaningless party platform in August of every gubernatorial election year. In presidential election years the state convention also has the duty of selecting the party's nominees for presidential electors. The method of selecting the state convention and its duties are so routine as to doom it to insignificance and isolation.

The County Central Committee is the only party organ that the party voters elect. Americans from the East and South are astounded by the absence of *any* precinct level party organization in California. Even here, interest among all but a handful of activists is minimal.

The State Election Code places fewer restrictions on the campaign activities of the County Central Committee than on other party organs. The committee may financially assist local candidates and may exercise considerable discretion in deciding where to allocate it money. But the committees cannot determine the outcomes of the party primary elections, and, therefore, often cannot hope to compete with the personal campaign organizations of the candidates. Only the death of a party nominee gives the county committee a limited sort of control over candidate recruitment. In that event, the committee bears the legal responsibility for choosing a new party standard bearer.

The State Central Committee consists of an ex officio membership prescribed by each party's by-laws. The state committees are so disorganized and underfinanced that they play little campaign role outside a few closely contested legislative races.

Substitutes for Parties

Organizational Substitutes: Extra-party Groups

Political activists in California have circumvented the weak and overly-regulated formal party structure with extra-party groups that can operate outside the law and at least attempt to perform traditional party functions like recruiting candidates, financing campaigns and formulating policy programs.

The oldest of these extra-party groups is the California Republican Assembly (CRA). Progressive Republicans organized the CRA in the 1930s, and the group can claim much of the credit for the survival of California progressive Republicanism into the 1950s. Not bound by the state regulations on party organizations, the CRA's local and statewide committees provided funding, expertise and a prestigious endorsement for Republican moderates facing primary opposition.

As the California Republican party moved to the right, so did the CRA. But this conservative movement was not rapid enough for many of the right-wing enthusiasts who flocked to Republican presidential nominee Barry Goldwater's banner in 1964. In that year, the rightists formed the United Republicans of California (UROC), whose endorsements and financing have since gone to the most strident variety of conservative candidate. As an organization attempting to force an expanding Republican party even further to the right than it already is, UROC faces a bleak future.

The same year UROC was founded; moderate Republicans formed the California Republican League (CRL). But the CRL has utterly failed to stop the rightward drift of the California Republican Party. In California, as elsewhere, moderate Republicanism seems a spent force. The CRL has adjusted, maintaining its influence by embracing the candidacies of more pragmatic conservatives such Pete Wilson and John Seymour.

The Democratic Party has never experienced a strong extra-party group to compare with the Republicans' CRA. The closest the Democrats have come is the California Democratic Council (CDC). Liberal Democrats, inspired by the presidential campaign of Adlai Stevenson, organized CDC in 1953. CDC was a more mass-based organization than its Republican counterparts, working through large conventions rather than selection committees. The CDC was undoubtedly important to the Democrats' revival in the late 1950's. But, in the 1960's, the CDC fell victim to the social and political divisions of the Vietnam era. Speaker of the Assembly Jesse Unruh tried to form a more moderate group, the Democratic Volunteers Committee (DVC). This newer extra-party group failed to establish itself, while the CDC's importance has waned. (Stone, 1991)

All the extra-party groups display a middle-class ideological fervor that isolates them from mainstream political power. Given this perspective, they are much more inclined to debate issues and to support the hopeless candidacies of "true believers" than to "pick winners" in the primaries. This tendency does not render the groups meaningless, but it does serve to limit their effectiveness as organizational substitutes for the political party.

Electoral Substitutes: Campaign Management Firms

California, with its weak parties and proximity to Hollywood, pioneered the use of public relations firms in the management of campaigns. The oldest campaign management firm in the nation, Whitaker and Baxter, got its start in California in 1933. Other famous California public relations firms involved in political campaigns include Baus and Ross, Spencer-Roberts, Cerrell and Associates, and Butcher-Forde, the Orange County experts in the last-minute campaign mail blitz.

Until the early 1960s, public relations firms were the "secret weapons" of a few sophisticated and well-heeled candidates. Today, nearly everyone employs them. Campaign management firms, as they are more commonly called today, may produce media advertisements, provide dramatic coaching for the candidate, poll voters, fabricate "issue positions" likely to resonate the popular attitudes the polls uncover, and schedule campaign stops.

The rise of the campaign management firms has bid up the cost of campaigning, making candidates all the more dependent upon large financial contributions. Moreover, the merchandising approach to politics has rendered obsolete old-style neighborhood political organization, the military approach to campaigning (Baer and Bositis 1988). Finally, candidates elected through the efforts of a campaign management firm owe the image makers nothing but money. The firm imposes no programmatic discipline on the newly-elected official. The disorganized voters reached via the media are in no position to demand anything of the candidate. Only the interest groups that paid for the advertising are able to exert any pressure in a politics of media campaigning.

Electronic Substitutes: Internet Based Grassroots

The newest trend in political parties in California is something that swept the country after people realized the political advantage to using something created right here in California. The information and electronic era brought forward—in part—by the success and creativity of Silicon Valley, slowly worked its way into the political scene.

At first, parties and campaigns used the Internet as an electronic version of the brochures they would produce and hang on people's doors. Now, throughout the country and in California political parties are finding ways to organize through building a small group dynamic for large groups of Californians. Political scientist Mancur Olson argued that one of the problems with effective group formation was that it was easy for individual members to avoid participating within large groups (1971). One way to overcome this *free-rider* problem was to form small groups within the larger organization. People had a stronger sense of identity to the small group and experiences direct peer pressure to maintain activity with the organization.

For groups as large as the California Republican and Democratic parties, using the internet to coordinate and promote small, specialized groups within the parties is an effective way to mobilize supporters and avoid losing the contributions of talent, money, and time that these people could give to the party. If you go to either party's web-site (*www.cagop.org* and *www.cadem.org*), you can easily find links to either county or local clubs for each party. Some of these clubs are identified by geography such as the Laguna Beach Democratic Club or the Irvine Republican Council. Other clubs identify particular constituent groups or interests within an organization such as the Rush Limbaugh Club of Southern Orange County or the Vietnamese American Democratic Club of Orange County. By being able to bring together a collection of small, niche groups throughout the state, the Internet has helped the parties build stronger resource bases. Much was written about the record sums of money that then-presidential candidate Barack Obama raised from small donations. The next step is to see if this technological approach to creating an effective small group dynamic can be applied to state political parties as well. As with many political trends and technological trends, California is often on the leading edge of this innovation and will be worth observing over the next few years for clues to its use.

Political Parties and the Future

California's political parties are less distinctively disorganized than they were forty years ago, but as noted the understanding of party organization is undergoing a change with the inclusion of new technologies. During the Clinton years, the national Democrats made great strides toward imitating the Republican organizational build-up of the 1980s. In the Bush years, the Republicans have taken steps to build stronger local organizations, even if they are evolving toward little more than administrative offices of the national party or outposts of strong Republican-oriented interest groups such as Christian conservatives or gun enthusiasts. The next step for party development may emerge as a result of the movement that led to President Obama's rise. As the core of the party decentralizes as a result of Internet based groups forming, parties can become more of a service organization to groups that wish to form. Political parties can help encourage small groups of like minded individuals to form and develop partnerships with them to help direct fundraising, find new talent for candidate recruitment purposes, and even as a way to generate new ideas that rise through the existing party organization to impact party direction and policy proposals. Even then, California's progressive legacy of legal restrictions and political independence will make it difficult to impose strong party organization upon the voters and political activists of the Golden State. Knowing this, political parties may find a way to incorporate the greater decentralization of the party in the electorate by using the ease of small group formation to help reinvigorate these organizations.

Chapter 6
CALIFORNIA INTEREST GROUPS
By Bert C. Buzan and Stephen J. Stambough

Introduction: The Nature and Importance of Interest Groups

At their core, interest groups are simply groups of individuals united to pursue a common political agenda. The group can be as stable, traditional, and organized as established business and labor interest groups which are constantly active or as seemingly non-political as a number of Elvis fan clubs who lobbied for an Elvis postage stamp in the early 1990s. Even though political rhetoric often paints interest groups in a negative light as Governor Schwarzenegger often does in his speeches, interest groups are a natural part of human behavior. The conflict in the view of interest groups has been well-documented by a number of scholars. Rozell and Wilcox (1999) show that although a majority of the public believes that government is run by a few powerful interest groups and that the public views interest groups as a threat to democracy, most Americans also say that they belong to an interest group. In this chapter we will explore the role, activities, laws, and trends related to interest group activity within California.

Why Study Interest Groups?

Interest groups gather together persons who share at least one need or goal, and who seek to influence policy-makers to act favorably. In this, interest groups may be similar to political parties, which also gather like-minded people together in order to achieve public policy goals. Political parties, however, seek to win and hold government offices. Interest groups do not, and this is a critical difference between them. As a result, interest groups need have no sense of accountability to the public at large.

Not being accountable at election time, interest groups are free to persuade policy-makers to act in ways that are apparently contrary to the general run of public opinion. For example, surveys for many years have consistently showed a majority of Americans in favor of stronger regulation and control over handguns, but one interest group—the National Rifle Association, representing a relatively small number of citizens who intensely oppose gun control in any form other than a "steady aim", has successfully blocked popular proposals for gun control at every level of government.

One useful criterion for understanding the varying effectiveness of different groups is to talk about the differences in the resources they possess. Resources include the size of the group and its number of members, the amount of money at its disposal, its level of organization and the skills and experience of its principal spokespersons. All of these resources combine to help interest groups attain their goals of gaining access to authorities, the ones making policy decisions which affect the group.

Another variable, focus, is most crucial in assessing interest group effectiveness at influencing policy. The most effective interest groups focus narrowly and sharply on a few issues that are of the utmost importance to the group itself (Olson, 1965). In the short run, the vast middle class majority may not possess enough cohesion to perceive any stake for itself in a given issue before the legislature. Even larger, more broadly representative interest groups such as the AFL-CIO, the Chamber of Commerce, Common Cause, or the Sierra Club cannot hope, usually, to match the effectiveness of narrower groups, particularly if the latter are well-financed. These large groups, with their diverse memberships and broad agendas, find themselves ensnared in so many disputes that they cannot engage in any one of them with maximum effectiveness. A business trade association, on the other hand, will single-mindedly pursue such an issue with a highly organized professional staff of interest group representatives known as *lobbyists*.

In summary, groups press their points of view to make new policy and also to prevent the making of new policy. In doing so, interest groups are so central to political processes that one cannot understand politics without understanding something about interest groups.

Interest Groups in the California Environment

Concern about special interests being contrary to the public good is as old as America itself. Writing in *The Federalist,* Number 10 (1787), James Madison warned of the dangers of "factions."

> The regulation of these various and interfering interests forms the principal task of modern legislation, and involves the spirit of party and faction in the necessary and ordinary operations of the government.

In the control of interest groups, as in so many other areas of life, California's greatest asset has always been its diversity. California is not exclusively dependent on either agriculture or industry. It is not as desperate to attract business as are formerly-impoverished Southern states, nor has organized labor dominated as in many areas of the East, nor does any extractive industry dominate, like oil in Louisiana or coal in West Virginia. If the power vacuum created by the Progressives' destruction of the parties resulted in strong California interest groups, at least no single interest group has ever dominated the Golden State in modern times.

Progressivism in California

The California "solution" to the problem of factions and parties is also a result of the "Progressive" movements that occurred in many Western states around the turn of the 20th century. A coalition of middle-class reformers, the *Progressives*, sought to eliminate what they saw as the corrupting influence of "special interests" on California politics. The Progressives were not radicals. They believed that corporations and other private interests had a right to prosper and to petition the legislature. Thus, a direct attack on "the interests" was out of the question.

The Progressives contented themselves with measures designed to weaken the strong political party organizations that "the interests" allegedly controlled with their money, contacts and favors (McConnell, 1966). They regulated political party activities, and denied party organizations control over government jobs. Loose coalitions of middle class reform groups superseded party campaign organizations. Direct citizen participation in party primary elections replaced conventions as the means of nominating party candidates. Civil servants replaced party "hacks" on the government payroll. Local officials were elected on a nonpartisan ballot, and even the California legislature came under the control of bipartisan cliques.

The Progressives hoped to replace the hated party "machines" with a purer and more direct form of democracy, leading to the adoption of such direct democracy techniques as the initiative, the referendum, and the recall (see Chapter 4). The Progressives could not predict that these tools—designed to permit more control by middle class voters—would instead become a mechanism for "special interest" electoral dominance in the later part of the century.

Progressive reformers dreamed of leading a morally outraged and perpetually aroused middle class in an endless crusade against "special interests". But as the middle class moral fervor of the pre-World War I period ebbed in the 1920s, the realities of political life shattered the Progressives' dream of America as a whole, but especially of California, as a moralistic middle class paradise. It now seems clear that the Progressives simply did not understand interest groups.

No potential group as large and diverse as the middle class can be organized into an effective interest group. The Progressives' dream of an aroused middle class majority competing as something like a "super-public interest" group turned out to be so much romantic fantasy: political parties, not interest groups, are the instruments that democracies have traditionally employed to mobilize great masses of citizens to greater levels of participation (Key, 1967). American reformers, in their zeal to "take the politics out" of government, virtually destroyed the party, until relatively recently, as a functioning organization in California. Interest groups, the province of well-organized and well-financed minorities, filled the vacuum created by the destruction of the party. It's a tale told in many states, but nowhere was this process of political disorganization more advanced than in California a generation ago. (For a discussion of California political parties, see Chapter 5.)

Hiram Johnson and the early California progressives, as noted, aimed at breaking the power of the railroads. Instead, they severely weakened the state's political parties. Indeed, the strength of California interest groups has long been an object of controversy in a state that prides itself on "clean government." One need not be obsessed with lurid, and all too often accurate, media reports of corrupt lobbying practices to be concerned about interest group influence. Even when they deal with the most upright public servants, interest groups distort the policy-making process. Interest groups, unlike elected officials, do not assume responsibility for the entire conduct of government. That is not their purpose. They exist to further narrow and specific interests, not a broad public policy program of the sort political parties—at their best—put forward and enact. Citizens cannot expect a collection of interest group demands to add up to the public interest. Nor can the electorate vote an interest group out of office for failing to serve the needs of the public. This missing element of political accountability is the main reason political scientists tend to favor the influence of party leaders over that of interest groups in the political process.

Through much of the state's history, California's weak parties invited a strong interest group influence over the state's policymaking process. Indeed, California during the 1930s and 1940s even had a lobbyist, a person hired to represent interest groups in Sacramento, as a "secret boss." His name was Arthur Samish, and even the governor of the state, Earl Warren, admitted that Samish had more influence in the legislature than he, at least on issues affecting Samish's clients (Samish and Thomas 1959).

Arthur Samish performed many of the functions of a political party. He collected funds for a great number of otherwise unrelated clients. He used the funds to help elect state legislators, often Republicans of the progressive stripe. When Samish's corporate clients urgently needed a bill passed, Samish cashed in his electoral chips. Otherwise, the befriended legislator was free to vote his personal or constituency interests. Samish shunned the spotlight and did not meddle in affairs that did not concern his clients. But his influence eventually made him a media celebrity. When Samish's antics became a national scandal, he could not account for the million of dollars he had so liberally dispensed, and he retired to the federal penitentiary (Velie, 1949a; 1949b). With that, California began its first serious effort to control lobbying by requiring spending reports from those seeking to influence public policy.

California Interest Groups and the Legislative Parties

In the 1950s, legislative power began to gravitate from the interest groups to the party leaders in the legislature, particularly Assembly Speaker Jess Unruh. "Money is the mother's milk of politics" was Unruh's motto, and he and his successors enlisted the lobbyists as party campaign fundraisers and eventually displaced them distributors. This sizable campaign treasure chest enabled the Speaker to impose a measure of discipline within the majority party, and the minority party found counter-organization a necessity. As a paradoxical result,

California, traditional home of weak parties, became a national exemplar of strong legislative party organization.

Willie Brown, Assembly Speaker from 1981 to 1995, continued the Unruh tradition of raising and distributing campaign funds with an eye toward enhancing legislative party discipline. By raising money from interest groups himself, then distributing them to Democrats on the basis of their needs, strategic importance, and adherence to the party program, Speaker Brown adapted the governmental party to the dominant institution of politics, the interest group.

As a result of this new union between interest groups and legislative parties, the Democratic legislative majority has not been capable of formulating a coherent party program on key issues, such as insurance reform. This was because the party leadership, to put it simply, took money from both sides! This pattern has continued beyond the Brown years, as the fragmentation and deadlock characteristic of interest group politics was exacerbated by the ever-increasing budgetary shortfalls that continued after Proposition 13.

Brown and Unruh's successes in adapting the governmental party to interest group politics have attracted imitators in the Senate and on the Republican side of both legislative houses. When a Republican Speaker, Curt Pringle, briefly held the leadership reins after Brown's departure, he continued the fundraising and distributing practices his Democratic predecessors pioneered, as have subsequent legislative leaders in both parties.

The Most Effective Groups in California Politics

The effectiveness of a group attempting to lobby policy-makers is dependent upon a number of factors. These include a narrow focus (see above) and available resources that include money, grass-roots membership, the skill and expertise of trained legislative advocates (another term for lobbyists), timing, and of course, the nature of the issue itself. Moreover, lobbyists have always been most effective when they wish to block a proposed action. Something like the law of inertia operates in politics to the benefit or those arguing against risky movement and painful change. Lobbyists who engage in negative action—preventing a proposed policy—rather than positive goals—attempting to initiate change—are in a better position to influence cautious decision-makers.

California lobbyists are highly professionalized, often with advanced educational degrees, competent staffs and well-run offices (Briscoe and Bell, 1986). The most successful lobbyists in California are those representing real estate interests (The California Association of Realtors), the alcoholic beverage industry, horse-racing interests, the health industry (including both organizations of medical personnel and hospital associations), insurance industry, and governmental agencies including associations representing cities, counties and governmental employees, particularly public school teachers (the California Teachers Association). Many of these groups are affiliates of national organizations (the AFL-CIO, manufacturers associations, and financial institutions).

After major political reforms were instituted in California (see below), a number of "public interest" groups have also emerged to counter the more narrow, economic interests of special areas such as insurance and real estate. Some of these groups devote themselves to governmental reform—the League of Women Voters, Common Cause—and others specialize in changing economic regulation—Consumer's Union, Taxpayers' Association. More narrowly focused groups, concentrating on specific issues such as the environment (Friends of the River, Sierra Club), or insurance (Proposition 103 Enforcement Project) are as likely to battle governmental agencies as they are to attempt influence on the legislature. Furthermore, recent reforms emerging from the initiative process continue to put more power in the hands of these groups at the same time as they weaken political parties even further.

Reforms in California and the Nation

Interest groups pursue all the available political processes to influence the outcome of public policy in their favor. They draft model legislation that they hope will be introduced by legislators and become law. They bring cases before the courts to obtain judicial relief and influence precedent. They work with governmental agencies to affect the regulatory process and ease administrative control over their enterprises. All these are considered the legitimate exercise of First Amendment protections of the "right to petition for redress of grievances."

The most controversial aspect of interest group participation in politics, however, has long been their involvement in the campaign and electoral processes. Political action committees (PACs) are, for many prospective and current legislators, the largest source of campaign contributions. As campaign costs have escalated with increasing dependence on expensive media—particularly television—exposure, the ability to attract substantial contributions becomes an overwhelming concern for potential office holders. Attempts to regulate interest group involvement, at both the national and state levels, have resulted in the unintended consequence of actually shifting more power into the hands (and pocketbooks) of interest groups.

The California Secretary of State reports that more than $300,000,000 is spent every two years to "educate policy makers and influence decisions that affect all Californians". One explanation for the growth in PACs and lobby groups lies in the growth of state government itself. As Richard Ziegler (1986, 71) points out,

> [There is] increased recognition that decisions made by the state—in the Legislature and in a myriad of state agencies—have substantial impacts on a growing number of businesses and professions. Even other government agencies now find the need for a Sacramento advocate to protect their share of the state's largesse.

Federal Reforms under the Federal Constitution

Political reform at the Federal level began in 1971 when Congress passed the Federal Election Campaign Act. The Act established the Federal Election Commission (FEC) and, for the first time, permitted corporations as well as labor unions the right to establish political action committees using corporate and union resources to underwrite the cost of raising and distributing money to political campaigns. While labor unions had always sponsored political activities—the American Federation of Labor-Congress of Industrial Organizations Committee on Political Education (COPE) had been a major supporter primarily of the Democratic Party—the Act represented an official blessing for corporations to become politically active.

The Act was amended in 1974 at the same time that Congress implemented public financing of presidential elections, and amended again in 1976 and 1979. The provisions of the Act allowed individuals to contribute a maximum of $1,000 to any single candidate for each election (primary, run-off, general) in any given year and a maximum of $25,000 to all candidates. Political groups (with the exception of the political parties) are limited to $5,000 per candidate per election as long as they contribute to at least five (federal) candidates each year. No maximum total expenditure is stipulated for PACs. In addition, stringent disclosure regulations were established to force political candidates to declare both their campaign donations and expenditures. Donors contributing more than $200 in a calendar year must reveal their names and professions, and no cash contributions larger than $100 are permitted at all.

The United States Supreme Court severely weakened the 1974 act and dealt a debilitating blow to campaign finance reform in the future in its (in)famous *Buckley v. Valeo* decision in 1976. At a philosophical level, limits on campaign spending were deemed to be regulations of the political **content** of speech itself, rather than mere regulations of the *manner* in which speech takes place. In more practical terms this meant that there could be no regulation of spending by (rich) candidates themselves and none on the spending of groups supposedly "independent" of the candidates and parties themselves.

Recently, the McCain-Feingold campaign finance reform bill attempted to restrict the influence of large money in politics. The legislation increased the amounts for contributions to candidates, but tried placing restrictions on large money donations to parties and for use in independent expenditure campaigns directly by individuals and interest groups. Instead, the reforms opened up a loophole called "527" named after the relevant tax code. In the 2004 election cycle, 527 organizations were incredibly influential with liberal groups like Moveon.org and conservative groups like the Club for Growth and Swift Boat Veterans playing important roles and spending millions of dollars during the election cycle.

Many thought the U.S. Supreme Court would strike down McCain-Feingold. It did not, upholding the law in *McConnell v. FEC* (2003). But proponents of meaningful campaign finance reform should not feel too relieved by the Court's rationale in *McConnell*. The Court upheld the act as a largely symbolic form of political expression on the part of the Congress, seen as attempting to prevent the "appearance", but presumably not the reality, of corruption. A member of the narrow majority upholding the act went out of his way to point out that regulating campaign spending was simply impossible. The Court, in short, seemed to say that *McCain-Feingold* did not restrict free speech because it was ineffectual on its face!

Finally, in 2010 the Supreme Court struck down much of the campaign reform movement in the *Citizens United v. Federal Election Commission* case. In this case, the Court ruled that past efforts to restrict corporate money in candidate elections was an unconstitutional violation of the 1st Amendment protections of free speech. This 5-4 decision was very controversial and even led to a high profile moment during the State of the Union speech when Justice Samuel Alito was caught in a breach of etiquette by signaling displeasure with President Obama's remarks about the case. Tradition held that members of the Court never publicly took sides in political discussions, especially at the State of the Union address. Like decades of court precedent, that tradition was a casualty of the *Citizens United* case.

California Reforms

Public ambivalence and a pervasive sense of futility about political reform in California are clearly reflected in the initiative and legislative history. Voters passed major reforms in 1974, 1990, and 1996, and in 2000, repealed much of what they had established in 1996. The major initiatives that have been passed by California voters include Proposition 9 (1974), Proposition 73 (1988), Proposition 140 (1990), Proposition 208 (1996) and Proposition 34 (2000). In between elections, voters have watched the courts overturn several reforms.

Proposition 9 established the Fair Political Practices Commission (FPPC) to enforce a broad array of political and campaign reforms. These provisions are set out generally in Table 6.1, below. In the 1988 primary, two campaign reform proposals were passed by the voters, Proposition 68, sponsored by Common Cause and Proposition 73 sponsored by elected officials of both parties. Since Proposition 73 outpolled Proposition 68, its provisions prevailed where the two were in conflict. Proposition 73 would have implemented much stricter campaign limitations from PACs (limited to $2,500 per candidate per year) and individuals ($1,000 per candidate per year), banned transfers between candidates and limited expenditures on the part of political parties as well. Additionally, it expressly prohibited public financing of campaigns. In 1990, the California Supreme Court, citing *Buckley* as precedent, overturned most of Proposition 73.

The 1996 election again found dueling propositions on the ballot. Proposition 208, which gathered more votes than Proposition 212, promised some serious reform, including stringent limits on contributions ($500 for statewide candidates; $250 for legislative races) and limited spending by political parties. Sponsored by Common Cause, it out-polled Proposition 212 that was backed by the California Public Interest Research Group (a Ralph Nader off-shoot). California legislators, faced with the possibility that the strict limits imposed by Proposition 208 might be upheld by the courts, placed Proposition 34 on the November, 2000 ballot.

Proposition 34 repeals much of Proposition 208. Voters may want reform, and may have thought they were voting for reform, but they undid the strict limitations on campaign spending they had authorized just four years before. Proposition 34 replaces Proposition 208's strict limits with much more generous amounts. It repeals

Table 6.1 Comparison of California Political Reforms

Type of Regulation	Proposition 9	Proposition 34
Establish regulatory commission	Fair Political Practices Commission	No change
Limits on contributions to candidates from individuals	No limits	$3,000/statewide candidates; $5,000 to statewide; $20,000 to governor
Limits on contributions from PACs and other groups	No limits	Repeals Prop. 208 limit of $25,000 to parties and candidates
Limits on total contributions	No limits	No limits
Disclosure	$100	Full disclosure required for $100
Loans	No limits	Restricted to $100,000 from candidate's own finances
Limits on spending	No limits	Voluntary limits, varies with race
Independent campaign organizations	Parties allowed to form such committees	No limits for political parties
Special provisions for small contributors	No special provisions	Limits doubled ($6,000 for legislators; $10,000 for statewide races)
Transfers	No restrictions	Transfers limited to $3,000 per candidate
Other provisions	Conflict of interest; lobbyist gifts limited	Increased penalties and disclosure requirements

the limits on political party contributions (so-called "soft money" expenditures), a major provision of 208. (A comparison of California's Propositions 9 and 34 is set out in Table 6.1).

The Effects of Political Reform: Money, Campaigns and Interest Groups

As a result of Propositions 9 and 140, public information about campaign contributions is now available (*http://cal-access.ss.ca.gov*). Likewise, there has been an enormous increase in registered lobbyists and PACs in the years following the passage of Proposition 9. More importantly, campaign contributions are now easily available from the Secretary of State's office. As mandated by the Legislature in 1997, all contributions are now reported electronically and made available over the Internet by the Secretary of State. The interested citizen will find PACs categorized by industry or interest affiliation and can track their campaign contributions and other expenditures.

Despite these reform efforts, contributions to political campaigns still constitute a major activity for California interest groups. If nothing else, interest groups contribute to campaigns because they believe it buys them access to legislators. A legislator may or may not vote on an issue the way a group wants, but few legislators will not listen to the plea of a significant campaign contributor.

The changing pattern of political contributions seemed to show that the organizations with the resources, usually business, labor and professional PACs, more recently conservative Christian groups, were providing the established political parties with a new tool for improving party solidarity and strength. If individual candidates were forced to rely upon the party for the distribution of election funds, the independent solicitation of PAC funds that characterized California politics always (but particularly since the Federal reforms of 1972-74) might become less significant than party sponsorship.

Things might have evolved differently if Proposition 34 had not repealed the provisions in 208 that would have limited both political party and candidate transfers of funds. Candidate transfers are now limited, but both propositions fail to limit independent expenditures made on behalf of candidates by parties or other interested groups. These are the "soft money" expenditures that are criticized by political reformers. As long as media advertisements or campaign brochures do not advocate the defeat of a candidate, organizations not technically affiliated with any candidate may spend without limit. This "loophole" in the law has profound consequences. David Townsend, a Democratic consultant who has run legislative campaigns, predicted one outcome:

> ... many interest groups that contributed large amounts to legislative and statewide candidates in past years now plan to wage their own campaigns on behalf of candidates.... There's a good chance that by the next election cycle, we'll [consultants] be working for independent expenditure committees rather than candidates." (Bernstein, 1997)

In short, reformers have been unsuccessful in their attempts to limit campaign spending. It is likely that no law imposing significant spending limits could be written that will conform to court guidelines. Any campaign finance law protecting the people from excessive interest group involvement in campaign finance would, somehow, at the same time, have to protect expenditures as a form of "free speech." while exempting "independent groups" and wealthy candidates from its spending provisions. Legislatures and the voters have improved reporting and disclosure requirements, created a watchdog agency, and imposed fines for campaign violations. An interested citizen is more able to track contributions to a candidate and public interest groups offer web sites that publish data about campaign contributions for all major races and ballot propositions. Other efforts to limit the influence of interest groups on elections, such as public financing of campaigns, are ideas whose time has not yet come.

Interest Group Politics in California

Much of what we know about interest group politics is California is borrowed from what we know about interest group politics in general. The types of groups are generally the same, the core functions are generally the same, and even the reasons why people join groups are generally the same. There are a few characteristics of the California political system which impact the way interest group politics operate within the state and differentiate it from other parts of the country. In this section, we explore the impact of two of the most important on California's interest groups: legislative term limits and direct democracy.

Legislative Term Limits

During the early 1990s, California joined most western states in adopting some form of legislative term limits. In 1990 California voters approved Proposition 140 to limit members to no more than six years in the State Assembly and eight years in the Senate. At the time, no one really knew what effect legislative term limits would have because no state had experienced the effects of legislative term limits. Since term limits were designed to alter the composition of the legislature: it was reasonable to believe that this alteration would have an effect on the use and balance of political power in Sacramento.

Since interest groups are rational actors, it is reasonable to expect that the interest group community would react to the new political environment with strategic changes suited towards the pursuit of their goals but reflective of the new institutional rules. Two political scientists (Gordon and Unmack 2003) examined interest group behavior in California in a post legislative term limits environment. Their study suggested that interest group behavior did change as a result of legislative term limits. They found that interest groups altered their patterns of campaign contributions.

While interest groups still based their donation decisions upon targeting their contributions towards positions of power, they acted as if the positions of power changed. In the pre-term limits era, money flowed to ranking members of important committees particularly committees overseeing the issues. In the post-term limits era, committee chair positions rotate quickly as membership rotates quickly. Therefore, a group is unable to establish a long-term political relationship with long tenured individuals who may serve on a committee for decades. Instead, it appears that the groups have changed their strategy and instead are basing their contributions upon political party affiliation and are using the party organization as a structure to guide their donations. These findings are consistent with findings in another study (Moncrief and Thompson 2001) which suggest that lobbyists believe power in post-term limits California shifted away from individual members and to permanent organizations like party, professional staff, and even the governor. Such activity may reinforce the trend towards greater party cohesion in the legislature.

Direct Democracy and Interest Groups

Like most of the western United States, California has a system of direct democracy (see Chapter 4). The progressive reformers believed, among other things, that direct democracy would provide a way for the citizens to thwart monopolistic control of governing by the entrenched special interests. Some recent commentators suggest that this progressive dream has been replaced with an initiative industry of high priced campaign firms hired by entrenched interest groups (Broder 2002).

However, an analysis of interest group use of the initiative process in California suggests a different conclusion (Donovan et al 1998). In their analysis of California general election initiatives from 1986-1996, the researchers found a substantial difference between the success rates of broad, diffuse interests and narrow special interests. The success rate for the initiatives pushed by broad and diffuse groups was much higher than the success rate for those measures sponsored by narrow, special interest groups. Only 14 percent of the measures supported by narrow groups passed while approximately 52 percent of those measures supported by broad, diffuse groups passed. These findings were preliminary but suggest that perhaps a certain type of interest group (narrow special interests) is disadvantaged while using the direct democracy system in California. Therefore, it is not surprising that these interest groups focus their energy on traditional lobbying and use of campaign contributions within the legislature itself.

These findings do not, however, suggest that interest groups—even narrow ones—avoid our system of direct democracy. In fact, some scholars have argued that California is in an era that can be described as *"Initiative-Centered Politics"* (McCuan and Stambough 2005). This new politics is in many western states but with California as the centerpiece. One part of initiative-centered politics is that there is an advantage to interest groups using the initiative process even if they are fairly certain they will lose on Election Day. Since politics is a repeated game, losing on Election Day is not viewed as the end of the process. Narrow groups also use the initiative process for many purposes other than passing a law. Some use it to help promote an agenda for long-term adjustments in public opinion. Some use it to demonstrate regional strength even in a statewide defeat in order to pressure regional legislators to support their agenda in the legislative process. Others employ a countermeasure strategy designed to confuse voters into not passing other, similar legislation. These strategies do not always work, but they provide an answer to why narrow interest groups continue to use the initiative process even with knowledge of the low success rate of such groups actually passing legislation directly by the voters.

Notes

This chapter is a revision of previous versions built upon contributions by Keith Boyum and Sandra Sutphen. We thank Keith and Sandra for their contributions.

Chapter 7
EXECUTIVE LEADERSHIP: THE GOVERNOR OF CALIFORNIA AND THE AMERICAN PRESIDENT[1]
Scott Spitzer

Introduction: Leadership in the United States and California

The California governor and the U.S. president have become synonymous with government leadership in their respective political systems. The similarities between them are many. Both are the centerpiece of the political process in their respective arenas, garner the majority of media attention, and are consequently our most visible political leaders. Each are elected, are limited to two four-year terms, and are checked by a bicameral representative legislature. Both are the chief agenda-setters in politics and policymaking. The issues that dominate the work of the Congress and the state legislature, and which are featured as the top stories of the day in the media, are most often initially their issues. Both dominate their respective budget processes: while they may not get all that they ask for, the tax and spending priorities are essentially first set by them, and then reacted to by the legislature and other political actors. Both are also chief administrators in charge of huge, sprawling sets of executive branch bureaucracies, and charged with appointing and managing the leaders of these bureaucracies. Finally, both have the power to appoint judges and huge numbers of executive branch administrators. Americans and Californians, however, are ambivalent about executive leadership. While we celebrate decisive and strong leadership from presidents and governors, we recoil at the idea of unlimited executive authority. Strong presidents and governors are lionized and revered: there is virtually unanimous praise reserved for the leadership from presidents Washington, Lincoln, and FDR; governors Hiram Johnson, Earl Warren and Pat Brown. But there is another side to this coin. Failed or corrupt presidents and governors receive strong repudiation from the public: consider the low approval ratings of President Nixon after 'Watergate', George W. Bush's low ratings

---

[1]This chapter is based on Vince Buck's chapter for previous editions of this volume. The section reviewing the powers of the various executive offices is drawn primarily from his ch. "The Governor and the Executive Branch," in J. Theodore Anagnoson et al., 2008, *Governing California in the Twenty-First Century* (New York: W.W. Norton), esp. pp. 111–113. I wish to thank Vince for his generosity in allowing me to draw liberally on his insightful work.

in the last months of his presidency, following a widely perceived failure of the military effort in Iraq, and in the midst of the worst economic crisis since the depression. Likewise, one need only refer back to the recent historic recall of Governor Gray Davis, or to the low approval ratings for Governor Schwarzenegger at the end of his second term for examples of the public's repudiation of unpopular governors.

It turns out that while the public's expectations of executive leadership are increasingly high, the punishment for failure is severe. As President Barack Obama heads into the third year of his presidency with the nation still struggling to overcome "the worst economic crisis since the depression,"[2] and as Governor Jerry Brown confronts a huge budget gap of $25 billion,[3] the demand for strong and effective executive leadership is even more intense, and the potential for failure ever more pronounced. How do we account for successful, effective presidents and governors? What factors produce effective leadership? What are the common reasons for failures? What resources can these elected executives draw upon to ensure that they succeed? The answers to these questions are difficult to come by, and political scientists and historians continue to plumb the historical record for answers. Here we can begin to assess the resources that each brings to their task, beginning with an examination of the similarities and the differences in their formal and informal powers, turning then to an assessment of the ways that their respective political environment, and individual leadership shape their success.

Formalizing Leadership: Executive Powers in the Nation and California

One of the great dilemmas that faced the founders of the nation, and the pioneers who chartered California's entry to the union as the 31st state, was how to provide for effective and strong leadership while protecting against the potential abuse of power. In both cases, there was a strong ambivalence towards executive power: on the one hand they feared unrestrained political power in the hands of a single man.[4]

---

[2]In the second presidential debate of 2008, Barack Obama said this in his opening statement. See *http://www.cnn.com/2008/POLITICS/10/07/presidential.debate.transcript/*, retrieved from the world wide web on February 15, 2009.

[3]This is almost 1/5 of the state's total projected expenditures in 2011-12: $127 billion. It comes on top of a much larger budget gap in 2009–10, of $60 billion. For state budget details, see the California Department of Finance website, at: *http://www.dof.ca.gov/budget.*

[4]While there are no formal prohibitions against women being President of the United States or Governor of California, there have been no women in either of these leadership positions as of 2011. Male pronouns are used throughout this chapter to reflect this history. It is worth noting that this is likely to change in the near term: In the 2008 Presidential election, Senator Hillary Clinton came very close to capturing the Democratic Party's nomination, and Governor Sarah Palin (R-Alaska) was the vice-presidential nominee for the Republican Party. Currently, moreover, there are six female governors in the U.S., leading Arizona, New Mexico, North Carolina, Oklahoma, South Carolina and Washington.

On the other hand, they also believed that the leadership of the nation or the state had to be lodged in an executive, not the legislature, and that strong executive leadership would be essential to the success of their nation and state. This ambivalence towards the executive was expressed in different ways in the national and state constitutions, and has evolved in both cases towards a far stronger executive than the original planners ever envisioned.

The constitutions of both the U.S. and California, as originally written, empowered their executives with broad grants of authority, while limiting them through a system of checks and balances (see Chapter 1). Still there are some important contrasts to take note of here: the Congress's checks on the president have been more serious than the limits that the state legislature has been able to place on the governor. A relatively weak state legislature has resulted in a stronger governor. At the same time, limits on the governor's powers come from two other places in California's political system. First, unlike the president who surrounds himself with his choice of the top executive branch leaders (his cabinet), the governor shares power with the leading executive officers, each of whom are independently elected in statewide elections. In addition, at the turn of the century, progressive reformers added a further check on the power of elected officials, by empowering the public directly. With the enactment in 1911 of the initiative, referendum and recall, the state's citizens were empowered to pass laws, amend the state constitution, and hold elected leaders accountable to the electorate before the end of their term *without* the involvement of elected officials (see Chapter 4). Still, neither of these checks has been strong enough to restrict the power of the governor relative to a fairly weak state legislature. In contrast, the presidents of the 19th century were largely restrained, with the exception of Washington, Jackson, and Lincoln. It was only with the presidency of Franklin D. Roosevelt, in response to the crises of the Great Depression and World War II, that the powers of the president were expanded to the point that we have become accustomed to today. As a result, the governor of California has been strong from the beginning of the state's history, while strong presidents have only become the norm in American politics since the 1930s.

What Are the Formal Powers of the Governor Exactly?

As the state's chief executive, the governor is charged with implementing the laws that are passed by the legislature or by citizen initiative. But there's more to his formal authority than simply this role. First, his formal powers can be understood best by taking a look at how they might be limited through the checks and balances designed in the Constitution. Beyond this, his formal authority can be divided into executive powers, legislative powers, and independent powers.

Checking and Balancing

The U.S. Constitution empowered the president with broad grants of authority, but limited him with checks and balances, chiefly coming from the Congress.

The governor is checked by the state legislature as well, but is limited further by independently elected executive officials—a *plural executive*.

We are all familiar with the separation of powers doctrine: the legislature—Congress and the state legislature both—pass laws which must be either signed into law by the president or governor, or vetoed. In both cases, their respective veto can be overridden by a 2/3 majority vote of the legislature. Beyond these more obvious checks and balances, it is worth noting that the President was not to be effectively checked by the power of the public. Presidents would not be directly elected: presidential elections emerged in the mid-19th century as an informal development. Not only would they not be elected by the public, they would also be singularly in charge of the nation's executive branch, checked only by the Senate, which would have to approve executive appointments and international treaties.

In California, by contrast, the state legislature was given a much weaker check on the Governor of California, especially in forging the state's budget (see below). By the 20th century, California's chief executive was seen by progressive reformers as an antidote to the political corruption in the state legislature. At the peak of their power nationally and in California, progressives elected Governor Hiram Johnson in 1911, and he led the state to institute a number of reforms designed to counter the dominance of big business (especially the railroads) and reduce the power of corrupt political parties, especially in the state legislature. Most importantly, Johnson led the charge to inaugurate the state's system of direct democracy—establishing the initiative, referendum, and recall. These instruments of direct democracy empower the state's citizens to make state laws, amend the state's constitution, and remove elected political leaders without the involvement of any elected official.[5] In California, the power of the public is strong, and acts as a check on the powers of the governor, as well as the state legislature.

On the other hand, while progressives wanted to empower the governor, especially as an instrument of reform and non-partisanship, they were cautious towards executive authority. California's progressives sought to check the power of the governor further, expanding the number of other independently elected executives. Currently, California's plural elected executive consists of seven additional state officials, all of whom are elected statewide: the Lieutenant Governor; Attorney General; Secretary of State; Controller; Treasurer; Superintendant of Public Instruction; and Insurance Commissioner. In addition to these seven, there are also four members of the Board of Equalization, elected in single-member districts.

This plural executive is a big contrast from the singular president, who appoints his own cabinet members with approval by a majority of the Senate, and many other top administrative officials on his own. In California, each of these

---

[5]Of course the Secretary of State and the Board of Elections would be involved in certifying initiatives, referenda, and recall petitions, in placing these items of the state's ballot, and in certifying the results. This is a neutral, administrative role, not one designed to influence the outcome in any way.

executives is elected independently, some may be from the opposition party to the governor, and frequently they have ambitions of their own to run for governor.

What follows is a short description of each of the offices in California's Plural Executive[6]:

The Lieutenant Governor (LG): The LG's purpose is to replace the governor if he becomes unable to govern. He also becomes the acting governor if the governor is out of the state, which can lead to some very interesting political shenanigans. Like the Vice President of the United States, he presides over the state Senate, breaking tie votes. Unlike the Vice President, he is elected independently of the Governor and is often from a different party.

The Attorney General (AG): The AG directs California's department of justice, which employs thousands, and which oversees law enforcement in the state. He or she oversees local district attorneys and county sheriffs; provides legal counsel to the state; defends the state in lawsuits; and sets the priorities for his powerful agency.

The Secretary of State: The Secretary runs the state's elections, publishes election pamphlets, certifies initiative petitions, and publishes the results of elections. He or she also oversees the records and archives of the state government.

The Controller: This is the chief fiscal officer for the state, and oversees the collection of taxes. The controller also sits on a large number of boards, including the Board of Equalization and Franchise Tax Board.

The Treasurer: This is not a powerful office. The Treasurer essentially manages the state's funds after they are collected but before they are spent—managing state investments and the sale of bonds.

The Superintendent of Public Instruction: This is the chief administrator of the Department of Education. The superintendent is elected on a nonpartisan basis (unlike the other statewide offices), and shares power with an appointed Board of Education and a Secretary of Education. The latter is appointed by the governor. These arrangements produce a great deal of confusion, controversy, and battles over education policy in the state.

The Insurance Commissioner: This is the only executive office established by citizen initiative (Proposition 103 in 1988). The commissioner regulates the insurance industry.

Board of Equalization: A four-member board elected in districts, overseeing the assessment and administration of property taxes, although most of this work is done at the county level. They also supervise collection and distribution of sales taxes and excise taxes.

---

[6]This section is based on Buck, 2008, "The Governor and the Executive Branch," pp. 111–113. See note 1.

Executive Leadership

Table 7.1 California's Executive Officers & their Vote Percentage in the 2010 Elections

Governor	Jerry Brown (D): 53.8% (5,417,731 votes)
Lieutenant Governor	Gavin Newsom (D): 50.2% (4,908,216 votes)
Attorney General	Kamala Harris (D): 46.1% (4,434,275 votes)
Controller	John Chiang (D): 55.2% (5,315,196 votes)
Treasurer	Bill Lockyer (D): 56.5% (5,423,219 votes)
Secretary of State	Debra Bowen (D): 53.2% (5,095,875 votes)
Superintendent of Public Instruction	Tom Torlakson (non-partisan): 54.7% (4,214,449 votes)
Insurance Commissioner	Dave Jones (D): 50.6% (4,756,969 votes)
Board of Equalization	Betty Yee (D) 1st District; George Runner(R) 2nd; Michelle Steel (R) 3rd; Jerome Horton (D) 4th

Other Formal Powers Legislative, Budgetary, Executive

Although the governor's powers are shared with the other elected executives, and although the state legislature also places limits on his authority, his power is still great. Aside from the power he draws from his visibility, and the size of the executive branch that he presides over, he has a number of formal powers which make him leader of the legislative process; leader in the budgetary process; and leader of the executive branch. Still, in each of these areas, the governor is limited by other elected officials, and by the constraints of contemporary political and economic circumstances.

Legislative powers:

The governor, much like the president, proposes the legislative agenda, usually outlining it in his annual "state-of-the-state" address. The governor sets out his administration's legislative priorities and calls on the state legislature to begin making his proposals into law. Governors have the power to call a special session of the legislature to address a specific issue, to veto legislation, and, in the case of spending bills (appropriations), the governor can veto or reduce single items in that bill without having to veto the entire piece of legislation. This is called the line-item budget veto, is perhaps the governor's most significant power, and is *not* available to the president. While President Clinton was given this power in 1996, in 1998 the Supreme Court declared the line item veto unconstitutional, as it gave the president legislative powers and therefore violated the constitutional separation of powers.

Budgetary Powers

The governor, like the president, proposes a budget. But unlike the president, the governor must present a balanced budget, which is required by the state's constitution. This is not quite as restrictive as it might seem, since it doesn't include bond indebtedness (the way the state borrows money). But, given the precarious budget situation that the state has faced since early 2009, it seems particularly relevant. The governor sends the legislature his budget by January 10, and revisions follow later in the spring (the May Revise), once there is a clearer sense of what the state's tax revenues will amount to, and how much the state's obligated spending will be.

Until 2010, the budget required a 2/3 majority vote in each house of the state legislature. Proposition 25 eliminated this requirement for spending measures, but not for taxes. In the past, once the legislature received the budget, the governor has had a major challenge in getting the required 2/3 majority in each house. This will become significantly easier for the new Governor Brown, but if he wants to combine tax increases with spending cuts to address the $25 billion budget gap he acknowledges in his 2011-12 proposed budget, he'll still need a 2/3 vote for those measures. This is another sharp contrast to the president, who needs only put together a simple majority to pass his budget bills, including tax increases as well as spending cuts. The 2/3 requirement for tax increases means that the governor not only has to get support from his own majority party – the Democrats: he'll also need the unlikely support of Republicans in the state legislature, who have been adamantly opposed to tax increases in the past couple of budget cycles.

Consequently, bargaining between Democrats and Republicans becomes necessary, which places more power in the governor's hands. He is the essential crafter of compromises that are necessary to forge the state's budget. His influence in the budget process is therefore greatly enhanced. One tool that significantly empowers the governor as he seeks to pressure the legislature to pass his budget is the line item veto. Once the legislature passes its budget, the governor can reduce any item, or remove any item completely, and then sign the changed budget into law. This line item veto, or its threatened use, is a most powerful tool of persuasion (see informal powers below). Governors use it regularly and threaten to use it even more often.

As the state struggles to close a yawning $25 billion budget gap in early 2011, the difficulty of bridging the divide between Democrats and Republicans in the state legislature has become particularly obvious, and the role of Governor Brown has become accentuated. In January of 2011, Governor Brown outlined his solution for the state's severe budgetary problems, including wide-ranging cuts in state spending, a "realignment" of local and state spending responsibilities that would reduce the state's spending obligations; and a series of one-time savings and borrowing measures. Moreover, in order to overcome the bitter partisanship that characterized Governor Schwarzenegger's budget negotiations among Democrats and Republicans in the state legislature, Governor Brown is proposing to put a set of ballot measures before the voters in June of 2011, whereby the state's citizens will be asked to approve the extension of temporary tax measures enacted in 2010 to close that year's budget gap.[7]

---

[7]"Governor's Message," "Introduction," and "Summary Charts," in *The Governor's Proposed Budget, 2011–12,* January 10, 2011. Department of Finance, California State Government at *http://www.ebudget.ca.gov*. Accessed on February 15, 2011.

Without the 2/3 requirement to raise taxes, the Democrats in the state legislature might be able to pass Brown's budget solutions without having to find a compromise acceptable to republican state legislators. Instead, Governor Brown is proposing to exploit the state's system of direct democracy to overcome the resistance of the opposition party. Brown recognizes that this is an unusual step to take: "This is not a time for politics as usual. The stakes are too high," he announced in his State of the State Address several weeks after introducing his proposed budget.[8] The fact that such an approach is essential, and very difficult to achieve, elevates Brown's role in this budget process, as he seeks to achieve a solution to the state's current and future budget problems.

The formal powers of the governor (the line item veto), and the formal requirements of the budgetary process (the 2/3 requirement for tax increases), act as limits on the governor's budgetary powers. His informal powers, however, are far more significant, and they act to expand his budgetary and political power (see below). The governor dominates the state's news media; he can appeal directly to the public through high profile speeches like his State of the State address; and he has a unique capacity to utilize the initiative process to pressure the state legislature to pass his budget proposal.

Executive Leadership

One more area of formal powers deserves discussion: the governor's leadership of the executive branch. Both the president and the governor head the executive branch of their respective governments. Both make appointments to top positions in executive agencies, the judiciary, and independent boards. Both have extensive staffs that help them manage the executive branch.

Over the course of his administration, a governor will appoint thousands of state employees. Like the president, who appoints the lead officials for each of the major federal departments—his cabinet secretaries—the governor appoints the secretaries of California's major agencies: business, transportation and housing; corrections and rehabilitation; environmental protection; food and agriculture; health and human services; labor and workforce development; natural resources; state and consumer services; veterans affairs; and emergency management. He also appoints the next level down – most of the department heads, such as the directors of the departments of aging; alcohol and drug programs; and of child support services. In addition, the governor appoints members to hundreds of independent boards and commissions, such as the Fair Political Practices Commission (FPPC), which regulates campaign finance. Many of the terms on these boards and commissions overlap the governor's 4-year term, and so no one governor will appoint all board and commission appointments. Like the president, who has to submit all of his political appointees for approval by the Senate, the governor must have the

---

[8]Governor Edmund G. Brown, "State of the State Address," January 31, 2011, full text at *http//gov.ca.gov/news.php?id=16897*. Accessed February 15, 2011.

state senate approve appointments to many of these high offices. Unlike the president, however, the governor must govern the executive branch with 7 other elected executive officials, as well as the elected Board of Equalization. This makes his ability to govern implementation of policies more complicated and politically challenging.

Summary of Formal Powers

In sum, the formal powers of the governor are significant. He sets the agenda for the legislative process, dominates the budget process by setting out a budget proposal for the legislature to react to, and by means of his powerful budget line item veto. In addition, the 2/3 majority requirement to pass the state budget ensures that the governor will be the leading broker of essential compromises between the majority and minority parties in the legislature. The governor is also the formal leader of the executive branch, and uses his power to make large numbers of executive and judicial branch appointments, all of which will shape the implementation of state policy. These formal powers are considerable. In the case of the line item budget veto the governor's power is perhaps even more potent than the president's. However, the fact that the governor shares power with a plural elected executive is a very important limitation on his power, one that is not shared by the president.

Informal Powers

Formal powers, however, are only one set of resources for executive leadership. It is in the marshalling of these formal powers in skillful ways, using the vast informal resources that accrue to both of these offices, that the *real power* of these chief executives can be found. It is telling that political skill is an essential ingredient in executive leadership. To the extent that the governor and president are effective in strategically marshalling their formidable formal and informal resources, they are effective as leaders. These same resources can be squandered ineffectively through poor political skill and strategic blunders. The informal resources for these executive positions come chiefly from their position as symbolic head-of-state, their high public visibility in the media, and from the weakness of other political actors.

Symbolic Head-of-State and Head of the State

The president's role as head-of-state is an enormous resource for him in exercising power. Above and beyond his roles as leader of the legislative process and the executive branch, the president is the symbolic representation of the nation's political identity. This gives him an enormous resource in leading the nation, particularly when confronting foreign crises. As Aaron Wildavsky (1969) wrote, there are two presidencies: one in foreign affairs, where the legislative branch and the interest groups recede from power; and the presidency in domestic policy, where both the congress and interest groups exert strong influence. To complement this, one might think of two other kinds of presidencies, a head of state, and a head of government. In foreign affairs, the president becomes head of state and head of government, and faces an arena very conducive to his exercise of power. There are few competing political officials to the president in foreign affairs, and therefore presidents act without any significant check to their authority. This is all the more the case because of their symbolic head-of-state status: presidents enjoy tremendous public support whenever the U.S. is threatened, or our military is involved in conflict. Governors don't benefit in the same way from their role as head of their "small s" state, and certainly don't have an arena of policy where they face only token competition from the legislature or from the enormously powerful interest groups in California politics.

And yet the governor is still the unique public leader representing the state of California when a natural disaster, such as wildfires or an earthquake, devastates areas of California's population. His ceremonial and symbolic appearances boosts public confidence, encourages rebuilding, and builds his political support, ultimately helping him with leadership of the legislative branch. In tough economic times, the governor's symbolic role as head of the state can be a particularly strong resource for exercising political leadership. Only the governor can speak to the interests of the state as a whole, over and above any special interests that have a particular claim on the state budget. Coupled with the weakness of the legislature, the 2/3 majority required to raise taxes, and the line item budget veto, the governor becomes the leading voice in the state's budget process.

The Governor's Powers and the Weak State Legislature

Probably the most interesting formally defined difference between California's governor and the president of the United States is found in the ways that they were originally intended to relate to their legislative branches. The presidency was to be limited by the Congress, who exercised this power effectively through the first 150 years of the nation's history, until President Franklin Delano Roosevelt, responding to the successive crises of the Great Depression and World War II, expanded the powers of the presidency and transformed his role in the nation's political system. California's governor, however, was viewed early on as the disciplinarian of the state legislature. While the president was to be above public politics, the governor was to be the great hope of the people. Governor Hiram Johnson epitomized this kind of leadership, as did other strong governors throughout the 20th century: Earl Warren, Pat Brown, and Ronald Reagan. In the 20th century, strong presidents have become commonplace, but they have assumed this power *despite* the formal limits coming from the Congress. The situation is just the reverse in California: strong governors are encouraged by the relatively weakly empowered state legislature.

The governor enjoys public visibility while state legislators are often unknown to the majority of their own constituents. Particularly in negotiating budget compromises, the fact that the legislature is often divided by partisanship, means that the governor is by default the chief mediator, or the "negotiator-in-chief". When he reaches an impasse, he can use his prominent media profile to place pressure on the legislature to reach agreement. When they agree, the governor can claim credit for rising above partisanship and bridging feuding parties with statesmanlike leadership.

In addition, the state legislature has been considerably weakened by the passage of term limits and budget cuts to the legislature. In 1990, with the passage of proposition 140, the legislature faced term limits, ensuring that the political and technical expertise that comes with long years of experience would no longer be held by members of the legislature. Term limits reduced the collective institutional memory and experience of the legislature, and guaranteed that the new members of the legislature were focused on their next political move, rather than of a long-term career in the legislature. As well, the staff resources that these legislators could turn to assist them were cut by half as a result of prop 140. Legislators often turned to interest group leaders in response (see Chapter 8). The less experienced the legislature, the more influence the governor attained.

Public Visibility and the Power to Persuade

Given the structure of a political system with separate institutions sharing powers, it is essential that the chief executive be effective at persuasion. If a governor or a president is to accomplish anything, he cannot just simply order people to obey, but rather must persuade others who control a share of the power to cooperate. This was the great insight of Richard Neustadt (1990), in his classic work *Presidential Power*,[9] but it is no less applicable to the governor of California. Neustadt did not mean that the president should be a good public speaker so much as that he be skilled at bargaining with others, especially the Congress, the other leaders of the executive branch, and the public. Governors bank on the fact that legislators cannot achieve their goals for budget increases or tax cuts without his intervention, which their priorities can be realized best by cooperating with the governor's agenda. These are his chief bargaining chips. With the executive branch, the governor is limited by the fact that many of the state's executive leaders are independently elected. This limits his ability to bargain with them. Still, the governor's dominance in budget politics gives him a distinct advantage with all members of the executive branch as well. Bottom line: when legislators and executive branch leaders go along to get along, they are no doubt going along with the governor.

---

[9]Neustadt, Richard E., 1990, *Presidential Power and the Modern Presidents: The Politics of Leadership from Roosevelt to Reagan,* New York: The Free Press. Originally published in 1960.

Going Public in California: A New Kind of Gubernatorial Leadership?

The linchpin in the governor's persuasive advantage over the other political actors in the system is his dominant profile in media coverage of state politics. Samuel Kernell (1997) observed that the modern presidency has a new strategy for leadership in his lexicon: he can use his command of the television air waves to speak directly to the American people, who will then pressure their elected representatives. President Reagan used this tactic perhaps better than any president before, or since.

Since the 1970s, however, California governors have had relatively benign if not downright poor media personas. Californians will not remember Governors Deukmejian, Wilson, or Davis as persuasive or inspiring leaders. But with the historic 2003 recall election of Governor Gray Davis, the only successful recall of a governor in California's history, the era of dull governors ended. After Davis was successfully recalled by the electorate, there was a new gubernatorial election. Arnold Schwarzenegger, blockbuster movie star, easily defeated Lieutenant Governor Cruz Bustamante in that historical election (49 percent to 32 percent, with Tom McClintock garnering 13 percent of the vote).[10] Schwarzenegger instantly made use of his media stardom in running for the governor's office in these unusual circumstances, attracting international news coverage to the state's politics.

Schwarzenegger attempted several times to use his heightened public profile to steer the state's agenda and priorities in his preferred direction. The first thing Schwarzenegger did on his first day as governor was to rollback the state's car tax, an enormously popular move, but one that also added another $4 billion to a budget gap that some analysts estimated to be approaching $38 billion at that time. Still, Schwarzenegger used his considerable persuasive skills to get voters to approve an additional $15 billion in bonds to refinance the state's debt, while cutting a number of deals with Democratic Party constituencies—including unions and educators—to push through his budget. Despite the fact that he recently called this original budget deal "a mistake", because it created more debt, Schwarzenegger was enormously popular at this point, with 65% of the public approving of his leadership in the fall of 2004.[11] Things quickly turned sour however. Facing a budget stalemate with the legislature in late 2004, Schwarzenegger became combative, calling legislators "girlie men" in an off-the-cuff televised comment. In 2005, Schwarzenegger confronted the legislature with an ultimatum: if they wouldn't accept his agenda of fiscal and political reforms, he would go directly to the public using the initiative

---

[10]See A.G. Block and Gerald C. Lubenow, 2007, *California Political Almanac, 2007–2008*, Washington, D.C.: CQ Press, ch. 1, "The Political Scene," for a brief description of California's recent political history. The details for the remainder of this chapter are drawn largely from this account.

[11]For Schwarzenegger's candid admittance that his first budget deal was "a mistake" see Evan Halper, January 2, 2011, "The Governor's Wins and Losses," *Los Angeles Times*, p. A1.

process. This was a new kind of gubernatorial going public strategy, coming on the heels of the recall election that brought him to power. The governor was using the tools of direct democracy to bypass a legislature that he felt was being uncooperative, and holding a special election to enact his priorities into law. It was also a huge political gamble, and in the end Schwarzenegger was the loser. The voters rejected every one of his initiatives, and some by substantial margins. Moreover, the voters were opposed to the whole exercise of holding a special election for this purpose, which cost the state an estimated $80 million. The rejection of the governor's agenda at the polls in November of 2005 corresponded with a tremendous drop in the "governator's" approval ratings.

The "Governator" was able to rebound from this by moving to the center in 2006. He achieved the successful passage of a landmark anti-global warming law; pushed successfully for voter approval of huge new spending on infrastructure; and nearly achieved the passage of a universal healthcare bill in California. Schwarzenegger also achieved some important political reforms: transforming the redistricting process from one dominated by the state legislative leaders to one controlled by a non-partisan citizen-based commission; and seeing through a move from a closed- to an open-primary system (both utilizing the initiative process to achieve these results). Still, Schwarzenegger left office with poor public approval ratings and a budget gap that was worse than when he arrived in Sacramento, despite promising to be the reformer that would force the politicians there to finally get a handle on the state's structural budget problems.

In 2011 Governor Brown has returned to the promise of the state's system of direct democracy, proposing to solve the difficult political challenges of the budget crisis by going public yet again. This kind of going public for Schwarzenegger was evidently too public in 2005, when all of his initiatives were defeated at the polls. Brown runs that same risk in 2011 with his proposal to extend the temporary tax increases of 2009 for five more years. Nonetheless it suggests that the role of the governor as a public leader has merged with the state's instruments of direct democracy to empower the governor further.

The Impact of Events

Another aspect of executive leadership should be mentioned: the role of political and economic circumstances. Political scientists have argued for decades that great presidents almost always emerge in the midst of a real crisis. Just think of Abraham Lincoln and the Civil War, or FDR and the Depression and World War II. More recently Steven Skowronek has argued that transformative presidential leadership emerges when the dominant governing party is discredited and defeated, leading to a widened opportunity for a new way of governing. Skowronek points out that presidentially led reforms of government and policy are often responses to the failures of the past, used by skillful presidents who take advantage of the opportunities presented by widespread dissatisfaction with current arrangements. Crises therefore empower presidents, but only if they take advantage of the moment. Do crises also empower governors? It would appear that major crises are less significant in promoting gubernatorial leadership. However, governors who recognize major social and economic changes underfoot, and respond to those changes by shaping state governance for the long-term, tend to be regarded as our most successful governors. The experiences of Governor Hiram Johnson, responding to the demands of the industrial revolution, and of Governor Earl Warren (the only governor to serve three terms), responding to the massive economic and social changes during and after World War II both suggest this interpretation.

Looking at the events of the last decade, one might argue that Schwarzenegger's unusual ascent to power in 2003 was based on a thorough repudiation of the administration and electoral campaigns of Governor Davis. The rapid increase in demographic racial/ethnic diversity in the state in the 1980s and 90s, coupled with the transformation of the state's economy produced a great need for effective gubernatorial leadership. Taking Davis's leadership as a failure, the state looked to the public leadership of Arnold Schwarzenegger for a response.

Governor Brown is in a position to repeat the successes of Hiram Johnson and Earl Warren: he faces a serious crisis with the state's economy and budget, and is seeking to restructure the state's budget and governance by relying on the voters' approval for measures that will significantly reform the state's governance. But he may be faced with the same problems that afflicted Governor Schwarzenegger in 2005. What will make the difference? Is there something about the personal qualities of the men that have led the state successfully that separates them from those who've not been as successful?

Character and Leadership

Unlike legislatures, presidents are frequently evaluated from the vantage point of their personality and character. What sort of person is our nation's leader? How is that translated into leadership for the country? James Barber has identified a typology of presidential character, based on two simple dimensions: whether the president is active or passive, and whether he takes pleasure in his role: positive—or takes it on more as a kind of burden—negative. Those presidents who are active-positive tend to be most effective leaders, argues Barber. Those who are active-negative are our worst presidents. Barber predicted Nixon's failed presidency at the height of Nixon's popularity, right after his landslide 1972 election, calling him an active-negative. Whatever one makes of Barber's typology, his observation that character matters in shaping presidential leadership is an important one. What can we learn about the success or failure of California's governors from a study of their character? It's a risky proposition to assess a man's character based on observations of his public activity, using information provided by the mass media. But one might argue that Gray Davis was a passive-positive governor, at a time when more active leadership was being demanded by the public.

Conversely, Schwarzenegger might be placed in the active-positive category. His effort to galvanize the public behind his reformist agenda in 2005 failed, but in 2006 he was able to make an extraordinary political comeback. He began by apologizing to the public for the unpopular special election, and promised to work more cooperatively with the state legislature. He followed this up with important changes in his staff. Schwarzenegger jettisoned his most conservative advisors, replacing them with moderates. He then pursued a politically popular package of infrastructure repair, financed by a large new bond measure. He publicly broke with his own party over the issue of global warming, signing a bill that imposed stringent air quality regulations. And he signed an increase in the state's minimum wage. All of these efforts signaled to the public that he was moderating, that he was embracing many of their concerns, and that he was effective. The result? Schwarzenegger easily won reelection in 2006, defeating State Treasurer Phil Angelides 56 percent to 39 percent.

One might take Schwarzenegger's successes in 2006 as evidence that his character is well-suited for effective leadership. On the other hand, his critics argue that Schwarzenegger's character is faulty, that he is willing to change his political views to curry favor with the public, that he can become combative and even insulting when he doesn't get his way, and that his successes reflect not so much leadership as effective public relations. Indeed, his approval ratings began to drop as he became more combative in facing an increasingly intractable budget situation after 2008, falling to the same historic low of 22 percent that his predecessor Gray Davis faced just before he was successfully recalled in 2003. In either case, it is clear that we need to consider not only formal or informal powers of the governor's office in evaluating executive leadership in California. We need to also think hard about the political circumstances facing the next governor, and the character and political skills of the person in the office. Governor Brown's considerable experience in state government, as a former governor, Attorney General and Mayor of Oakland, and his reputation for being willing to venture outside traditional solutions may have explained his appeal in the 2010 election, as the state faced another in a series of daunting budget challenges amidst high unemployment and a wounded state economy. Brown's experience may be what the voter's were searching for, as he bucked a national trend towards the Republican party in the 2010 elections, winning against an extremely well-financed moderate Republican opponent with a solid majority of 53.8 percent to Meg Whitman's 40.9 percent.[12]

---

[12] California Secretary of State, Debra Bowen, January 6, 2011, *Statement of Vote, November 2, 2010, General Election*, http://www.sos.ca.gov/elections/sov/2010-general/complete- sov.pdf, accessed on February 15, 2011.

Conclusions: Executive Leadership in California and the Nation

The governor faces a relatively weak legislature, filled with term limited politicians who have limited staff resources. The president, on the other hand, faces a Congress dominated by career politicians, with considerable resources to counter the power of the presidency, particularly in domestic policymaking. The Vice-President of the United States is the president's campaign "running mate" and works to assist the President in fulfilling his agenda. The lieutenant governor of California, however, is elected independently of the governor, and is frequently a political adversary of the governor. Likewise, so too are the state's other executive officers: the Attorney General, Controller, Treasurer, Secretary of State, Superintendant of Public Instruction, Insurance Commissioner, and the 4-member Board of Equalization. This 'plural executive' has significant powers that can limit the governor. The executive officers in the federal government, however, are appointed by the president, with the approval of a majority of the Senate, and can be removed at his will.

Probably the most significant differences in their formal authority can be found in the arena of the budget process. Both the president and the governor propose a unified executive budget to begin the process, and the legislative branch then goes to work on his proposal. The similarities end there. The Congress breaks up the federal budget into 15 appropriation bills, which the president must either sign as law or veto in their entirety. The governor's formal powers in this arena are more formidable. First, he responds to the state budget as a whole, and is given authority to reduce or veto any specific spending line in the budget, without vetoing the budget as a whole: a line-item veto. Moreover, in California, the legislature must pass any tax increases that are part of a budget package by a 2/3 super-majority, which makes it even more difficult for the legislature to offer a disciplined clear budget alternative to the governor's proposal. The U.S. Congress need only pass budget bills by a simple majority.

But the real differences between the two offices run deeper than these institutional parallels and divergences. They are rooted in the very different founding impulses. While the Presidency was founded by men who were ambivalent towards executive authority, seeking to arrive at a functional executive that would be limited, the powers of the California governor were designed by reformers intent on empowering the public directly. The presidency was in fact established as a kind of bulwark against a rawer form of democracy, and the electoral college itself was adopted in great part to separate the public's voice from the choice of this powerful new executive. In California, the voice of the people was intended, as a result of the progressives, to be the dominant voice in the government. The governor, to the extent that he positions himself as the people's tribune, therefore, governs effectively against the perceived political class, embodied by the state legislature. When he ignores the people's concerns, or misreads them, he faces sure retribution in the polls.

Table 7.2 Comparisons between the Governor of California and the President of the United States

	California	The United States
Designation:	Governor of California	President of the United States
Shape/Design:	Plural Elected Executive	Single Elected Executive—appoints the others
Special Features:	• State's symbolic leader • Line item budget veto • 2/3 requirement on tax increases strengthens governor • Can use mass media & direct democracy to "go public", to persuade the public	• Nation's symbolic leader • More powerful in foreign policy than in domestic policy • Uses mass media to "go public" to persuade Congress
Importance:	• Governor leads budget process • Appoints many executive branch leaders • Appoints state judges • Responds to long-term social/economic trends	• Leader in national security • Appoints all executive branch leaders • Appoints federal judges • Responds to economic and foreign policy crises

Summary

In understanding the governor of California through a comparison with the president of the United States, we can focus on these similarities and differences.

Similarities:

Five important similarities may be noted.

1. They are both the single most powerful individuals in their respective political circumstances, each of which is characterized by checks and balances.
2. Both must seek their goals by persuading other powerful individuals to go along with their ideas.

3. Both rely upon their formal powers and informal resources, especially their influence over public opinion, to lead effectively.
4. Both are constrained by the checks and balances of the legislature.
5. For both presidents and governors, success depends on their formal and informal powers, the political and economic circumstances they inherit, and their political skills and abilities.

Differences:

In terms of formal powers of office, four important differences are especially important.

1. Unlike the president, the governor of California must share executive power with other independently elected executives, such as the Attorney General and Lieutenant Governor.
2. With respect to the budget process—always crucial to any government—the governor must win approval of any tax increases by a two-thirds vote in each house of the legislature. The president, on the other hand, needs only a majority vote from each house of Congress.
3. Also with respect to the budget process, the governor has a line-item veto, the importance of which is hard to overestimate.
4. The legislative term limits in California weaken the legislature even further, empowering the governor. There are no such term limits for the Congress of the United States.

Three final observations on executive leadership are worth making:

1. Media power in contemporary politics is especially important for the president and the governor. Going public is becoming a strategy for leadership that presidents and governors both must learn to use to lead effectively.
2. Crises as well as long-term social and economic changes cannot be avoided or sidestepped. Executives must lead effectively in responding to these, for they will be evaluated based on their effectiveness in doing so.
3. Character and political skill matters. Wise use of one's considerable resources towards the end of political persuasion will go far in achieving one's leadership goals. Leaders who find ways to lead actively and positively despite major challenges will be more effective than those who find their leadership task burdensome.

Chapter 8
THE CALIFORNIA LEGISLATURE
Matthew G. Jarvis[1]

Broadly, the legislature is for the state of California what Congress is for the nation. It is the state's principal lawmaking body. Many features of the legislature are modeled on Congress: the California legislature has two houses, like Congress; its lower house, called the Assembly, is headed by a Speaker, and the upper house (the Senate) by a President pro tempore. Yet there are plenty of differences, and in this chapter we will be concerned with comparisons, calling forth both similarities and differences. Great changes since 1990 mean that we begin with some differences.

Great Changes in the California Legislature

No state government institution has changed more since 1990 than the California legislature. In that year, voters adopted Proposition 140, which amended the state constitution. Proposition 140 did three important things. First, it installed term limits for legislators. After 1990, members of the Assembly were restricted to three two-year terms, after which they could not be reelected to the Assembly. Members of the state Senate, similarly, were restricted to two four-year terms. Second, Proposition 140 cut legislative staffs by about half, meaning that the number of workers who might supply research, advice, and general help to legislators was greatly reduced. Third, Proposition 140 cut off most legislators from retirement benefits that they previously could have received. In fact, in November 2000 California voters again said no to legislator retirement benefits, defeating a proposed constitutional amendment to allow legislators to participate in the state's public employee retirement system.

With these three extraordinary changes California had turned its back on a *professional model* for state legislatures. It makes sense for us to explore that model, in order to understand what the California legislature once was, and where the California state legislature stands today.

The Professional Model for State Legislatures

Proponents of a professional state legislature see strength in full-time, veteran, expert legislators. Making the legislative job full-time can mean more time studying issues and staying abreast of constituents' wishes. Over time, legislators would

---

[1]This chapter is an updated version of the same chapter in previous editions of this book written by Harvey P. Grody and Keith O. Boyum.

have an opportunity to develop experience and knowledge, enormously helpful as lawmakers strive to grapple effectively with complex modern policy issues.

Those who want veteran, expert legislators, therefore, would favor a system that built in encouragement for talented people to build legislative careers. Good salaries, generous pensions, and other benefits make sense in that framework. Such things attract people to careers. Without them, people would not want to stick with the legislative job. Legislative staff also support the general idea. If veteran lawmakers were given a large, expert, and secure staff to help them, there would be still more knowledge and perspective available. The legislature as an institution might be an appropriate match or balance to the governor—who has a very substantial staff. The state could have the benefit of careful scrutiny—by experts—of the governor's proposals for new laws.

When California adopted these concepts in 1966, this professional model made California's legislature more like Congress than any other state's legislature. It seemed a great reform. Indeed, in the next decade other progressive states sought to follow California's lead, moving away from the part-time, amateur legislatures that many small states still maintain. It seemed that modern, complex issues would be better addressed by strong institutions.

Why California Spurned the Professional Model

Why, then, did California voters abandon the professional model in 1990? What might be the virtues of a term-limited legislature with a smaller staff? And were the voters wise or foolish in the choice that Proposition 140 represented?

Notice first that Americans—Californians very much included—have changed a basic orientation toward all institutions of government in the years since 1966. In the mid-1960s, roughly three-quarters of Americans, when asked in a survey, would *agree* that government was made up of people who usually tried to do the right thing. Confidence in government was high. But there had been a virtual turn-around in attitudes by the 1990s. In the mid-1990s, roughly three-quarters of Americans, when asked in a survey, *disagreed* that government is made up of people who are competent and well-motivated. Politicians were equated with incompetence and venality in the American (and Californian) mind. Amid all of this, few institutions drew more scorn than legislatures. Thus California's voters in 1990 were ready to express their dissatisfaction by voting for Proposition 140.

Proponents of Proposition 140 also argued that term limits would keep legislators oriented to the people "back home" whom they represented. Fresh faces regularly would be drawn from the district, they argued, as term limits required incumbents to retire. The argument was that these new people would better understand the needs and interests of the district. The proponents, in essence, were arguing that legislators should behave as *delegates*—legislators who simply vote the way their constituents prefer, rather than exercising the legislator's own judgment. The new people would not be as reliant on Sacramento lobbyists for either information or campaign donations, it was said.

Opponents of Proposition 140 raised several concerns, in addition to the loss of institutional strength that came with abandoning the professional model. The most basic was democracy. How can it be appropriate to forbid voters from electing the people they wish to elect, opponents asked? "Stop me before I vote again!" some joked. Furthermore, the opponents of Proposition 140 argued that amateur legislators would be *more* dependent on interest groups and bureaucrats. Where professional, long-time members of the legislature could develop real expertise in public policy, both in them and in their staffs, amateurs would have to look to the governor, to the state bureaucrats, and to organized lobbying groups for basic information and perspectives. A weak legislature rather than a strong one was the real outcome of Proposition 140, opponents argued. The opponents of Proposition 140 supported a legislature composed of trustees—legislators elected to craft legislation that *they* saw as being in the best interests of their district, state, or country.

As the twenty-first century began, it was clear that a weak legislature was California's fate. The governor stood tall in state policymaking, while the Assembly was especially hobbled by fast turnover of members and even faster turnover of leadership. A weak legislature, then, indeed seemed to be in California's future for some time to come. On one hand, the federal appellate courts have refused to find Proposition 140 unconstitutional. On the other hand, California voters, mistrustful of politicians, seem to be in no mood to change things. In 2002, for example, the voters rejected a proposed constitutional amendment to allow some legislators to extend their legislative tenure by one term, and in 2008 voters rejected another constitutional amendment to allow legislators to serve 12 years in either chamber as opposed to six in the Assembly and eight in the Senate.

California thus finds itself with a legislature composed mostly of fairly inexperienced legislators who have one eye on their next job. As we will discuss below, this interacts powerfully with the nature of California's electoral districts to create a system whereby legislators are at the whims of the extreme wings of their parties and interest groups.

Basic Characteristics of California's Legislature

The Essential Functions of Legislatures

Generally, of course, legislatures do for the states what Congress does for the United States: they enact legislation (i.e., new laws) via *statutes*. Beyond this *lawmaking* function, political scientists usually define three other functions that legislatures perform: representation, oversight, and the so-called constituent functions. *Representation* is the notion that policy choices are made with our interests in mind, either those interests that we have communicated to the legislator or those interests that he or she can recognize without being told. *Oversight* amounts to keeping watch on the implementation of policies and programs that already are on the books. That is, legislators try to (a) insure that government employees (especially within the executive branch) carry out the wishes of the legislature as expressed in the laws that were adopted, and (b) review policies and programs to see whether or not they need to be altered in some way so as to more efficiently achieve their intended goals.

The *constituent* function involves individual casework, that is, investigating and trying to resolve problems that ordinary citizens may have with government bureaucracies. State legislators and members of Congress perform some of this function, for example, helping with a Social Security problem or trying to resolve a mix-up with the Veteran's Administration.

The Essential Structures of Legislatures

Congress and the legislatures of every state except Nebraska are bicameral (composed of two houses). The larger of California's two houses is the Assembly, which is composed of eighty members elected to two-year terms. Under the terms of Proposition 140, each California Assembly member is restricted to serving only three terms, that is, a maximum service of six years. The state Senate includes forty members elected to four-year terms, with half of the members elected every two years. State senators represent about twice as many constituents as do members of the Assembly. Under the terms of Proposition 140, senators are limited to two terms, or eight years. The differences in size and term lengths invite comparisons to the U.S. Congress, where the House of Representatives consists of 435 members each elected for a two-year term, and the Senate consists of 100 members elected for six-year terms. There are no term limits for members of the U.S. Congress. In both the California legislature and the U.S. Congress, the larger house elected for a shorter term is considered the "lower house." Each Senate is considered the "upper house."

Most observers consider the upper house to be a better job. In the first place, running for reelection is hard work, and in any given election voters might, after all, choose one's opponent. Thus, politicians like it when they must run for reelection less frequently. Second, longer terms seem to connote greater trust in senators. Some see in this an implication that senators are expected to use their own judgment in reaching decisions more than members of the lower house, who are expected to pay closer attention to the views and opinions of constituents. That implication is reinforced by some differences in duties. For example, U.S. senators and California state senators are asked to vote to confirm (or not to confirm) some high-level appointments proposed by the president or by the governor, respectively. By and large the lower houses are not asked to offer their judgments about nominees. Third, as a member of a smaller body, the influence of one person increases, for example, one California state senator is one of forty whereas one Assembly member is one of eighty.

Legislative careers often begin in the lower house and conclude in the upper house. It makes sense: begin with a smaller constituency, take a short term in office, and let the voters and your colleagues take your measure. At the same time, however, some elected members of the U.S. House of Representatives keep seeking reelection to that body, and often seek leadership jobs as their careers mature. Here we see the professional model. Veteran leadership and expertise can be found. The same was true for California—until Proposition 140 brought in term limits. Until 1990, the Assembly had its share of veterans whose careers and essential orientations were to that body. Facing being termed-out in 1996, many of these "veterans" began looking toward other political careers.

As of 1996, when the term limits adopted in Proposition 140 fully took effect, no members of the Assembly elected in 1990 could run again for that body. Some key Assembly veterans, however, ran for and were elected to the state Senate, a pattern that continued through the 2002 elections. By 2004, however, all of the long-term, pre–Proposition 140 legislative veterans who had moved to the Senate were termed out of the Senate. Three-term Assembly members, that is, those with a maximum of six years' legislative experience, now would be the "Assembly legislative veterans" making their way to the upper house. Thus the two houses of the California legislature over time may become more different from each other, at least to the extent that many "freshmen" senators may come to the upper house with up to six years prior legislative experience. The twenty-first–century California legislature truly is no longer an example of the *professional model* discussed earlier.

Elections and Redistricting

California legislators, as in most states, are elected from single-member districts. The geographical boundary lines for the eighty Assembly and forty state Senate districts are created every ten years (after the national census), and are based roughly upon equal numbers of people per district.

However, while obeying the principal constitutional requirement for essential population equality, it is possible to draw district lines favorable to Republicans or to Democrats. Thus politicians regard the drawing of district lines—the process is called redistricting—as enormously important. It is no surprise that Republicans and Democrats have had some bitter fights about redistricting over the years. Where Democrats cried foul after the redistricting which followed the 1950 census, the redistricting that followed the 1980 census left Republicans grumbling. Governors (who have the power to veto a redistricting bill) and often the courts (with the power to judge constitutionality) are important players in the redistricting game, too. In fact, courts had the last word following both the 1980 and the 1990 censuses. With the governor and large majorities in both the Assembly and Senate in the hands of the Democrats after the 2000 general elections, control of the next decennial redistricting was securely in their hands.

Term limits, however, also impacted the 2001 redistricting. With little opposition from the Republican minority, a bipartisan redistricting was accomplished with very few competitive districts created at any level (Congressional, Assembly, or Senate). State legislators in both parties seemed more interested in creating safe districts not only for their next election, but also for where they could run when they were termed out of their current seats.

The consequences of redistricting and term limits combined are rather severe. Long-serving legislators have the ability to cultivate name recognition and goodwill among their constituents; term-limited legislators are deprived of these advantages and must cater to the majority in their districts. At the same time, these term-limited legislators have to keep an eye on the next job they might run for, whether it is the Assembly, Senate, or Congress. However, since the last wave of redistricting created districts that are safe for each party for all three, what this means is that legislators have to worry about the primary election for their current seat and their next one. Either one will cost a great deal of money, which will have to come from interest groups located on either end of the political spectrum.

In 2008, Californians voted for Proposition 11 to create an "amateur" redistricting commission to create new districts for the 2012 elections and beyond. The hopes of supporters are that private citizens don't care about protecting any particular legislator's interests. Opponents charged that Proposition 11's requirements for commissioners (no electoral experience and no large campaign contributions, among others) would lead to a commission made up of people who had no idea how to satisfy the many constitutional requirements on redistricting. It remains to be seen which side is right, but voters were in no mood to change the policy before it went into effect, and retained it at the ballot in 2010.

Primary Elections

The first task of a candidate for the legislature is to win nomination in the March primary election. The winner of a primary election becomes his or her party's nominee in the November general election. California saw changes in the rules for primaries, and then a return to the previous rules as the 1990s closed, and finally, completely different rules go into effect in 2012.

For over a century, in most of the nation, party voters in closed primaries have chosen general election candidates. In closed primaries, voters who registered as Democrats choose Democratic candidates, while voters who registered as Republicans choose Republican candidates. Voters who "decline to state" a political party for themselves may not vote in a partisan primary election. California, though, has often been just a little different than other states. Cross-filing from 1913–1959 allowed candidates to run for the nomination of multiple parties; the blanket primary in the late 1990s allowed voters to vote for anyone they wanted in any party's primaries; and in 2010, voters approved Proposition 14, where the top two vote-getters in the "primary" election, regardless of party, would be the only candidates in the general election (for more on the history of nominations in California, see Chapter 5). The argument for Proposition 14 was that, in very partisan districts, moderates or members of the opposite party have little voice, and this system will force candidates to "run to the middle." Opponents noted that voters, robbed of knowing which party a candidate is from, actually know very little about the candidates; the information that is likely to swing them would come from campaign ads, and this would increase the influence of moneyed interests.

Election scholars tend to find these claims dubious. State legislators are polarized mostly because our residential patterns give us fairly homogenously liberal and conservative districts. Moreover, in primary elections, only the most motivated voters tend to show up, and these are people with strong opinions. Nothing about the top-two primary system changes these realities, and California is likely to see two candidates facing each other in the general election who are either a conservative and a liberal, or both on the same side of the aisle with an established incumbent and a fringe challenger. Neither of these scenarios produces moderation.

Organization

Both legislative houses usually are organized by the political parties in terms of committee memberships and leadership positions. As with the U.S. Congress, California's legislature does most of its significant work through its many standing committees, the most important of which are the committees that screen the budget and other money bills. Although partisanship traditionally had been less important in the organization of the state Senate than in the Assembly, since the late 1960s the role of political parties in both houses has increased. Political party organization in California's legislature, especially in the Senate, however, remains less significant than in some other states or the Congress.

Bills must be introduced by a member of the legislature. Once introduced a bill is referred to an appropriate committee, which reviews and frequently amends the original version before recommending passage by the full house. Most bills never make it past the committee stage. To become law, a bill must be passed in identical form by an *absolute majority* in both houses (i.e., twenty-one in the Senate and forty-one votes in the Assembly) and signed (or not vetoed) by the governor. This process is essentially similar to that of the U.S. Congress except no absolute majority of either house is required. Another major difference is that an "absent" or nonvoting California legislator has his or her vote tabulated as a "nay" vote. Legislative critics point out that nonvoting is a way for legislators to avoid taking positions on controversial subjects and that many bills are defeated as a result of nonvoting.

California required a two-thirds majority vote on passage of the annual budget bill from 1933 until 2010, a provision that enhanced the bargaining position of the minority party. In 2008, for example, minority Republicans refused to vote for budgets that had tax increases, while majority Democrats wanted to balance the budget with a mixture of spending cuts and tax increases. During the budget negotiations, Republicans even wanted the Democrats to revoke nonbudgetary legislation that had already passed! In 2010, voters passed Proposition 25, however, which made the budget a majority decision again. In the very same election, however, voters also strengthened restrictions on the ability of legislators to raise revenues, passing, Proposition 26, which requires that fee increases receive a two-thirds vote in the legislature. Thus, the new legislature should be more amenable to majority party control, if only for measures that don't increase revenues.

Senate Leadership

One significant difference between the leadership positions in the two houses is found in the different roles played by the Senate president pro tempore and the Speaker of the Assembly. Many significant *formal powers* held by the Speaker are not held individually by the Senate leader. The president pro tempore shares the leadership power and management functions of the Senate with the Rules Committee. The president pro tempore, a member of the majority party, chairs the Rules Committee, which among other things assigns members to Senate committees, appoints the chairs and vice chairs of committees, and refers (assigns) bills to committees. Although the Rules Committee majority reflects the partisan alignment in the whole Senate, in the past chairs of other committees were not always members of the majority party. In recent years, however, this pattern has changed as partisanship has increased in both legislative houses.

One similarity between the state Senate and the U.S. Senate is that formally each body is presided over by a nonmember, the lieutenant governor and the vice president, respectively. The functions of the formal presiding officer are limited, with the most significant item being the rare casting of a vote to break a tie.

Assembly Leadership

As is the case with the Speaker of the U.S. House of Representatives, prior to term limits, clearly the most significant political figure in the California legislature was the Speaker of the Assembly. The Speaker is elected formally by a majority of the entire Assembly: the winning candidate must receive 41 votes. In practice this usually means the majority party selects one of its members in a party gathering (a *caucus*), and then votes as a unit for that candidate.

With one party firmly in control of the Assembly, the politics of who should become the Speaker is restricted to members of that party. Assembly members do political favors for each other, bargain with each other, and make agreements—and a winner emerges. This bargaining and agreement-making process happens frequently in this era of term limits, and the job of Speaker turns over every couple of years or so.

The Power of the Leaders

Even though the Senate president pro tempore has become a more powerful political figure in recent years, the Speaker is not necessarily a politically weak leader. Depending upon rules agreed to by one's party caucus and then adopted in a vote on the Assembly floor, Speakers can exercise varying degrees of power. Speakers typically have the significant power to assign bills to the committees of their choice. Speakers also commonly determine committee memberships, and these powers taken together—to assign bills to committees and to determine who will serve on committees—mean that the Speaker is in charge of legislation. The Speaker also controls all Assembly space in the Capitol building, meaning he or she can award good offices to friends and bad ones to adversaries.

Given these formal powers, it is not surprising that interest groups as well as Assembly members pay special attention to the Speaker. Because these groups pay such attention, Speakers also can find ways to encourage campaign contributions to their friends, or to discourage contributions to those who are not so friendly. Imagine, then, that you are a member of the Assembly. The Speaker might (a) help you win election by helping you to raise money for your campaign, (b) help you be effective in your job by giving you choice committee assignments, and (c) through his or her influence upon other members, help you win passage of legislative proposals that you consider important, especially for your home district. Or the Speaker might withhold any or all of this help. How likely would you be to do what the Speaker wants you to do whenever you could? In addition, the Speaker and Senate president pro tempore are two of the "Big Five," which also includes the governor and the leaders of the minority party in each chamber. This informal group meets often to discuss pending legislation, especially the budget. Party leaders can represent their party in these informal negotiations, where it is often easier to make concessions and deals.

In some other states, strong political party organizations compete for influence with legislative leaders. Legislators in those states may look to their parties, not to their legislative leader, for such things as help with campaign contributions. In California, however, statewide political party organizations are weak (see Chapter 5). The Speaker's power is thus not as frequently or effectively challenged. Note, however, once again the importance of term limits. Speakers come and go every couple of years in this era of limited terms. This has two very important consequences. First, leaders lack experience and contacts that might give them more power. More importantly, though, because leaders are going to be replaced soon, others (legislators, interest groups, and the governor) don't have to worry about how the leaders might react in the future, and the leaders cannot promise any future actions. In contrast, a governor elected twice can serve eight years. The advantage is decidedly to the governor, and he or she, not the Speaker, is the principal leader and spokesperson for the governor's party.

Money and Elections to the Legislature

Californians, like most Americans, have a hard time figuring out what they would prefer for a relationship between politics and money. Ordinary citizens know that it costs a great deal of money to run for political office, and even alert 11-year-olds know that people who want something—for example, interest groups (see Chapter 6)—are typical sources of that money for candidates for office. Americans hate that system. It seems like selling the government to the highest bidder. On the other hand, ordinary citizens are not willing either to donate the money themselves, or to support legislation that would provide public money—tax dollars—to candidates for office. Remember, in our times, ordinary citizens have little respect for politicians. Who would give money to those they scorn?

In that context, Californians have been ready to say yes to initiative constitutional amendments that would artificially limit the influence of money on politics.

Propositions 208 in November 1996 and 34 in November 2000 both won by wide margins. Yet the limits are relatively generous. And in any event, such limits will not end the link between money and politics. Campaigning will always take money.

Let us note just one reason why campaigning takes money. Most ordinary citizens get most of their news from television, but California television stations do a remarkably poor job of covering politics in the state capital. This is true partly because ordinary citizens have little interest in policymaking in the legislature. They prefer local television coverage of weather, sports, crimes, fires, lost children and pets. The result, however, is an electorate that rarely knows the name of its member of the Assembly or of the Senate. To break through that inattention requires campaign advertising, and advertising takes money. In California, this is very costly, as our legislators are competing over very many voters and media costs are very high.

It also is crucial to note that the courts are certain to have the last word on campaign finance restrictions. The principal reason for that is American freedom of speech. Individuals and interest groups alike cannot be prevented from telling the world their point of view, through advertising or in any other way, even if laws may limit direct contributions to political campaigns beyond certain dollar limits. Freedom of speech means that interest groups will continue to be able to spend any amount at all to tell the world whom they support as a candidate for office.

The twenty-first century thus began with Californians unhappy about the perceived influence of money on politics and willing to vote for restrictions on campaign donations. Yet these restrictions could not end the money and politics relationship, given fundamental needs to communicate with inattentive voters, and given freedoms of speech. At the same time, Californians are a long way from being willing to spend tax dollars to take the place of willing interest groups in writing large checks to support campaigns for office. Continuing dissatisfaction with little opportunity to resolve it is in store, a negative for a legislature already weakened by term limits and other Proposition 140 restrictions.

The Governor and the Legislature

The governor of California has both political strengths and weaknesses when it comes to dealing with the legislature as state laws affecting public policy are produced. Significant strengths include the governor's initiative in proposing the annual budget, the item veto on money bills, and a strong position in making appointments. Furthermore, although the governor cannot formally introduce bills, he often requests the introduction of bills, which initiate major policy proposals to which the legislature must react.

The legislature primarily reacts rather than takes the initiative in preparing the annual budget proposal. As in all states and in the United States, the chief executive takes the lead in proposing the budget. There also are some specific, constitutionally mandated deadlines—regularly ignored in recent years—on the legislature for getting a budget measure enacted. Note also that the governor has the power to reduce or eliminate through item veto any appropriation made by the legislature. Some other states also give their governors the item veto. The U.S. president does not have this authority.

The key point is this: budgets are the most important policy documents considered by legislative bodies, and executives dominate the budget process. We can say that the governor of California is "the most important legislator," even though he is not a member of the legislature. The same point is true for the president: he is the most important person in congressional deliberations, even though he is not a member of Congress (see Chapter 7). The potential for discord between a legislative body (a state legislature or Congress) also is more likely when the political parties of the chief executive and the legislative majorities differ.

A Concluding Perspective

For about twenty-five years, it seemed that a professional California legislature had a genuine opportunity to tackle the problems of the nation's largest state. Not that the legislature ever was triumphant or preeminent. On one hand, the policy-making function was never fully conceded to the legislature, as in normal American style the governor sought leadership and vigorously advanced his ideas, and the courts and the bureaucracies exercised extremely important influence over laws and policies at the point of implementation. On the other hand, new departures in public policy for California were frequently enacted via the initiative route, using ballot propositions to gain the lawmaking consent of ordinary voters.

Still, even while hobbled by internal weaknesses—importantly, the lack of discipline brought about by the astonishing weakness of California political parties—most observers thought the California legislature worked. The legislature accommodated large changes, some like property tax cuts or mandates on state spending brought about via ballot propositions (13 and 98 in these examples). The legislature grappled with changing demographics and changing economics in the state. The legislature responded to earthquakes, fears of crime, recessions, and more, never pleasing everybody (no one ever does in politics) but at a minimum creating a real dialogue in the state capital. Interest groups and the governor had a legislature armed with a strong staff, long memories, and expertise to engage these issues. It seems likely that California public policy was better for having had twenty-five years of a strong, competent legislature.

As the state began the new century, however, its legislature had been weakened by term limits and sharply reduced staff. Feeble political parties were no support for a legislature of newcomers. The inexperienced, understaffed legislators have few incentives to learn about complex issues, term limits and uncompetitive districts encourage them to be very liberal or very conservative as they run for the primary in the next seat, and with supermajority budget rules, this ends up paralyzing the legislature in partisan gridlock. The influence of governors, bureaucrats, and interest groups has increased, and governors and others running for office increasingly join interest groups in mounting public relations campaigns on behalf of ever more ballot propositions. Within less than a year of his election as governor in 2003, for example, Arnold Schwarzenegger became a regular advocate of initiative proposals. With a weakened legislature, the public policy conversation in California seemed likely to be lean rather than abundant, mean rather than generous, and too frequently imprudent rather than wise.

As a new decade dawns in 2011, the legislature has again been born anew. Redistricting is now in the hands of a supposedly non-partisan commission, primaries now yield the top two vote getters and the budget rules have changed for the first time in nearly 80 years. It remains to be seen what the effects of these changes will be; the first two changes are argued to reduce partisanship, whereas the last one empowers the majority party. All of the effects of these changes are theoretical, however, and it is unclear how these new rules will impact the legislature.

Table 8.1 Comparisons between the California Legislature and the United States Congress

	California	**The United States**
Designation:	• The California Legislature	• Congress of the United States of America
Shape/Design:	• Composed of two houses, or "bicameral": a *Senate* (40 members, 4-year terms); and an *Assembly* (80 members, 2-year terms)	• Bicameral: a *Senate* (100 members, 2 from each state, 6-year terms); and a *House of Representatives* (435 members, 2-year terms)
Special Features:	• Both houses apportioned by population • *Speaker of the Assembly* is important figure; state *Senate president pro tempore* has become as important, if not more so • Absolute majorities to pass bills and two-thirds vote on budget bill • Absent member's vote counts as a "nay" vote • Chairs of standing committees are powerful figures in both the California legislature and the United States Congress	• No term limits • Only the House of Representatives is apportioned by population • The *majority leader* is the most important figure in the U.S. Senate; the *Speaker* is the most important figure in the House of Representatives • Only a simple majority of members "present" needed to pass most bills

Table 8.1 *Continued*

	California	The United States
Importance:	• Takes up key state and local issues, including education, transportation, crime, and environmental quality • Proposition 13 shifted key decision making about many issues, such as education, away from the local level to the state, because the state must supply the money • By weakening the legislature, Proposition 140 increased the influence of the governor, bureaucrats, and interest groups • The chief executive—the governor or the president—although not a member of the legislative branch, is much more influential than any other figure inside or outside of the legislature or Congress.	• Both houses of Congress play a major role in making domestic policy, including taxing and spending decisions • The U.S. Senate is much more influential than the House of Representatives in making U.S. foreign policy

Chapter 9
THE COURTS OF CALIFORNIA
By Pamela Fiber-Ostrow

Introduction: The Essential Independence of State Courts

Very basically, courts resolve disputes between parties. These parties may be private citizens, a citizen and a public entity like a city or state or government agency, or even the public against a person accused of a crime. The role of the courts is to *apply* the laws that legislatures and others enact. State courts apply state laws and constitutions while Federal courts apply national laws and the national constitution. This is not as simple as it sounds. The principles of federalism mean Americans are subject to both their state's constitutions and the federal constitution and there are significant areas of overlap. From time-to-time under some circumstances, Federal courts may enforce state laws and state courts may enforce national laws.

An important area of overlap involves the Constitution of the United States. The Constitution stipulates that "Judges in every State" shall be bound by its provisions. During the early part of the twentieth century the United States Supreme Court began to apply the rights and liberties guaranteed in the U.S. Constitution to the states through the Fourteenth Amendment, known as selective incorporation. This incorporation expanded into the 1960s and state judges put national constitutional requirements into practice. Fundamental liberties that most Americans prize are among these, including freedoms of speech and of religion. Guarantees of certain standards of fairness in criminal proceedings in the Bill of Rights and the Fourteenth Amendment, which also requires that all persons be equally treated in crucial ways, were applied to the states changing the way state judicial proceedings were conducted in a variety of ways.

When questions of law that turn on national constitutional provisions arise in state proceedings, the Federal courts can ultimately override state courts' rulings. This, then, amounts to a limited oversight that the Federal courts may exercise over state court decisions. However, two key points should be kept in mind as we seek to understand the relationships between the two systems:

1. Most cases do *not* raise constitutional issues.
2. Most cases in which national constitutional issues *are* raised in fact never reach the Federal courts, but instead are finally decided in state courts.

The most important lesson in this is that *state courts are substantially autonomous and independent of Federal courts*—because very few issues raised in state courts are subject to Federal court review, and even when such issues are subject to review, they usually are not reviewed. It follows that if the state courts are essentially autonomous, state constitutions and laws also are fairly independent of any Federal court intervention providing they do not violate the national constitution or laws

Kinds of Law and Numbers of Cases

Important differences between California courts and Federal courts can be traced (a) to the kinds of law that prevail in each system, and (b) to the numbers of cases processed in each system. Different kinds of law help to explain the different numbers of cases—and in turn, different numbers of cases require variations in the structure of trial courts.

Kinds of Law: Criminal and Civil

Criminal law involves the government as a party to the dispute. When criminal laws are broken—when I hit you on the head—the public via the government considers itself aggrieved. Prosecutors in criminal cases, therefore, are government employees and public defenders (again, government employees) often provide court representation for persons accused of crimes when the defendant cannot afford a private defense attorney. *Civil law*, by contrast, covers transactions primarily between private parties in which the government usually has no direct involvement (although it may be called upon to enforce outcomes in civil cases). In 1996 and 1997, the trials of O. J. Simpson taught the public a lesson about the differences between civil and criminal trials. The state of California (the "People") prosecuted Mr. Simpson in a criminal trial that ended in a finding of "not guilty". The family of slain Ronald Goldman sued Simpson in a civil trial that ended in a finding that he was liable for the wrongful deaths of Goldman and Nicole Brown Simpson. The state had sought imprisonment; the family sought damages. The state acted according to criminal law; the family acted according to civil law.

Kinds of Law: Public and Private

A second distinction useful for this discussion is between public law and private law. Public law involves general rules for broad classes of people, and typically the state is either a party to public law transactions, or considers itself substantially affected by the outcome. Technically, criminal law is in the public law sphere, but better modern examples include civil rights laws, welfare laws, antitrust laws, environmental laws, and social security laws. Governments secure civil rights for people, and thus are involved in the transaction. Governments provide welfare to people in need, and thus are involved in the transaction. Private law, on the other hand, manages relationships between individuals, in which usually it is thought that the government has no direct stake. For example, most contract law is private, and if you wanted to change your name, it would be a private law matter.

Structure and Jurisdiction

Table 9.1 generally sets out the organization of courts in California and in the United States. Of interest are the ways in which courts are organized, and the qualifications and tenure of judges.

Like the federal courts, California's courts are divided into two jurisdictions: trial courts and appellate courts. Trial courts are the fact-finding courts because their jobs are to determine the facts of a case; this may include determining whether a crime occurred (criminal court) or settling disputes between two parties or individuals, like whether a person is responsible for damaging another's property (civil court). These courts have original jurisdiction; this means that they will be the first court to hear a case. The courts of appeal, which include the California Supreme Court, review questions of law and due process and have appellate jurisdiction, hearing cases on appeal, or in certain cases may have original jurisdiction. Jurisdiction here refers to the authority of a court to interpret and apply the law. Article VI of the California Constitution creates trial and appellate level courts and authorizes the state legislature to fill in some details. The legislature, however, does not have as much discretion in the creation of state courts as is given to Congress regarding the creation of the Federal courts.

The national constitution authorizes the creation of courts in two places. Article I authorizes Congress to create "tribunals" (sometimes called legislative courts). Such courts have limited jurisdiction (that is, limited authority to hear cases). The national constitution in Article III creates "one Supreme Court," and authorizes Congress to create other courts inferior to the Supreme Court. These Article III courts (sometimes called constitutional courts) exercise "the judicial power of the United States," and have been given general jurisdiction (that is, broad authority to hear cases).

Trial Courts: Fact finding

California follows the hierarchical, pyramid pattern of the national system and most states. There are fact finding trial courts, appellate courts and a Supreme Court in both systems. Both the federal district courts and California's superior courts require juries in order to meet the Constitutional demands of the Sixth and Seventh Amendments, and call upon citizens to serve as jurors, before hand to decide whether probable cause exists to indict (accuse) individuals or corporations on criminal charges based upon the evidence presented (grand jury) and in trial (petit jury). Both Superior Court and District Court juries require a twelve-person panel.

The Federal trial court of general jurisdiction is the U.S. District Court. Congress has created 94 U.S. District Courts including at least one district in each state, the District of Columbia and Puerto Rico, the Virgin Islands, Guam, and the

Table 9.1 The Organization of Courts in California and in the United States

	California[*]	The United States[**]
Constitutional Varieties:	California has no "legislative" courts comparable to those created by Congress. Article VI of the state constitution provides for all California courts.	The U.S. Supreme Court and the lower Federal courts are based upon Article III of the U.S. Constitution. Congress also creates Article I "legislative" courts to hear some administrative matters.
Trial Courts General Jurisdiction:	58 Superior Courts with 1,872 judges; about 9.5 million cases/year.	94 U.S. district courts (including territories & Puerto Rico) with approximately 678 judges; about 300,000 cases/year; in addition over 300 bankruptcy judges are assigned to districts.
Intermediate Appellate Courts:	6 district courts of Appeal with 105 authorized justices; nearly 25,000 case filings/year	13 U.S. courts of appeal with approximately 179 judges; about 60,000 cases/year
Courts of Last Resort:	California Supreme Court composed of Chief Justice and 6 Associate Justices; about 9,000 filings and dispositions/year	Supreme Court of the United States composed of Chief Justice and 8 Associate Justices; about 10,000 cases filed/year but most denied review
Judicial Selection and Terms of Office:	All trial court judges appointed by the Governor or elected in nonpartisan election; 6 year term Appellate and Supreme Court Justices are nominated by the Governor and confirmed by Commission; retained by nonpartisan, noncompetitive election; 12-year terms	All Article III judges nominated by the President of the United States and confirmed by U.S. Senate; these judges serve during "good behavior" (i.e., for life unless impeached); "Legislative" (Article I) court judges serve varying fixed terms

Table 9.1 *Continued*

	California*	**The United States****
Methods of Removal:	Impeachment, or by commission, or by defeat at election, or recall election	Impeachment for Art. III courts; nonreappointment for Art. I "legislative" courts
Formal Qualifications:	Member of the bar for a number of years (varies with court level); certain residence requirements	No constitutional criteria
Informal Qualifications:	Political background; appellate justices often have trial court experience.	Political background; by tradition only attorneys have been appointed; "Senatorial courtesy" often applies to trial court nominees.

In both systems, the chief executive normally selects judges from his or her own political party and of similar philosophy and ideological persuasion.
*California data: Judicial Council of California, *Annual Report* 2008.
**U.S. data: Administrative Office of the United States Courts, *Annual Report* 2008.

Northern Mariana Islands. In total, there are 678 authorized judgeships (not including bankruptcy) (2008 Judicial Facts and Figures). In addition Congress has established several specialized courts. The U.S. Court of Claims hears cases over most claims for money damages against the United States, disputes over federal contracts, and unlawful "takings" of private property by the federal government. The U.S. Court of International Trade addresses cases involving international trade and customs issues. Finally, U.S. Bankruptcy Courts handle bankruptcy cases since bankruptcy is a federal issue; therefore the federal courts have sole jurisdiction over bankruptcy issues, and cannot be heard by a state court.

California's trial court is the Superior Court, which is empowered to hear any cases arising under California law. They are established in each of the 58 counties in more than 450 locations, with about 1,872 judges to deal with both civil and criminal matters, but the number of judges per Superior Court varies with case load. In 2004 the Judicial Council of California requested the legislature to add 150 new judgeships over three years to meet the demand of increasing case loads. The legislature passed SB56 in 2006 creating 50 of these judgeships, and AB159 in 2007 for an additional 50 judgeships; however, given the budget shortfalls, the Legislature has now twice deferred funding the second set of judgeships most recently in July 2010, and did not pass the third bill for the remaining 50 judgeships. (Judicial Council of California, Annual Report, 2008).

Given the abundance of issues that state courts address, California has established several specialized subdivisions of superior courts including traffic court and small claims court. If the amount of money involved in a claim is $7,500 or less, citizens or legal entities may utilize small claims courts. Individuals must represent themselves in small claims court, as they do not involve lawyers or juries. While there is no limit on the number of claims an individual who seeks less than $2,500 may file in a year, California law limits the number of claims a person may file over $2,500 to two cases a year. There are three additional subdivisions which include courts addressing inheritance and probate, families, and juveniles. Probate court involves the administration of wills and estates. Family law courts settle domestic disputes including divorce and child custody. Finally, juvenile courts deal with matters affecting children under the age of 18 years. An exception occurs when prosecutors choose to try young individuals accused of particularly heinous crimes as adults. There are no juries in juvenile proceedings. If punishment includes incarceration, juveniles are sent to the California Youth Authority (CYA).

Numbers of Cases

While the courts of every state hear both civil and criminal cases, the ratio of criminal to civil filings and disposition will vary from state to state. In total, California's Superior court case filings totaled 10,255,360, and dispositions totaled 8,733,177 in FY 2008–2009. Of these, civil filings accounted for over 1.7 million, and civil dispositions nearly 1.5 million leaving over 8.35 million criminal filings and 7.07 million criminal dispositions. However, If you eliminate parking tickets, misdemeanors, and other minor "ticket" cases (i.e., "infractions"), the number of civil and criminal filings and dispositions evened out around one-and-a-half-million each (Judicial Council of California, Annual Report, 2008). In Federal trial courts, there is a clear preponderance of civil cases with about 78 percent of them civil and 22 percent criminal (282,307 filings between March 2009–2010 compared to only 282,307 criminal filings) inasmuch as crimes are predominantly state matters.

Most civil cases are private law matters. Smith may sue Johnson about a contract, or Mrs. McGregor may sue her husband Mr. McGregor for divorce. A moment's thought makes it clear that there are more of these private law transactions in society than there are public law transactions. If we add to that insight the knowledge that regulating private transactions is overwhelmingly state business, and if we further remember that criminal law is overwhelmingly the business of the states, we can correctly conclude that *state courts hear more cases* than do Federal courts. Indeed, in any given year the state trial courts located in Los Angeles County alone do more business than *all* of the Federal trial courts in all of the states combined! A fair conclusion is that when ordinary citizens find themselves involved in court cases, those cases are very likely to be heard by state courts.

By way of summary, we can explain the large number of cases brought to California courts by remembering these points:

1. Ordinary "private law" transactions are numerous, and are brought primarily to state courts rather than to Federal courts.
2. Criminal cases nearly always go to state courts.
3. California (unlike many states) is active in the public law area, and thus California courts hear state-level cases based on such laws.

In contrast, the central business of the Federal courts is public law. Comparatively few private law and criminal cases are heard there. Even though substantial growth has been experienced in Federal case loads over the past three decades, the numbers are dwarfed in comparison with state court case loads. Note, too, that the cost of operating the California courts is no small matter: 3.8 billion dollars proposed for 2008–2009.

Appellate Courts

Following a trial parties may appeal the decisions reached by the jury. These cases are handled in the Courts of Appeal. Appeals must be based on a legal question which may include the constitutionality of a law, or the procedure followed in trial among other questions. There are two levels of courts at both the state and federal level: appellate courts and a supreme court. California has a court of last resort with seven members (state Supreme Court), and six intermediate appellate courts (105 justices). The number of authorized appellate court justices increased approximately twenty percent from a decade earlier. Appellate courts usually sit in "divisions" of three justices whereas the Supreme Court sits en banc (as a whole group). These courts also have some original jurisdiction as well as non-trial functions, e.g., the Supreme Court has discretionary authority to review disciplinary action taken against judges and lawyers. In 2009 there were 24,048 filings for the Courts of Appeal. During the same period California's Supreme Court issued 116 written opinions; filings for the California Supreme Court totaled 9,274, and dispositions totaled 9,513.

California's Supreme Court hears cases on appeal, and by law, must hear all cases from a capital case (one in which the death penalty has been ordered). According to the California Commission on the Fair Administration of Justice (2008) between 1992 and 2002 the California Supreme Court upheld the death penalty 90 percent of the time, compared to 14 other death penalty states who combined have a 73.7 percent average. Additionally since 1978, 70 percent of the cases upheld by the state and then appealed to federal courts have been overturned. For Californians, this means the most populous state has the largest population of death row inmates but the longest time waiting on appeal. The Commission reports that the California Supreme Court is so backlogged that just one appeal from a conviction after 1997 has been resolved. Among the recommendations made by the Commission, one would be to permit intermediate courts of appeal to decide capital cases, but this would require a Constitutional Amendment. Posing the question before the voters would likely open a floodgate of debate, not over the rights of the courts to resolve death penalty sentences, but on the death penalty itself.

There are thirteen Federal Courts of Appeal, distributed throughout the country and one for the District of Columbia in addition to the Federal Circuit which hears cases on subject matter and not by geographic location. The number of judgeships for the Circuit Courts is established by Congress in Title 28 of the U.S. Code, Section 44. The current total is 179, with the Ninth Circuit (includes California) the largest with 28. The United States Supreme Court is comprised of a Chief Justice and eight associate justices. This number was established in 1869. In 2009–2010 there were 56,790 filings in the U.S. Circuit Courts and 8,159 cases in the Supreme Court which includes petitions for certiorari. The number of cases filed in the Court's *in forma pauperis* (cases in which normal court costs are waived due to inability to afford or pay for the costs) docket accounted for 6,576 of these cases, while paid cases consisted of the remaining 1,583 cases. Of these Supreme Court cases, the Court heard oral argument in 82, issuing 73 written opinions.

Courts of Limited Jurisdiction

The structure of court systems can change, in response to population growth and change, for example, or in response to best current thinking. Thus, like most states, California had rural courts throughout most of the twentieth century. There, often non-law trained judges served very small, rural counties in an informal process via Justice Courts (akin to the "Justice of the Peace" in many states). By the late 1970s, however, these California judges had to be law trained. Hearing only cases of small consequence, they kept a general peace in the community in light of community norms and values. Serious criminal matters and civil cases of large dollar values bypassed these courts for the Superior Courts.

The structure also changed in the 1950s with the creation of urban courts of limited jurisdiction called Municipal Courts. These courts provided expeditious access for civil cases in which dollar compensation was small, and also handled preliminary hearings in criminal cases. In time the Justice Courts were entirely replaced by the Municipal Courts which in turn (between 1999 and 2004) were unified completely with the Superior Courts making one comprehensive trial court structure for each of California's counties. All trial courts functions, therefore, now are Superior Court functions.

Regarding limited jurisdiction, then, California is different from the Federal system (which has limited jurisdiction Article I courts) and most (but not all) of the other states (which typically have such limited jurisdiction courts).

Selection of Judges

In the United States judges are either elected or appointed, though the details of the election or of the appointive process vary substantially from state-to-state. All Federal judges are appointed. They are nominated by the President of the United

States, and confirmed by the U.S. Senate. California uses a combination of appointment and election to choose judges.

Superior court judges are elected countywide on a nonpartisan ballot for six-year terms. Vacancies are filled through appointment by the governor. Candidates must be attorneys who have been members of the California bar for 10 years. In order to avoid cluttering the ballot, the name of an unopposed incumbent does not appear. If a vacancy occurs between elections, the governor may appoint a qualified replacement who must then be voted on by the electorate at the next general election. When the workload of a court exceeds the capacity of the existing staff, the judges may appoint attorneys to serve as temporary judges, called commissioners.

The Governor nominates Justices of the California Courts of Appeal and of the California Supreme Court when vacancies occur. The three-member Commission on Judicial Appointments must confirm such nominations. The Commission is composed of (a) the Chief Justice, (b) the Attorney General of California, and (c) either the statewide senior presiding Courts of Appeal justice (when a Supreme Court nominee is considered) or the presiding justice of the affected appellate district (when a Court of Appeals justice is nominated). At the next gubernatorial election the new justice must be retained by the state's voters. The election is noncompetitive, i.e., the state's voters simply mark "yes" or "no" on the ballot question of whether the justice should be retained in office.

The electoral defeat of a sitting justice rarely happens, although three sitting Justices of the California Supreme Court were defeated in 1986. In that year, Chief Justice Rose Bird, and Associate Justices Cruz Reynoso and Joseph Grodin received decisive "no" votes following a long and acrimonious campaign that featured, among other things, partisan attacks on the Court for having failed to send convicted murderers to the gas chamber. This electoral experience is discussed in more detail below in our segment on "Judicial Politics."

Most California trial court judges initially are appointed to vacancies resulting either from judges leaving office before the end of a term, or because new judgeships have been created by the Legislature. These trial court judges, however, must face election at the end of their first term (and subsequent terms) if they wish to continue in office. The election is competitive but nonpartisan, *i.e.*, two or more candidates may contest for the office, but none seek office as a party nominee. The first part of this election process occurs at the spring primary election, in even-numbered years. If no candidate receives a majority vote at the primary, the two leading candidates face each other in the November general election.

Terms of Office

California trial court judges serve six-year terms, while California appellate court and Supreme Court justices serve twelve-year terms. Article III Federal judges are appointed for a term of "good behavior," which essentially means until retirement, death or, rarely, impeachment. Article I judges serve fixed terms and are subject to reappointment. In California persons frequently are appointed to complete unexpired terms when a state judge leaves office before the end of a full term.

"Discipline": Handling Judicial Wrongdoing

The state Commission on Judicial Performance is responsible for the discipline of judges. The Commission is composed of a majority of lay (non-lawyer) members plus judges and lawyers. In 2009, there were 1,755 judgeships within the Commission's jurisdiction. In addition to jurisdiction over active judges, the Commission has the authority to impose certain discipline upon former judges. The Commission handled about a thousand complaints against judges annually during the 1990s. While Commission actions ranged from reprimand to removal from office, in fact very few complaints led to disciplinary actions of any kind, and removal from office was especially rare. In 2009 there were 1,161 new complaints about active and former California judges considered by the Commission. These complaints named 856 different judges alleging legal error not involving misconduct or expressed dissatisfaction with a judge's decision.

In addition to action by the Commission, California judges may be removed in three further ways: reelection loss, impeachment, and recall. (See Chapter Four). In a small move toward such a system at the national court level, Congress has provided for procedures for investigating complaints of unfairness or incompetence against Federal judges. Providing methods other than formal impeachment for removing Federal judges, however, would take an amendment to the U.S. Constitution. Informal avenues, however, exist for dealing with errant Federal trial judges, e.g., reducing of case loads or assigning minor matters to them.

How Trial Courts *Really* Work: Settlements and Plea Bargains

The very large number of cases in California would require a staggering amount of court time if they all actually were to be tried. But nearly all of the cases filed in courts are not tried. Civil cases, as a result of negotiations between the plaintiff and respondent, usually end in settlement. Criminal cases, as a result of plea bargaining (negotiations between the prosecutor and defense counsel), usually end in guilty pleas. Pleas of guilty to a criminal charge, whether or not the product of a "bargain" or other negotiation, usually result in shorter sentences than the theoretical maximum allowed by law. There is no compelling evidence, however, that those who plead guilty receive shorter sentences than they would have received at a trial. Nonetheless there is controversy over negotiations, in civil and criminal cases alike.

Support for Negotiations

The practice of negotiating settlements and plea bargains has been the subject of controversy. On one hand, some observers argue that nontrial dispositions are normal, expected, and even desirable. When private issues in civil cases are settled, the parties at least must be reasonably happy, these observers argue. Furthermore, the state is spared the expense of a trial (the full cost of which is not paid by the parties to the essentially private dispute).

As to plea bargaining, some observers note that most persons arrested for a crime usually, in fact, are guilty of something. The judicial process addresses not only whether the arrested person is guilty, but also concentrates on the question of exactly what legal definition of unlawful behavior is the right definition for this instance. The small proportion of arrested persons who in fact did nothing at all is usually quickly weeded out of the process, and those cases are dismissed.

Criticisms of Negotiations

Critics worry that at least some civil settlements are unfair, as when one injured party feels it necessary to settle for a smaller payment than might have been won at trial. Monthly bills may have begun to pile up, and parties cannot afford the cost or time involved in fully pursuing the suit. A tenant, for example, may be at a particular disadvantage versus a landlord in this regard.

Some critics of criminal case plea bargaining worry that persons accused of crimes may be pressured unfairly into guilty pleas. Others express the concern that some accused persons escape too lightly, by offering to plead guilty to a lesser crime than in fact they committed. For example we all have heard criticisms about the "revolving door of justice" or the criminals that get a "slap on the wrist." In the two decades ending the twentieth century it was clear that critics of criminal case processing were persuading voters. Various efforts, some by initiative ballot proposition, were mounted in the 1980s to curb plea bargaining. The 1990s also saw "Three Strikes and You're Out" legislation adopted both as a ballot proposition and as a statute passed by the legislature. In March 2000, voters adopted a statutory initiative providing in murder cases for the trial as adults of children as young as 14 years.

The popularity of getting tough on crime occasionally spills over to proposals for taking all persons accused of crime to trial. Yet negotiations are the only possible way that cases can be moved through trial courts. American states take about five percent of all cases to trial. California is right in line with this figure. In the 2008-2009 fiscal year, about 3.8 billion dollars has been allocated to the court system. If the state doubled the number of cases taken to trial, the courts' budget also would roughly double. Negotiations continue, and they are inevitable.

Issues and Value Conflicts

Judicial Participation in Private Law Issues

Marriage is ancient. The rules about marriage, however, can be marvelous examples of value conflicts surrounding private law. One of the most contentious issues in California has been over the definition of marriage, involving every branch of California's government as well as the initiative process. Same-sex marriage has become an ongoing legal battle in California, which has taken its cues as well as leading the way for other states. Advocates for same-sex marriage argue strenuously that they ought to be legal. Nothing else would fulfill the U.S. Constitution's mandate for equal protection under the law, activists argued. In their view, it was simply unfair, unequal, and unconstitutional, to give inheritance, beneficiary, income tax, employment benefits, hospital visitation, and other good things to spouses of standard opposite-sex marriages while withholding all of those things from same-sex couples who would marry if only the laws permitted it.

The recent story regarding same-sex marriage began in 1993 when Hawaii's Supreme Court declared that denying the right for same-sex couples to marry constituted discrimination and sent the case back to trial court for a rehearing. The trial court judge ruled that denying gays a right to marry could not be supported by the Hawaiian Constitution. However, the decision unleashed a tremendous backlash and voters in the state passed a Constitutional amendment defining marriage between a man and woman only. But the Hawaii legislature passed a landmark "Reciprocal Beneficiaries" law that created some of the protections same-sex couples could not access through marriage. How did this affect California? The United States Constitution declares that states must honor contracts from other states, known as the Full Faith Credit Clause of Article IV, Section 1. This clause means that traditional marriages must be recognized in the states, even if the marriage license was issued in another state.

Fearful that couples would soon have the right to marry, California picked up the debate in 2000, passing Proposition 22, denying through statutory law the right of same sex couples to marry by defining marriage as "a personal relation arising out of a civil contract between a man and a woman." A number of parties attempted to overturn the law in court, and in March 2006 the California Supreme Court agreed to hear argument regarding the issue. As discussed below, the debate rages on. Clearly, the courts have a tremendous role in the private lives of its citizens, as well as significant law making powers.

The point is not to argue that same-sex marriages are good or bad. The point is that courts interpret as well as change the rules about private law. Some observers, mostly on the conservative side of politics, thought that courts probably weakened the institution of marriage and had done great mischief. Others, mostly on the liberal side of politics, thought that the courts had advanced the cause of justice. Let us notice that courts had taken a side, had made rules, and had supported some values while turning away from other values. The short label for all of that is politics. In ways just like these, courts can be regarded as significant participants in the American political process. Issues surrounding same-sex partnerships, by the way, have continued in California, as discussed below.

Judicial Participation in Public Law

Courts have a critical role to play in at least some of the political issues of our times. Examples include how races should get along, and how society should treat illegal immigrants. Surely the participation of state and Federal courts in resolving the November 2000 presidential election disputes in Florida sharply illustrates the point.

In fact, judges have made many rules about how the races should get along in American history. The most famous of these is probably the decision in 1954 in the case called *Brown v. Board of Education*. In that case the U.S. Supreme Court declared that racial segregation in public schools was unconstitutional.

Controversial public issues in California in the past decade or so, for example, included ballot propositions seeking to end certain "affirmative action" benefits for racial minorities (proposition 209) and to withhold a variety of public benefits, such as access to schools and universities, from undocumented (illegal) immigrants (proposition 187). Same-sex marriage and related issues (domestic partners' rights) were and continue to be "hot" political issues brought before the courts. Both propositions 187 and 209 were approved by the voters and also immediately challenged in the courts.

Opponents asked that the judges prevent public officials from putting the propositions into effect, because the propositions were unconstitutional infringements of every person's right to equal protection of the law. Some cases challenging these propositions went to state courts, while others went to Federal courts. Both state and Federal courts, recall, are sworn to uphold the U.S. Constitution, and must (if asked) decide whether laws are unconstitutional. This is the great power called judicial review.

California voters clearly opposed affirmative action as well as wanted to withhold benefits from undocumented immigrants. It also was clear, however, that ordinary voters through ballot propositions were unlikely to have the last word. Judges, interpreting ballot propositions in light of state and Federal constitutional requirements, were going to have the last word.

The same may be said regarding laws enacted by the legislature and lower level governmental actions. In August 2004, for example, the state Supreme Court (in *Lockyer v. City and County of San Francisco*) nullified the city's issuing of marriage licenses to same-sex partners. The issue of same-sex partners also was before a Sacramento Superior Court a month after the marriage license case. Here the Superior Court upheld as constitutional the state's domestic partners law. It had been challenged by supporters of the successful 2000 initiative Proposition 22 which defined marriage as being between a man and a woman. However, the story continues. In May 2008, the California Supreme Court overturned Proposition 22 in a 4–3 ruling declaring that the state Constitution protects a fundamental "right to marry" that extends equally to same-sex couples. In November 2008, voters passed a Constitutional amendment to California's Constitution defining marriage as a union between a man and a woman only. The California Supreme heard challenges to Proposition 8 under Constitutional procedural grounds and held that the proposition had been passed constitutionally. However, the Court's ruling did not settle the question of gay marriage in California; instead it merely continued an ongoing state and national debate that both the courts and the voters will again play a large role in deciding. In August 2010 a Federal district court struck down the law under the Equal Protection Clause of the U.S. Constitution's Fourteenth Amendment. However, just weeks later the Ninth Federal Circuit Court stayed the district court ruling to allow the proponents of the ban to organize an appeal. The point is that California and many other state courts exercise a state based constitutional judicial review function very similar to that of the Federal courts.

One also should note that when courts exercise the judicial review authority, it often generates political reactions. This especially is true where the issues at hand are emotionally charged. For example, there was considerable criticism as well as support voiced when Florida's Supreme Court in September 2004 unanimously struck down as unconstitutional a statute prohibiting the removal of a feeding tube from a woman who had been in a vegetative state over a decade. These cases illustrate the authority and role of courts as the final interpreters of state constitutions and the constitutionality of any statutes or other enactments by local governments. Consequently, we will say it again, reader: state and Federal courts are significant participants in the American political process.

The Nonpartisan Tradition of Judicial Politics

Californians no less than other Americans prize a notion that judges are and ought to be uninfluenced by partisan political considerations. There is no conflict in that with the dimensions of judicial politics that we identified earlier. Although values surely conflict and though that surely amounts to politics by any reasonable definition of the word, there is no necessary fight between Democrats and Republicans implied.

Ways of insulating judges from partisan politics are consciously present in California as well as U.S. judicial structures. Strong tradition is a part of this: judges and other observers alike agree that partisan elections are inappropriate for California. Furthermore, long terms of office help to insulate judges from partisan fights. Schemes like retention elections usually insulate judges from electoral challenge, too.

For all of this, there are some traditional political elements found in the judicial selection process that have been accepted if not always cherished. These include such things as making judicial appointments that reward former legislators or other political party supporters for faithful service, or indeed other friends, like former law partners or law professors. But other political activities, e.g., using the ballot initiative process, have appeared to be attempts at lessening the traditional independence of the judiciary.

Judicial Politics at the Beginning of the Twenty-First Century

From the mid-1970s through the mid-1980s, conservative political groups mounted serious efforts to unseat both trial court and appellate court judges in California. In the most remarkable assault, Governor George Deukmejian, other Republican candidates for office, and a remarkable variety of ad hoc groups joined a campaign in 1985 and 1986 that resulted in the landslide defeat of Chief Justice Rose Bird (who received a 66 percent "no" vote), and Associate Justices Cruz Reynoso and Joseph Grodin. The incumbent justices and their supporters were out-spent in the campaign by roughly $5.5 million to $2 million (Wold and Culver 1987:350).

Observers differed on the question of whether the incumbents deserved to be cashiered by the voters. But the process, which relied on large amounts of money and heavily negative television advertising, disturbed professional observers. The inability of judges to engage in heated, high-priced election contests, and indeed, the view that they should not even try, dominated the arguments of those who were critical of the 1986 judicial retention elections. But others not critical of the contests responded that this was just the kind of situation for which retention elections were designed. The people spoke—as the system was designed to allow them to speak. By 1988 it was clear that the newly-constituted court led by Chief Justice Malcolm M. Lucas was deciding cases differently from its Rose Bird-led predecessor. With the exception of several decisions that affirmed sentences of death imposed by trial courts, the changes were subtle, in most instances gradual yet discernible.

Nationwide the capital punishment debate rages on. The use of DNA technology in recent years, for example, has been used to reverse convictions of a number of individuals convicted of capital crimes. These new findings have led opponents of the death penalty to amplify their argument that innocent people have been sentenced to death. Proponents, however, continue to argue that the number of mistakes, while unfortunate, is very small. Furthermore, future mistakes are less likely because technology has advanced in such areas as DNA.

By the mid-1990s in California, it seemed that a new consensus about the proper political role of the courts had been established. The overtly partisan strife that had marked the 1980s was gone. It was clear, however, that judges would continue to take part in the policy process—from making decisions about custody disputes to putting on hold ballot propositions while their constitutionality was being determined. It also was clear that the courts would continue to be the subject of political if not partisan scrutiny. For being involved in the policy process, judges have been reviled as well as praised. But that is, inherently, the nature of the judicial process.

Chapter 10
CALIFORNIA PUBLIC ADMINISTRATION
Yuan Ting

Since the founding of our nation, Americans have been reluctant to give government too much power because we are suspicious of elected officials abusing their power and government agencies wasting tax dollars. Nevertheless, over the course of our nation's history, Americans have increasingly depended on government at all levels to provide services to meet their needs. This is especially true at the state and local levels. Take the example of an average businessman, who owns a restaurant in a Southern California city. He does not like government and signs every petition that seems to be aimed at curbing government growth. But the reality is that government plays an important role in creating and running his business.

Before he embarked on his business venture, he contacted the city's economic development office and visited the county public library to find out demographic information about the local market, like age, gender, education, income level, ethnicity, and spending patterns. He used this information, collected by the government, to identify prospective customers and develop menu items and service levels to meet their tastes and needs. He picked an eye-catching name for his restaurant. Before he could file the name with the county, he asked the California Secretary of State to do an online search to see if the name had already been taken.

He had to fill out different forms to get licenses and permits from the city, the state of California, and the Internal Revenue Service. He needed to get a public health permit from the county because he runs a restaurant. Public health inspectors look at his kitchen regularly and issue him certificates of compliance with various health laws. He displays these licenses, permits, and certificates on the walls next to the autographed pictures of famous clients. His establishment is subject to inspection by the city and county governments for compliance with fire and safety laws. Because beer and wine are served he had to obtain a liquor license from the city, which was granted to him in exchange for his promise of compliance with state liquor laws.

His relationship with government does not end there. The water he uses comes to his restaurant through the California Aqueduct. It has traveled hundreds of miles through a complex delivery system of cement channels and tunnels. Before delivery to his establishment, the food he serves has been inspected according to regulations enforced by the California Department of Food and Agriculture and other government agencies. The procedures used to hire and supervise the workers who picked the tomatoes he serves were established and enforced by the California Agricultural Labor Relations Board. He carefully accounts for the money he takes in, and returns a portion to the state as sales taxes. Because of his minority status, he applied for a state-supported low-interest loan available to minority business enterprises. He deposits his receipts in a bank licensed and regulated by the California Department of Financial Institutions. His restaurant benefits from a state-financed freeway, which exists only two blocks away from his business. There is a state-supported public university and a county-run hospital nearby, which supply a constant stream of customers.

This example shows that without the actions of government agencies, many common activities like dining at a restaurant would be impossible or unsafe. It also points out that government has to hire a large number of employees to provide a variety of services, and many services are mundane and less visible to the public. Public employees are referred to by some people as the "fourth branch of government" (the executive, legislative, and judicial branches are the other three). We don't elect them and many work outside the public eye, so we usually don't know them unless we have had the occasion to deal with them directly. Who are these people hired to provide public services, and why do they act the way they do? Are they destroying our rights and liberties, or are they protecting us from foreseeable harm while helping us realize our potential? This chapter examines California's public administrators. We will look at who these people are, how they make important decisions, and the arrangement of the organizations in which they work.

Former Governor Arnold Schwarzenegger criticized the state bureaucracy and made reform of state agencies a major tenet of his campaign during the recall election in 2003. Through a broad reform program, he expected to achieve great gains in efficiency and cost savings. Upon his election, he signed Executive Order S-5-04 creating the California Performance Review (CPR) to conduct a rigorous examination of state government and recommend changes to improve efficiency and effectiveness across all aspects of state government. This chapter will also look at the CPR and recommendations for reform.

Who Are California Public Administrators?

There are four groups of people performing and providing public services to our citizens. First, there are a small number of high-level officials appointed by the governor to state agencies, departments, boards, and commissions. These political appointees serve at the pleasure of the governor. Their numbers have increased in recent years to about 750. Some of these positions are salaried and others are non-salaried. About 150 of them are important management positions, like the Director of Finance and the Secretary of Corrections and Rehabilitation, which must be confirmed by the State Senate, similar to the way in which high-level federal officials must be confirmed by the United States Senate. These officials are appointed on the basis of their political connection and loyalty to ensure the political (executive) control of state bureaucracy and make state employees more responsive to the policy and will of the governor, and ultimately to the public.

Second, more than 335,000 people work for state agencies, and these numbers include 45,000 people employed by the California State University system and 86,000 people by the University of California system (California Department of Finance 2008, Table C-5). Their job is to implement state laws, enforce regulations, and provide services to the public. Their ranks include highway patrol officers, public defenders, college professors, agricultural inspectors, personnel officers, environmental planners, maintenance workers, and many others. Practically any imaginable occupation can be found in the state government somewhere. These employees have to pass examinations to get their jobs, and they are protected by the state law with greater job security than political appointees and private sector employees. This principle is called the merit system, under which civil servants are hired, evaluated, and promoted on the basis of their job-related competence and performance.

Third, a large number of employees in other levels of government, including cities, counties, and special districts, are responsible for the enforcement of state laws. While they do not work directly for a state paycheck, their duties are partially or completely defined by state laws and regulations. For example, Los Angeles County Department of Public Social Services hires people to manage the CalWORKs program, which provides temporary financial assistance and employment services to low-income families with dependent children. The job of these county employees is to enforce the state law to determine if a family is eligible to receive the assistance.

Fourth, people work for private or nonprofit organizations that carry out services paid for by the State of California. In the last several decades, there has been an increasing trend among the states and local governments to contract out services traditionally performed by public employees (i.e., social services, health care, and solid waste) to the private or nonprofit sector. While aimed to control the cost and improve the efficiency of public services, the trend has raised concerns about the negative impact for public employee morale (Nigro, Nigro, and Kellough 2007, 329). It also has raised the issue of accountability and equality since private and nonprofit organizations are not subject to the same public scrutiny and transparency as government agencies (Behn 2001, Chapter 2).

These four groups of people have several common traits. All are paid a salary directly or indirectly by the state; all are responsible for the enforcement of state laws and rules; all but the first group is likely to carry out their duties regardless of the ideology of the elected officials; and few will change their duties when elected officials change.

Obviously, we are talking about spending a lot of money to employ large numbers of people to perform services for the public. In fact, the State of California, measured in terms of either the amount of money spent or the number of people employed, is one of the world's largest organizations. It is responsible for many of the most essential services to the public, and the trend in recent years from both the federal government and the courts is likely to give more responsibilities to the states.

Why is Public Administration Important Politically?

Size does not always dictate importance. If state employees simply carried out the wishes of their elected officials, there would be little reason to study them in detail. They are extremely important, precisely because their task is not simply to do what they are told. Public administrators make policy as well as carry it out.

Power Is Delegated to Public Administrators

Traditional public administration scholars tried to reconcile democracy with the idea of professional administration by conceiving of government divided between politics and administration. The job of politics (elected officials) is to express the will of the people by making laws, and the job of administration (public administrators) is to execute the will of the people by carrying out the laws. In theory, this concept of a dichotomy between politics and administration assumes that politics should have a general superiority over administration, and public administrators should be separated from the influence of politics to promote professionalism and efficiency (Wilson 1887).

In reality, however, carrying out state laws requires the making of numerous decisions that must rely on the judgment of those implementing them. Public agencies have to create administrative rules to implement laws passed by elected officials. Going back to the example of the restaurant owner, who can best decide whether his restaurant will provide enough parking for its customers and therefore not contribute unduly to traffic congestion in the city? Who can decide the specific criteria and procedures used to determine if his restaurant meets the public health and safety requirements? Legislators could make the determination, but to do so would require extensive knowledge, professional expertise, and hours of fact-finding on the subjects. Instead, the lawmakers establish general guidelines and rely on public agencies to create their own rules and apply them to specific cases. Therefore administrative rulemaking becomes an important way in which public agencies create policies, and public administrators are given much discretion in how laws and policies are to be interpreted and implemented because legislative guidelines are usually vague. Do police officers arrest everybody who travels faster than the speed limit? Are all students with low grades automatically disenrolled from the university? Plainly the answer is no, yet decisions like these directly affect the lives of those involved. Most often, they are based on the best judgment of public administrators, who are not elected by the public, but instead are appointed to their jobs based on their job-related qualifications.

There are limits to the discretion of public administrators. General guidelines have been established by elected officials. Agency rulemaking also confines administrative discretion in individual cases by establishing specific standards and procedures that public administrations have to follow (West 2005). Often courts rule on whether administrators are correctly interpreting the law. An administrator who seriously violates the intent of a law can be reprimanded and the decision altered. There also are appeal mechanisms for most administrative decisions. If you are arrested, the courts, not the police officer, will decide if in fact the charge is warranted. Your house cannot be condemned by the government to widen a street unless good cause can be shown, a public hearing held, and a fair price offered. You as the owner of the house have the right to protest such decisions and take the government to court. Administrative decisions must be made in an open and transparent manner, following legal procedures.

These constraints affect administrative decisions but much leeway remains for public administrators. Laws are often vague and the direction of high-level officials to the administrator who implements the law usually gives the person at the bottom of the organization considerable discretion to exercise his or her best judgment. This has raised the important question about how we hold public administrators accountable to elected officials and ultimately to the people.

As Experts, Public Administrators Are Given Power

Elected officials delegate decision-making power to public administrators because they assume administrators' knowledge will lead them to preferred decisions. For example, we trust doctors to decide on the best course of action on the basis of their expertise. So will legislators rely on the knowledge of engineers for the design of a bridge and the determination of the best way to build it, although the legislature may determine when and where to build it. In our culture, knowledge is often thought to be the best way of making decisions. It follows that elected officials delegate authority to appointed officials (public administrators), within the area of expertise of those appointed officials.

Career public administrators, who handle general management functions like personnel and financial administration, also are given deference because they are familiar with the functions and procedures, and have established trust with their elected superiors. Public administrators are on the job daily and have usually worked for their organizations much longer than have the elected legislators. Therefore, their institutional memory and professional knowledge prompt their suggestions to be frequently taken seriously and implemented based on their understanding of the way things have been done in the past. For example, the city council asks staff in the planning department for their recommendations on land use and redevelopment issues, and is likely to be influenced by the recommendations.

As Members of a Large Organization, Public Administrators Are Part of a Large Machine

We like to use the word *bureaucracy* to describe complex and large government agencies. Literally speaking, bureaucracy means a form of rule by offices and desks, that is, each member of an organization has an office with a set of responsibilities, rules, and tasks. Therefore, specifically defined tasks generally are found in large organizations and employees perform their tasks routinely and repetitively to increase their efficiency. These tasks need to be coordinated and supervised by mechanisms to make sure that the narrowly defined tasks are completed in timely fashion. As long as tasks are performed to specification, goods are efficiently produced. The more repetitive the tasks, the easier it is to coordinate and supervise the job and produce the desired product efficiently. This concept is based on the work of classical organization theorists like Frederick Taylor, Max Weber, and Luther Gulick. They compared large organizations to large machines, considered organizations as a rational tool, and attempted to find the best way to accomplish organizational objectives in the most efficient way (Shafritz, Ott, and Jang 2005, Chapter 1).

According to classical organization theorists, specialization and repetition are essential to the efficiency of any organization. A machine stops and starts frequently to make changes in its parts, but will not produce as efficiently as one that does not stop. Like machines, large organizations want to do repeated tasks and react badly to anything that may disturb the prescribed routine. Any attempt to radically change organizational routines and existing operations can expect to meet resistance because rank-and-file employees and their managers are convinced that the way things are running is the way things ought to run. Therefore, day-to-day decisions of those in large organizations will rely on standard operating procedures to maintain and reinforce the status quo. Managers who wish to operate efficiently will oppose any major change.

Managers also want their organization to grow, so they will hide funds from view and inflate their budget if they fear that resources may decline to threaten the future of their organization. This concept is taken from the early economic analyses of bureaucracy by Gordon Tullock (1965), Anthony Downs (1967), and William Niskanen (1971) that public administrators are difficult to control because they are self-seeking individuals who like to take advantage of their informational and expertise advantages to manipulate elected officials for their own gain.

This section explains the reasons why California public administrators are powerful and politically important. Many of the most basic decisions of government are made by those who are appointed to their jobs. They are not tightly restricted to the application of laws and rules passed by the elected officials because in most instances the laws and rules are only very general guidelines. Public administrators are most likely committed to the missions of their organizations. For example, agriculture policy analysts believe in a strong and healthy farm sector for the good of the state and nation. Highway administrators believe that road repair is an urgent public priority. Educators in public universities fear that the future of our state and nation will not be secure without increases in education budgets.

California Public Administration Reflects American Political Values

The organization of the state bureaucracy is confusing and complicated. The place of the states in the federal system, the values embedded in California history, and the rapid social and economic changes of recent years all have had an effect on the organization of state government.

California Public Administrators Operate Within a Larger Political and Administrative System

The U.S. Constitution created two layers of government: the federal government and the states. At the beginning of our nation's history, the federal government was quite small compared to the states and most governmental functions were performed by the states. This federalist system of government prevailed in the first 150 years of American history during which the balance of power favored the states. However, this balance began to shift when the states and local governments realized that they could not cope with the demands brought on by the Great Depression at the beginning of the 1930s. As a result, the federal government, under the leadership of President Franklin D. Roosevelt, created many relief and public works programs to help the states and local governments in fighting the Depression. This signaled the expansion of the federal government and the need for more intergovernmental cooperation among the federal, state, and local governments. As the federal government expanded its grants-in-aid and other programs, it gained more influence over state and local government affairs. However, the critics argued that federal grants-in-aid do not allow for enough flexibility to address local needs. In response, since the 1970s the states and local governments have been given more responsibility from the federal government to govern their own affairs through general revenue sharing and block grants, which provide federal money to state and local governments with little strings attached.

These days California public administrators operate within this system of government. Rules, laws, and administrative decisions of the federal government and local governments all influence public administrators in the state bureaucracy. Judicial decisions and even international agreements may also influence administrative decisions. The functions of government are fundamentally intertwined. State and federal officials often work together on similar tasks in which a program is funded by the federal government and administered by state and local agencies. Interest groups concerned with a given problem know the most effective strategy to influence policymaking is to try to influence all levels of government.

The term "picket fence federalism" aptly describes this system of federal-state-local government relations. It describes a political system where policy is made by many different public administrators, affected by many different interest groups, at many different levels of government. In this system, interest groups become more influential in some policy domains than public administrators who are supposed to interpret, coordinate, and implement government policies (see Chapter 6 for further discussion of California interest groups). For example, health policy is made at all levels of government by public health administrators, health care professionals, and supporters of the health industry (the "pickets"). The elected officials and public agencies work together to coordinate the various policies the government implements (the rails of the fence). Within this context, state agencies must deal with public administrators and organized groups that are concerned with policies at other levels of government.

Local governments also play a critical role in the state administrative system. Legally speaking, local governments are creatures of the state, and the state can create or dispose of them at will. In practice, however, local governments are important partners with the state and federal governments in implementing state and national laws and have strong political support through their elected representatives. Many California cities and some counties have been granted charters (see Chapter 11), which provide them with independent legal standing and greater control of their own operations.

Local governments, however, are directly tied to state policy through the ability of states to mandate localities to carry out certain state functions. Most of what counties and school districts do, for instance, is the result of state laws. For example, school districts must uphold certain standards, a given number of days are required in the school year, teachers must meet state qualification requirements, and certain subjects must be taught while other subjects may not be taught. State administrators rely on local school districts to carry out these requirements. State officials in this process are effectively limited to inspecting the operations of individual districts and schools to verify their compliance with state laws. Therefore, state government delegates the actual job to another level of government (school districts) to implement its education policy.

As mentioned before, government responsibility is also delegated to private and nonprofit organizations. In this case, the state oversees but does not directly take part in the provision of public services like mental health care. That makes it hard to precisely define the administrative branch of California government. It seems to be more than just state employees, who themselves work for the state, since policies are delegated to and carried out by other levels of government as well as private and nonprofit organizations, and since some policies are made by the federal government with implementation delegated to the states. With that in mind, we will turn our attention to important principles and values governing the structure of government agencies and the activities of public administrators in the state of California.

Accountability, Professionalism, and Public Control

Structure of government refers to how political and administrative functions are arranged and organized in public agencies. When change in government is proposed, structure is usually the first element to which people look. This was certainly the case with the CPR, which proposed a major consolidation of departments and commissions in the state government.

All governmental structures reflect our beliefs about basic questions, like who ought to make important decisions, who should be hired and fired from the civil service, and how important one feels elected officials, the public, and professionals ought to be in making policy. Generally speaking, American governmental structures represent compromises between three basic values, including *accountability*, *professionalism*, and *public control*. Some people have argued that the most important purpose of governmental organization is *accountability* to the wishes of elected officials, and through them, to the people. Supporters of this position assume that elected officials should make policy for most issues and be allowed to hire people they feel are most loyal and able to carry out their policy. They wish to organize public employees to effectively carry out the policy, and by doing it this way, public employees can be held more directly accountable to elected officials.

But another group of people believes that organizations should be structured and run on the basis of *professionalism* to encourage the application of professional expertise to the solution of public problems. They would like to establish an administration that recruits the best trained and most qualified employees and provide conditions that would encourage them to stay with the organization. The hope is that professional experts would find the most effective and efficient solutions to the issues at hand by applying their knowledge, skills, and insight. Hiring employees who perform well on examinations and protecting employees from political intrusion or removal through a civil service system are based on this perspective. From this standpoint, elected officials should provide broad policy guidelines only, leaving technical details and implementation to the experts to handle.

Finally, others are most concerned with the potential abuses of power that can occur when authority is delegated to public administrators who have the informational and expertise advantages to manipulate elected officials for their own gains. This group of people desires to organize the bureaucracy to minimize the power of administrators and maximize *public control*. The proponents of this position support strict rules and procedures to control administrative initiative, improve organizational transparency, and require public hearings and input of citizen groups before major actions may be taken by public agencies.

Conflicts among these values, *accountability, professionalism,* and *public control,* permeate the discussion of how to organize government. California's structure, like most governments in this country, incorporates features of all three values. The Progressive Reform Movement that started in the early twentieth century has emphasized professional expertise and brought the large number of public employees under the protection of the merit system. In California, the State Personnel Board was established in 1934 to administer the civil service system and ensure that state employment is based on merit and free from the influence of political patronage. The popularity of the initiative and referendum and many actions of the legislature designed to limit administrative discretion emphasize popular control (see Chapter 4 for further discussion of different ballot measures). Accountability is achieved through the governor and other statewide elected officials and the legislature as they provide direction to the bureaucracy through political appointees and policy guidelines (see Chapters 7 and 8).

In the state government, administration of most functions begins in the office of the governor. The governor appoints major agency heads and other important officials, sets the tone for most of what occurs during his or her time in office, and prepares the state budget. But the legislature is also closely linked to public administrators through the writing of legislation and oversight responsibility. Surveys of state administrators, in fact, find that the legislature is perceived as a more important influence on administrators than is the governor (Abney and Lauth 1986).

Unlike the federal government, California also elects several department heads in statewide elections, including the Lieutenant Governor, Secretary of State, Attorney General, Controller, Treasurer, Insurance Commissioner, Superintendent of Public Instruction, and the Board of Equalization. For example, the Attorney General is elected statewide to serve as the chief law officer of California. The Attorney General carries out his or her responsibilities through the California Department of Justice. Public administrators in the Department of Justice report and are held accountable to the Attorney General and they are subject to less influence by the Governor and State Legislature (see Chapter 7 for further discussion of these officeholders).

The major functions of California government are carried out by six superagencies and more than eighty departments. The creation of superagencies allows the Governor greater capacity to hold agency secretaries accountable, who are in charge to coordinate, supervise, and hold the departments and offices inside their agencies accountable (see Table 10.1). These agency secretaries and department heads are appointed by the Governor and confirmed by the State Senate. These appointees are political supporters of the Governor, serving at his or her pleasure, and therefore an emphasis on *accountability* is achieved. Most other employees are recruited through civil service examinations, and the emphasis represented here is on the value of *professionalism*.

Independent Boards and Commissions Separate Policy from Political Direction

Another outgrowth of the Progressive reform tradition is the creation of independent boards and commissions. California undertakes certain functions at the direction of an appointed board or commission whose members are sometimes selected for terms longer than a governor's four-year term. Therefore, policy direction of an independent board or commission is shielded from direct partisan control, and the office operates more independently of the political influence of elected officials. Board members and commissioners are considered experts in the area of concern and are assumed to be neutral arbitrators in instances of conflict. To a large extent, the value emphasized here is *professionalism*. Some boards and commissions are housed within a superagency, but are authorized to exercise independent powers (see Table 10.1). Housed in the Natural Resources Agency, the California Coastal Commission is responsible for the development of land and water in the coastal zone and has the power to issue building permits for construction that may change the use of land or public access to coastal waters. Others, like the Public Employment Relations Board and the Public

Table 10.1 Superagencies in the State Government

Agency Name	Departments Within the Agency	Boards and Commissions Within the Agency
Business, Transportation, and Housing	California Highway Patrol Department of Alcoholic Beverage Control Department of Corporations Department of Financial Institutions Department of Housing and Community Development Department of Managed Health Care Department of Motor Vehicles Department of Real Estate Department of Transportation Housing Finance Agency Office of the Patient Advocate Office of Real Estate Appraisers Office of Traffic Safety	California Film Commission California Travel and Tourism Commission Small Business Board
Environmental Protection	Department of Pesticide Regulation Department of Toxic Substances Control Office of Environmental Health Hazard Assessment	Air Resources Board Integrated Waste Management Board State Water Resources Control Board Regional Water Quality Control Boards (9)
Health and Human Services	Department of Aging Department of Alcohol and Drug Programs Department of Child Support Services Department of Community Services and Development Department of Developmental Services	Managed Risk Medical Insurance Board

(*continued*)

Table 10.1 *Continued*

Agency Name	Departments Within the Agency	Boards and Commissions Within the Agency
	Department of Health Care Services Department of Mental Health Department of Public Health Department of Rehabilitation Department of Social Services Emergency Medical Services Authority Office of Statewide Health Planning and Development	
Labor and Workforce Development	Business Investment Services Department of Industrial Relations Economic Strategy Panel Employment Development Department Employment Training Panel	Agricultural Labor Relations Board Unemployment Insurance Appeals Board Workforce Investment Board
Natural Resources	CALFED Bay-Delta Program California Conservation Corps Department of Boating and Waterways Department of Conservation Department of Fish and Game Department of Forestry and Fire Protection Department of Parks and Recreation Department of Water Resources	California Coastal Commission California Energy Commission California State Lands Commission San Francisco Bay Conservation and Development Commission Delta Protection Commission Colorado River Board of California State Reclamation Board Board of Forestry Fish and Game Commission Mining and Geology Board

Table 10.1 Continued

Agency Name	Departments Within the Agency	Boards and Commissions Within the Agency
		Native American Heritage Commission
		Parks and Recreation Commission
		State Historical Resources Commission
		State Off-Highway Motor Vehicle Recreation Commission
		California Water Commission
		California Boating and Waterways Commission
		Wildlife Conservation Board
State and Consumer Services	California African American Museum California Public Employees' Retirement System California Science Center California State Teachers' Retirement System Department of Consumer Affairs	California Building Standards Commission Fair Employment and Housing Commission Seismic Safety Commission State Board of Control State Personnel Board

Utilities Commission, stand outside any superagency. Among the issues handled by these boards and commissions are political practices, utility rates, teacher preparedness, employment practices, and the lottery. The number of boards and commissions has increased significantly since 1970, today totaling over 300. The Governor appoints more than 2,500 members to commissions and boards.

Although the CPR was highly critical of this array of boards and commissions and proposed to eliminate some and consolidate others, the proposal generated concern among important interest groups and stakeholders that see these boards and commissions as an important source of access to the state policymaking process (see Chapter 6 for further discussion of California interest groups). Supporters of the current system stress the importance of *public control* through these boards and commissions.

Rulemakings, Procedures, and Court Rulings Emphasize Public Control

The state constitution and statutes passed by the legislature create and grant power to various state agencies, departments, boards, and commissions. These powers often include rulemaking, the creation of rules and regulations to carry out their duties. These rules and regulations are designed to limit the discretion of public officials. To ensure public control and fairness in the rulemaking process, administrative agencies must follow the procedures set forth in California's Administrative Procedure Act when adopting, amending, or repealing regulations. The act is an important legislative weapon designed to promote democratic accountability in the state bureaucracy. It limits arbitrary actions and requires that the administrative process of making rules and regulations be open to public scrutiny. The act requires administrators to make public their proposed regulations and activities, contact persons who are affected by the proposed administrative actions, and permit the public to comment on the proposed policies and regulations. Any action by a public body that affects the environment, for example, must include an elaborate and detailed evaluation of its impact called an Environmental Impact Statement. Affected parties are invited to contribute to this report, and failure to adequately account for environmental impact in such reports can ultimately become the basis for court cases. In such cases, the courts have the authority to halt public projects. Moreover, many administrative decisions require direct public participation by affected groups. Hearings are required for cases where land is to be condemned for public purposes, and the public is invited to appear. In California, the Office of Administrative Law is responsible for reviewing all proposed regulations by state agencies for compliance with the standards set forth in California's Administrative Procedures Act as well as other legislative and judicial rulings.

In addition to regulations, state law requires that the budget process be formal and detailed. Once a budget is appropriated, departments have the responsibility to operate within budgeted levels and to comply with any restrictions enacted by the legislature. The Department of Finance approves budget changes, and these changes are forwarded to the State Controller's office, which maintains and monitors the statewide appropriation accounts after the budget is adopted. However, change in budgeted amounts beyond a certain limit cannot be made by departments without legislative approval. The Governor has certain powers to adjust expenditures, but not appropriations. For example, in the past governors have issued executive orders to implement hiring and purchase freezes and delayed capital expenditures under emergency conditions. Rules and regulations also limit the manner in which budgeted money may be spent. Large purchases must be based on competitive bidding among potential suppliers. Purchases at the lowest feasible unit cost are required. All financial transactions must be carefully documented.

Together these methods of public control are the "red tape," which is the time-honored complaint about public administration. They are not necessarily arbitrary or capricious, nor are they simply the product of a large organization. By and large they are serious attempts to promote *public control* and transparency in the administrative process. Such regulations and procedures do in fact slow the decision process and may add considerably to the workload and the efficiency of public administrators. But they also ensure that public administrators operate within the law and listen to what the people most affected by their decisions have to say. In other words, these regulations and procedures promote democratic accountability in public administration.

Who Manages State Employees?

Which kinds of people are best to implement public policies? The answer to that question has a good deal to do with how one might evaluate the way an organization hires, fires, and promotes its employees. Three perspectives that we previously discussed define methods of recruiting and evaluating employees. One perspective assumes that *accountability* should dictate public personnel policy. Advocates of accountability maintain that newly elected leaders ought to be able to select people who will follow the leader's point of view. The test of accountability is whether one will follow the direction of a political superior or clearly know what that direction might be. The premise of this perspective is that making personnel decisions on the basis of political loyalty and support for the elected officials ensures that public administrators are responsive to the will of elected officials, and through them, to the public (Nigro, Nigro, and Kellough 2007, 22).

Others maintain that government employees should be selected by skills, knowledge, and abilities needed for particular tasks. These people support selection by *merit*, defined as the skills and qualities necessary to perform the task regardless of personal values or political attitudes. This perspective supports the value of *professionalism,* which means that individuals must be hired, trained, evaluated, and promoted based on their job-related qualifications and performance only. To retain the most competent, government employees must be protected from political interference. This perspective led to the passage of the Civil Service Act in 1913 and established a merit-based civil service system in the State of California. Under this system, personnel decisions should be made on the individual's merit, which could be determined through formal and objective appraisal, evaluation, and tests.

Merit or professionalism-based personnel policies should be run by a neutral agency (usually called a Civil Service Commission) and employees should be retained unless proven to be incompetent. A new governor in this system would work with the same employees that the previous governor had. It is assumed that neutral hiring and political protections will assure the governor of a more highly skilled workforce. While a strong and neutral civil service system has the advantage of attracting and retaining highly skilled employees, a disadvantage of a civil service system is the increased power of public administrators. As a result, elected officers are less able to change the direction of policy and find it increasingly difficult to dismiss civil service–protected employees for doing poorly on their jobs.

Organized Employees

A third perspective to the managing of public personnel involves the organization of public employees. State employees expanded their influence in policymaking through employee organizations and unions in the 1970s and 1980s. Laws adopted, especially during the years in which Edmund G. "Jerry" Brown served as the thirty-fourth governor (1975–1983), provided for collective bargaining over wages, salaries, and working conditions for the first time for public employees. Employee organizations also influenced the making of personnel policy by the legislature. Further, public employee organizations and unions vigorously expanded their activities in elections, work stoppages, and in a few instances, strikes. By the early 1990s, over 75 percent of public employees in California were members of unions or employee associations that have the right to bargain over wages and working conditions, among the highest number in the country (Ban and Riccucci 1995).

Organized employees advocate greater control by employees and unions in the managing of personnel matters. They support group decision making with the particular influence of lower level employees, and broader laws and regulations protecting employees from management abuses. Critics wonder if organized employees, through collective bargaining, gain unwarranted influence on policy and needlessly increase "red tape." Others wonder whether public employees, now provided with most of the rights afforded to workers in the private sector, should continue to enjoy the protection and job security afforded to them by civil service system in California and other states. For example, Republican Governor Scott Walker in Wisconsin signed measure passed by the legislature in March 2011 to eliminate most collective bargaining rights for many state employees, although the issue is likely to be tied up in court for some time. Leaders of employee organizations, on the other hand, argue that public administrators' influence on policy is complementary to a democratic system. They represent the concerns of public service recipients who aren't represented well by elected officials, for example, parents of children in need of better educational facilities or citizens who are the victims of crime. Employee unions may increase communication between the top and bottom of the organization. In the midst of these debates, the newly elected Governor Jerry Brown is expected to have a tough job balancing the critics and supporters of state employees and their unions as he tries to address the State's severe budget problems.

State Personnel Board and the Department of Personnel Administration

The organization of personnel management in the state of California reflects different perspectives on how we should handle personnel issues. Currently California state government's personnel functions are split between the State Personnel Board (SPB) and the Department of Personnel Administration (DPA). The five-member

SPB, appointed by the Governor, was created in 1934 to revise classification plans, develop examination techniques, and hear employee appeals of disciplinary actions. It is charged with administering the state's civil service system to ensure that state employment is based on merit and free of political patronage. Created in 1981, the DPA reports directly to the governor and is responsible for negotiating salaries, benefits, and other employment terms with unions and overseeing the administration of collective bargaining contracts under the State Employer-Employee Relations Act (also called the Ralph C. Dills Act). It also administers compensation, evaluation and training programs, and layoff and grievance procedures. Since each body represents a different perspective on how state employees should be managed and both are headed by gubernatorial appointees, conflicts between these two organizations are common. For example, while the DPA handles voluntary resignation, the SPB is responsible for appeals of dismissal during probation and classification appeals. In the mid-1990s, the Little Hoover Commission issued a report which described the split personnel management structure as constrained by procedures that discourage change, and recommended that the SPB be abolished (Little Hoover Commission 1995). However, this recommendation was never passed into law by the legislature because of the strong resistance from state employee unions and the lack of consensus and leadership to reform the state civil service (Naff 2006).

How Employees are Hired and Fired

In theory, policy and administration should and could be separate. In reality, however, few people today argue that public administrators are simply following orders. As the example of the restaurant owner indicates, many public administrators, although not elected by the public, make important decisions with little or very general direction from their superiors.

Civil Service and Fairness

Followers of the Progressive reform tradition argue that hiring employees through a civil service system protects the public from problems thought to be particularly associated with the appointment of officials based on patronage, like corruption and lack of competency. Under a merit system, job-related knowledge and expertise frame decisions made by people who were neutrally recruited via an examination process. Civil servants are insulated from politics.

One of the most important features of the civil service system is its use of examinations to hire people for public service as well as the objective methods used to evaluate performance and determine who should be promoted. Therefore, the merit system emphasizes political neutrality and objectivity in making personnel decisions (Nigro, Nigro, and Kellough 2007, 97). Recently the neutrality of civil service procedures has been called into question by the courts because in many instances what personnel officials thought were neutral and valid methods for recruiting or promoting employees were actually biased. For example, education, not job-related skills, was often what civil service exams in fact measured. Not surprisingly, those with access to better education systems were more likely to be selected. Still other seemingly neutral job requirements, such as minimum height and weight, discriminated against women and certain racial and ethnic groups. Some testing procedures, while appearing neutral on the surface, were designed to ensure that only certain kinds of people were selected. In a landmark case, *Griggs* v. *Duke Power Company* (1971), the U.S. Supreme Court ruled that even if there was no discriminatory intent, if a selection test had an adverse or disparate impact with regard to race, color, religion, or national origin—if it eliminated disproportionate numbers of minority applicants—and its validity had not been established to serve a legitimate business necessity, its use might constitute unlawful discrimination under Title VII of the Civil Rights Act of 1964.

If we cannot show with complete confidence that our testing process selects the most qualified, the question of exactly who is chosen for the job becomes a more intense source of concern. This concern arises because government jobs are regarded as a commodity that should be fairly apportioned among major groups in the community, and people ask to what extent the groups of appointed public officials should approximate the ethnic, regional, sex, and other makeup of the community. The presence of significant differences between the characteristics of public administrators and the general public they serve may imply that administrative decisions might not meet the test of fairness because decisions are made by those who are less representative of the people most affected.

Affirmative Action

Studies of government employees show that while significant numbers of women and minorities are employed by the states, their numbers in the upper ranks, where more important decisions are made, are much smaller (Greene, Selden, and Brewer 2000). In an attempt to bring hiring patterns in the state government more closely in line with workforce characteristics, state agencies have in the past implemented affirmative action plans to redistribute employment opportunities from those who have been historically advantaged to other groups that have been subject to discrimination in the past. The plans include increased advertising for positions in media more accessible to underrepresented groups, removal of employment restrictions that inhibit minority employment and are unrelated to the characteristics of the job, and a setting of goals and timetables for hiring and promotion of underrepresented groups. While most people do not oppose efforts to broaden recruitment and remove employment restrictions unrelated to the job for underrepresented groups, numeric goals and timetables are often challenged by those who believe such preferential treatment amounts to reverse discrimination.

Table 10.2 Representation in the State Civil Service

	Prior to Prop. 209 in 1996	2007	Change from 1996 to 2007
Men	52.6%	52.8%	+0.2%
Women	47.4%	47.2%	−0.2%
African American	11.5%	11%	−0.5%
American Indians	0.3%	0.4%	+0.1%
Asian American	6.1%	8.5%	+2.4%
Hispanic	17.4%	21.1%	+3.7%
Pacific Islanders	0.4%	0.5%	+0.1%
White	58%	50%	−8%

Source: California State Personnel Board, *Annual Census of Employees in the State Civil Service, 2006–2007 Fiscal Year.* http://www.spb.ca.gov/WorkArea/showcontent.aspx?id=3962

This issue of affirmative action has generated considerable debate in California. In 1996 California voters approved Proposition 209 to amend the state constitution to prohibit public institutions in the state from discriminating against or giving preferential treatment to any individual or group in public employment, public education, or public contracting on the basis of race, sex, color, ethnicity, or national origin. After its passage, the opponents of Proposition 209 immediately filed a lawsuit to block the implementation. In 1997, the Supreme Court refused to hear an appeal case on Proposition 209 and allowed the decisions of the lower courts to stand, which means that the prohibition on affirmative action in California has been upheld. We can expect that different groups will continue to speak out both for and against the passage of Proposition 209. While the future of affirmative action is difficult to predict, data collected by the California State Personnel Board (2007) seemed to suggest that the passage of Proposition 209 has not had any significant impact in reducing the employment of minorities and women in the state government (see Table 10.2).

Evaluating and Reforming California Public Administration

Are Californians well served by the state government? In his letter to the Little Hoover Commission (2005), Governor Schwarzenegger declared that:

> The current framework of state government is antiquated and unsustainable. Reform of California state government—its practices, processes and organization—is a daunting but long-overdue task.

Upon his election, the governor created the California Performance Review (CPR) in 2004 to review state agencies and develop recommendations to increase the performance of state government and make it more responsive to the needs of the state's people. The CPR had four major components:

1. **Executive branch reorganization**—The Review will consolidate common functions and responsibilities in single departments, ensure departments with similar responsibilities are grouped together for effective leadership by cabinet secretaries, and eliminate and/or restructure many boards and commissions.
2. **Program performance assessment and budgeting**—California needs to undertake regular and rigorous evaluations of program performance focusing on prioritization of program needs, return on program investment, and effective program management.
3. **Improved services and productivity**—California must pursue a customer-focused transformation to provide timely, responsive, and cost-effective services to the public. Local, state, and federal governments must join collaboratively to design a more integrated process for delivering services to the public.
4. **Acquisition reform**—The State's acquisition process is in desperate need of a complete overhaul as systemic failures can be found in every area of California's acquisition practices.

The need for major changes in California state government seems to be supported by the findings from the Government Performance Project (GPP), which is the most comprehensive analysis of all state governments. Since 1996, the Pew Center on the States has supported the project, led initially by the Maxwell School of Citizenship and Public Administration at Syracuse University. One of the most important products of the GPP is a 50-state report card, which examines the use of contemporary management tools and processes in all 50 states and provides comparative state information on government performance. The GPP focuses on four management areas, including money, people, infrastructure, and information—money refers to budgeting processes, people refers to human resource management practices, information refers to data collection for management decision making and performance measurement, and infrastructure refers to government assets and infrastructures. Table 10.3 shows that California receives relatively low grades in overall performance and performance in individual areas (Pew Center on the States 2005, 2008).

Both the CPR and GPP suggest that major change is needed in California's executive branch including the elimination of many boards and commissions, better coordination with local governments and the implementation of innovative methods and techniques that have improved management in the private sector and other states. On the other hand, it should be noted that the state of California serves a population of over 37 million people, and when we look at the number of

Table 10.3 Report Cards on the State of California

	2005 Report Card	2008 Report Card
Overall Performance	C−	C
Money	D	D+
People	C−	C−
Infrastructure	C	B−
Information	C	C+

Source: Pew Center on the States. *Grading the State 2005. http://www.pewtrusts.org/uploaded Files/wwwpewtrustsorg/Reports/Government_Performance/GPP_Report_2005.pdf* & *The State Management Report Card for 2008. http://www.pewcenteronthestates.org/uploadedFiles/ Grading-the-States-2008.pdf*

government employees on a per capita basis, a different picture emerges. The number of state employees per 10,000 people ranks forty-ninth among all fifty states (Bureau of Census 2006, Table 456). State and local employees per capita are the seventh lowest among the fifty states. These numbers suggest that the accomplishments of the state bureaucracy come to us at a comparatively low cost and acceptable efficiency. With this comparatively small administration, the state government appears to be able to provide public services to its people. Yet both the CPR and GPP point out many areas in the state bureaucracy that can be improved to make it more efficient and responsive to its citizens. Policymakers in the state government have to critically assess the merit of different proposals to determine if proposed solutions can effectively address the problems and result in greater efficiencies and improved services in the state government.

Conclusion

Let us reflect once more on our restaurant owner with whom we began this chapter. He may not be happy with the amount of tax he must pay to California government. Perhaps he dreams of the California of his grandparents' time, where a very small state government supplied a few services, required less tax money, and left small businesses alone. He also wishes that his interests were better served by the public administrators with whom he must deal. He reads the newspapers and sees calls for greater state government efficiency and responsiveness to citizens; he hopes for lower taxes and improved services. The news reports mention the waste, poor management, and high salaries earned by public administrators, which will undoubtedly make him mad.

The public administrator also reads the newspaper with hope for improved service delivery, but with concerns that her efforts are not properly appreciated. The public administrator knows that an increasingly complex society must be served with fewer resources to meet increasing demands and that organizational change is necessary. She hopes, however, that the restaurant owner comes to understand that public administration is a difficult task, especially in California where the demand for services is complex and enormous. That is also the reason why she is likely to find her public service job both demanding and gratifying.

Chapter 11
CALIFORNIA LOCAL GOVERNMENTS
Yuan Ting

In addition to being a citizen of the United States and California, an average Californian also lives within the jurisdiction of perhaps ten or more local governments. Residents in the city of Fullerton, for example, are governed by a city government, a county government, three school districts (elementary, secondary, and community college), and several special districts (air quality management, sanitation, transportation, vector control, and water). These local governments are given responsibility for providing the most basic governmental services like health, public safety, education, water, public transit, recreation, and commerce, to name just a few.

The importance of local government increases as more people settle in urban areas. At the beginning of the twentieth century, 60 percent of the American population lived in rural areas and most of them lived their lives without too much involvement with government. By 2000, almost 80 percent of the population lived in cities. This urbanization trend is even more startling in California, where over 94 percent of Californians lived in cities as of 2000 (see Table 11.1). As more and more people moved into urban areas, people living in close proximity had to work together to provide their communities with fresh water and waste management. They had to create police and fire departments to protect lives and private property from crime and natural disasters. So we have to create local governments and hire people to provide more public services as our communities grow.

As we entered the twenty-first century, the needs and problems of our communities have become more complex and require governmental solutions across political jurisdictions. For example, the cars that leave the bedroom communities in the morning produce traffic jams and pollution for major employment centers in other cities later in the day. The crime of the central city affects suburban residents who travel to see a baseball game or a concert. Intergovernmental cooperation has become more important as governments from different jurisdictions and levels seek solutions to solve their problems.

In addition to the impact of population change on the growth of local governments, there is a long history of grassroots democracy in our country. Many Americans believe that government closest to the people governs best. Therefore, we arrange our local governments in small units and divide responsibility and authority among many governmental units in the same area. We try to coordinate public policies among these separate governments. The result is a complex maze of many jurisdictions with different duties and powers, and a system that makes coordination and common policies

Table 11.1   Rural and Urban Population in the United State and California, 1900–2000

	1900	1950	1990	2000
United States				
Rural population	60.4%	36%	24.8%	21%
Urban population	39.6%	64%	75.2%	79%
California				
Rural population	47.7%	19.3%	7.4%	5.6%
Urban population	52.3%	80.7%	92.6%	94.4%

Source: Bureau of Census, *Urban and Rural Population: 1900 to 1990.* Released in October 1995. Retrieved on January 18, 2009 http://www.census.gov/population/www/censusdata/files/urpop0090.txt; *Statistical Abstract of the United States: 2006,* Table 29. Washington, DC: U.S. Department of Commerce.

difficult to achieve. Behind these conflicts are differences over basic perspectives on how to create the best kind of government to serve the needs of people.

This chapter will discuss the origin and constitutional basis for local governments, the particular features of California local governments, and political values that affect the way decisions are made in local governments. The chapter will attempt to answer one key question: can local governments be held accountable to deal with the needs of an increasingly complex urban society?

Why Local Governments?

The American Revolution of 1776 has been called a revolt against a strong central government: revolutionaries sought to create governments that citizens could directly influence. Throughout American history, prominent thinkers have argued that the most basic governmental functions should be handled by governments physically close to the citizens they serve. Thomas Jefferson, for instance, believed strongly in the principle of local control. The gentleman farmer from Virginia and the author of the Declaration of Independence envisioned small units of local government in which every citizen becomes "... an acting member of the government, and in the offices nearest and most interesting to him, will attach him by his strongest feelings to the independence of his country, and its republican constitution" (Jefferson 1999, 213). In Jefferson's view, small areas like five miles by ten miles are the ideal size for the most important unit of government. In these neighborhoods, all important decisions can be made in a meeting of the people living in that territory, where issues can be decided by a show of hands.

The Jeffersonian tradition features faith in local government and distrust of the national government. Local governments are thought to be more responsive to the interests and desires of the people in a given area and easier to change if significant numbers of residents object to the ways things are done. Moreover, the idea of community held by Jefferson and others included not just physical proximity, but also common values and feelings of those who live near one another. Such common values, interests, and desires would be shared by local government officials and reflected in governmental decisions.

When a French political thinker, Alexis de Tocqueville, visited America in 1831, he observed this unique tradition of grassroots democracy and wrote:

> "These Americans are the most peculiar people in the world. . . . In a local community in their country, a citizen may conceive of some need which is not being met. What does he do? He goes across the street and discusses it with a neighbor. Then what happens? A committee begins functioning on behalf of that need. All of this is done by private citizens on their own initiative. The health of a democratic society may be measured by the quality of functions performed by private citizens. (1956, 201)"

This tradition is shown in the U.S. Bureau of Census' count of local government. According to Table 11.2, there were more than 87,500 local governments in the United States as of 2002. Between 1982 and 2002, the number of county governments has remained relatively constant, decreasing by only 7 or 0.2 percent. In 2002, there were 353 more municipal governments than in 1982, a 1.8 percent increase. Township governments have decreased by 230 or 1.4 percent in the same period. However, counts of special-purpose governments have undergone greater changes than general-purpose governments. The number of school districts has decreased by more than 9 percent, from 14,851 in 1982 to 13,506 in 2002. This decrease reflects a continuing trend since the 1950s resulting from school district consolidation and reorganization. The number of special districts has increased by almost 25 percent from 1982 to 2002, which is in response to the increasing demands for services that traditional governments (townships, cities, and counties) cannot provide. The large number of local governments reflects the Jeffersonian tradition of grassroots democracy, but it raises an important question about the financial burden local governments place on citizens.

Table 11.2 Local Governments in the United States

Type of Government	1982	2002	% Change 1982–2002
All local governments	81,780	87,525	+7.0%
County	3,041	3,034	−0.2%
Municipal	19,076	19,429	+1.8%
Township	16,734	16,504	−1.4%
School district	14,851	13,506	−9.1%
Special district	28,078	35,052	+24.8%

Source: Bureau of Census (2006). *Statistical Abstract of the United States: 2006*, Table 415. Washington, DC: U.S. Department of Commerce.

The U.S. Constitution of 1789 was also supported by those who saw too much state and local power in the Articles of Confederation. Its authors, James Madison and most particularly the influential Alexander Hamilton, wanted a powerful central government capable of defending the borders and regulating the economy. Madison, the most important voice in crafting the Constitution and the principle of separation of powers, feared the evil power of the "mischiefs of faction" that he felt were common in smaller governmental units (1787). Only a central government with sufficient checks and balances could protect individual rights and liberty. Hamilton believed that the Articles of Confederation clearly demonstrated the weakness of decentralized government, and argued for a powerful national government. In his view, Americans need a national government strong enough to protect their interests and fulfill their dreams.

These traditions created the constitutional government in the United States, and they both support and are leery of strong local governments. This explains the reason why our history is one of conflict over these traditions of how best to make governmental decisions and serve the needs of citizens. Should we divide our country into small local units that may represent the view of the average citizen more effectively, or should we be more concerned with the potential tyranny of such small units? Can those small governments adequately handle concerns that may span beyond the boundaries of local jurisdictions? Will larger urban governments be sensitive to the needs of individual neighborhoods and communities? California local governments can be described as conflicts over these perspectives.

Local Governments Are Creatures of State Governments

The U.S. Constitution leaves to the states all governmental functions that are not assigned to the federal government. Local governments are nowhere mentioned in the Constitution, even though local governments existed when the Constitution was signed in 1787. The organization of local governments was left for each state to determine. State constitutions and laws can create local governments and can abolish them. State-level legal provisions determine what local governments can and cannot do. Obviously, officials of local governments must work closely with state government officials.

In the early years of California's history, cities were dependent on the state for their powers, and the legislature was accused of running the state for the benefit of large companies, like the Southern Pacific Railroad. The railroad company forced many local governments to pay subsidies for the privilege of having a station built in their communities. The lack of concern for local government led to a series of reforms to make government more responsive to the people, dating back to the early California Constitutional Convention in 1879, through the Progressive movement in the early twentieth century (see Chapters 4 and 5 for further discussion of the Progressive movement), the adoption of the Brown Act and other state laws in the 1960s, and most recently the reinvention reforms to make government more accountable for performance and results.

Charter vs. General Law Cities

Local governments are the creatures of the state and the state law regulates local government services. School districts, for instance, are regularly inspected by state education agencies to ensure uniformity of standards that the state law requires be met. There are two kinds of cities in California: charter and general law. As part of reforms to maximize local control, the state constitution gives cities the power to become charter cities. The charter city provision in the state constitution, referred to as the "home-rule" provision, is based on the principle that a city, rather than the state, is in the best position to know what are the needs of its people and how to satisfy those needs. A city charter is a special document that, in many ways, acts like a constitution for the city. By adopting a charter, the home-rule provision allows the city greater autonomy to make its own decisions and enhanced ability to conduct municipal affairs, like election matters, land use and zoning, and how to spend its tax dollars. To become a charter city, a city's voters elect a charter commission to draft the charter, which has to be ratified by a majority vote of the city's voters. A city charter can only be changed by a vote of the city's voters, not by the city council. Of 481 cities in the state, only 112 of them are chartered. In general, charters are more common for the larger cities than the smaller ones.

The 369 cities that have not adopted a charter, called general law cities, are bound by the state's general law with respect to municipal affairs. These general law cities are permitted to do only those things prescribed by the state law and little else. The state law governing general law cities is clear because it has been subjected to judicial scrutiny and tested over many decades; however, city charters can be more complicated, and it is not always a straightforward process to determine what can and cannot be done under the state law.

The Federal Government Influences Local Governments

The federal government influences local governments in several ways. Congress provides direct financial aid to local governments and the amount of federal aid has varied in different periods of time. The federal government has become active in assisting local governments, and by the 1970s it was common for 10–15 percent of a city's budget to come from Washington. Generally speaking, cities with larger numbers of poor residents were more heavily dependent on federal funds. During this period, costs for providing public services might be shared among the federal, state, and local governments, with state and local officials working within federal guidelines to provide many public programs. And the federal government began to increase its influence on state and local governments. For example, public education is considered traditionally a state and local responsibility—to establish schools, develop curricula, and determine requirements for teacher qualifications, enrollment, and graduation. The Cold War stimulated the first comprehensive federal education legislation, when in 1958 Congress passed the National Defense Education Act in response to the Soviet launch of Sputnik. As a result, the federal government began supporting public elementary and secondary education to improve science, mathematics, and foreign language instruction. In 1965, Congress passed the Elementary and Secondary Education Act, which provided federal aid to disadvantaged children from poor urban and rural areas. In the same year, Congress passed the Higher Education Act to provide federal aid for needy college students. Today, the federal government's influence is everywhere. Almost all school districts receive some federal aid, which requires them to comply with federal rules and regulations.

The relationship between the federal government and local governments took a turn during the Reagan presidency. Reagan wanted to end the federal government's role in domestic programs and shift some responsibility back to the states. As a result, the Reagan and subsequently George H. W. Bush years brought a significant reduction in federal funds for local government programs, and little increase occurred during the Clinton administration. One consequence of this shift of responsibility is that we find our older central cities are facing the problems of declining city life with fewer resources. During the George W. Bush presidency, the role of the federal government expanded significantly after the terrorist attacks in 2001. The passage of the Patriot Act greatly increased the surveillance powers of the federal government. President Bush also expanded the role of the federal government in domestic policy areas like education and social services. For example, Congress passed the No Child Left Behind Act in 2001, which introduced further federal involvement in public education, traditionally the responsibility of the state and local governments. In addition, since the September 11 attacks, the federal government has expanded its role in emergency management. For example, Congress has authorized several assistance programs, including grants, training, technical assistance, equipment, and exercises to help first responders in local governments-such as fire service, emergency medical service, and law enforcement personnel-prepare for potential terrorist attacks.

The federal court system also influences local governments. The U.S. Supreme Court has been asked frequently to determine the constitutionality of local government practices. Since local governments are considered creatures of the state, many of their actions, like police practices, zoning laws, and restrictions on commerce are frequent subjects of state and federal court cases. For example, in 2003 California passed a law to establish the medical marijuana program, which is administered through county governments. The program allows patients, upon obtaining a recommendation from their physicians for use of medical marijuana, to apply for and be issued a medical marijuana identification card. The program allows qualified patients and their caregivers to possess, grow, transport, and use medical marijuana in California. In the Supreme Court case *Gonzales* v. *Raich* (2005), the court ruled that the federal government has the power to arrest and prosecute patients and their suppliers even if the marijuana use is permitted under state law, because of its authority under the Federal Controlled Substances Act to regulate interstate commerce in illegal drugs. This ruling has an important impact on local governments enforcing the medical marijuana program because such practice is subject to federal prosecution. On the other hand, in 2008 the U.S. Supreme Court refused to review a landmark decision in which California state courts found that its medical marijuana law was not preempted by federal law and that it was not the job of local enforcement to enforce the federal drug laws (*City of Garden Grove* v. *Superior Court (Kha)* 2007). This example shows how the federal court can influence the actions of local governments.

California Local Governments

All of the various kinds of local governments in California share some common characteristics:

- They are governed by elected officials.
- They have the authority to raise money through taxes and fees.
- They can borrow money, hire people, and administer certain public services.
- They have the power to enforce certain laws made by state or local elected officials.

We can divide California local governments into counties, cities, and special districts.

Counties

California is geographically divided into fifty-eight counties of varying sizes and shapes. Originally counties were the primary vehicle through which the state performed many important functions including law enforcement, public health, welfare, transportation, and the administration of elections. Generally speaking, California counties don't have the broad powers of self-government that cities have. The state legislature has more direct control over counties than cities and may delegate to the counties any functions that belong to the state itself. For example, if the state legislature passes a law to require land use zoning by a certain method, it will be binding on all the counties. On the other hand, the county may adopt its own if the state didn't require a method. Counties can also be more than simple agents of the state government. At the direction of elected county officials, other functions beyond those mandated by the state can be undertaken.

The state constitution recognizes two types of counties: general law and charter. General law counties stick to the state law as to the number and duties of county elected officials. Charter counties have a somewhat greater authority to determine the election, compensation, terms, removal, and salary of the governing board and other officers. Currently, there are 44 general law counties and 14 charter counties. In California, charters are more common for larger counties than smaller ones—of the ten most populated counties, eight of them are chartered (see Table 11.3).

Table 11.3 Ten Most Populated Counties in California

County	Population (2008)	Type
Los Angeles	10,363,850	Charter
San Diego	3,146,274	Charter
Orange	3,121,251	Charter
Riverside	2,088,322	General law
San Bernardino	2,055,766	Charter
Santa Clara	1,837,075	Charter
Alameda	1,543,000	Charter
Sacramento	1,424,415	Charter
Contra Costa	1,051,674	General law
Fresno	931,098	Charter

Source: California Department of Finance (2008). *California County Population Estimates.* Sacramento, CA: Department of Finance.

The governing board of each county is called the Board of Supervisors. Counties typically have five supervisors, elected from separate districts. County residents also elect other officials, including the sheriff, the coroner, the district attorney, and the county clerk. Unlike the separation of powers that characterizes the federal and state governments, the Board of Supervisors is both the legislative and the executive authority of the county. The board performs its executive authority by setting policy priorities for the county; overseeing county departments and approving their budgets; supervising county employees; and appropriating money for programs to meet the needs of county residents. As the legislative body of the county, the board may pass and enforce within its limits all police, sanitation, public health, social service, and other ordinances that do not conflict with the state's general law.

County government also mirrors California's great diversity. For example, Los Angeles County is one of the nation's largest counties with 4,084 square miles and has the largest population (over 10 million in 2008) of any county in the nation. It had a budget of $22 billion for the 2008–2009 year, which is more than the expenditures of twenty states. San Bernardino County is larger than any other county in the nation with 20,160 square miles and is larger than nine states. Alpine County, on the other hand, had only about 1,200 residents in 2008.

Counties have major responsibilities for many social services as required by state and federal laws, including health care and public defenders for the indigent, aid to the homeless, and welfare to the poor. They are major providers of jails and juvenile halls. They are the assessors and collectors of property tax. They keep and issue official records and administer elections. In recent years the demands for these services have increased, just as the economy has declined. This has presented a tremendous challenge to local governments seeking solutions to meet increasing demands with fewer resources. In particular, counties in urban areas have faced considerable financial problems in recent years as the need for these services increased while state funding declined. Orange County declared bankruptcy in 1994, sending shock waves throughout the nation's local governments and financial community. How could one of the nation's wealthiest counties have insufficient resources to cover its expenditures? One reason was the increasing pressure placed on county officials to pay for social services while state and federal funds for these services declined and the numbers of people in need increased. Another reason was the reluctance of Orange County officials, responding to voters' perceptions of high government spending, to increase taxes. To solve these problems, the county treasurer's office tried to raise needed funds through speculative investments, which seemed to be a "low-cost" solution at the time. Many cities and school districts in the county found the temptation similarly promising and added some of their money to the Orange County investment pool. Eventually this high-risk investment led to one of the largest local government bankruptcies in United States history. More recently, Los Angeles County has faced serious fiscal problems, and elected officials have threatened to close the county-run hospitals and drastically curtail medical and social services to the poor.

Cities

There are 481 cities in the state. Cities are formed at the request and consent of the residents in a given area. It is easier to form a new city than a new county because forming a new county would require majority approval by the voters in both the proposed new county and the remaining portion of the old county. By contrast, the process of forming a city within a county requires only the voter approval of those living within the proposed city's boundaries and the new city does not take territory from other cities. Normally, residents create cities when a settlement of people becomes large enough to need more public services than the county government can reasonably provide. For example, the city of Menifee in Riverside County was incorporated in October 2008 after decades of growth and became the youngest city in California. There are also examples of cities formed by major landowners, like the cities of Irwindale and Industry in Los Angeles County, which contain large industrial properties and less than 2,000 residents. Incorporation as a city permits these industries to be well served by local governments without significant changes or taxes. Other cities such as Villa Park in Orange County and several small cities on the Palos Verdes Peninsula in Los Angeles County consist of small numbers of wealthy homeowners. Incorporation as a small city allows these residents to avoid being burdened with the costs of serving poorer residents.

The residents who want their community to incorporate as a city usually are looking for more local control. As we have discussed earlier, the state constitution, under the "home-rule" provision, gives cities greater authority for self-government by adopting their own charters. The state law giving cities their legal authority provides for two different forms of municipal government: the mayor-council form and the council-manager form. Residents can choose their own form of government and elect people from their own community to run it.

Council-Manager Government

The most common form of city government in California is the council-manager government in which most administrative responsibilities are delegated to a professional manager. In the council-manager form of government, residents elect a city council of five or more members, which is the legislative body of the city. Often a mayor is also elected. He or she is a voting member of the council and presides at council meetings and performs ceremonial functions, but has no specific executive duties. Council members and the mayor are generally part-time officials. They are paid salaries varying from nothing to several hundred dollars per month. Some cities elect their council members in small districts designed to represent different sectors of the population. More commonly, council members are elected citywide or at large. Other cities employ some combination of these two methods, electing some council members by districts and some at large or requiring council members to live in various districts but be elected at large. The council meets frequently to enact local laws, adopt the budget, and give policy direction to the city manager.

The city manager is appointed by the city council and acts as the chief executive officer. The day-to-day tasks of running the city government are placed in the hands of the appointed city manager. She or he is guided by the council but is given the responsibility of hiring employees, seeing that the work of the city is being carried out, and providing plans for future growth. City managers serve at the pleasure of the council, which means that they can be fired by a majority vote of the council, and the council is free to determine their salary. Their relationship to the council is similar to that of a chief executive officer to a corporate board of directors. City managers may have learned about municipal government and management skills in graduate programs like the Master of Public Administration and on the job as a department head or assistant city manager. Ideally, in the council-manager form of government, different departments are coordinated and led by the city manager, and the entire city government is responsive to the city council and, through these elected representatives, to the people.

Mayor-Council Government

This form of government rules San Francisco, San Bernardino, Los Angeles, and several small cities in California. Citizens in the strong mayor-council cities elect a city council, which is the legislative branch of municipal government, and a mayor, who is the executive head of the government. The mayor and city bureaucrats who report to the mayor are responsible for executing council-approved policies. The mayor is also involved in legislation and normally can veto bills passed by the council. He or she appoints department heads with the advice and consent of the council. The strong mayor-council system has the advantage of clearly defined political leadership. A directly elected mayor with executive powers can more easily introduce innovations in city policy.

In theory, a mayor's position with respect to the city council is analogous to a governor's position with respect to the state legislature or to the president of the United States' position with respect to Congress. But, historically, a mayor's powers compared to the city council are typically weaker in California than those of the president compared to Congress. The city of Los Angeles, for instance, is usually referred to as having a weak mayor-council form of government. The mayor does not have direct authority over several important operating departments like police, fire, and public works. Commissioners appointed by the mayor and confirmed by the city council directly govern these departments. Los Angeles city council members also have considerable control over public decisions that are made in their districts.

Special Districts

Special districts are the most numerous form of government in both the nation and the state. As the community becomes more densely developed, more special districts are created to provide separate services. In California, there are about 3,400 special districts, including almost 1,000 school districts. This number is far greater than all the counties and cities combined. Special districts are governmental units created to perform a single or limited set of services to the community. Although school districts may have received the most public attention, other districts provide air pollution control, coastal management, fire protection, libraries, mosquito control, recreation and parks, waste management, and other important services.

As independent governmental units, special districts may have the power to levy taxes and issue bonds. Special districts have no specific boundary requirements. Some cover only portions of a city, while others may cut across several cities and counties, resulting in a layered public sector of considerable complexity. The Metropolitan Water District of Southern California, for example, serves 26 cities and water agencies with nearly 19 million residents in six different counties in Southern California, which allows the district to achieve economies of scale and avoid problems of coordination between cities and counties with respect to their need for water.

Special districts are occasionally created as a response to problems common to several cities or counties. Air quality management, transportation, and water districts are good examples, since traffic congestion, smog, and water problems do not stop at city or county boundaries. Other special districts are formed to provide services before a city is created. School districts are common in most of the United States and seem best explained by a widespread feeling that school decisions should be made locally and separate from other governmental decisions.

Special districts may be governed by elected boards or by boards appointed by elected officials. Most special districts have five-member boards, but some special districts are governed by a large board. The Metropolitan Water District, for example, is a consortium of 26 member cities and water agencies, and each member is entitled to elect at least one director to its governing board. In most cases, board members do not receive any compensation or receive only a nominal salary. While special districts are created to provide specific services and promote local control, the increase of special districts in a densely populated area may create a fragmentation of government and make it difficult for citizen participation because overlapping boundaries and different layers of local governments are likely to make special districts less visible than city and county governments. This explains why voter turnout in special district elections is usually lower than in municipal elections.

Local Government Finance

Given the increasing demand for public services, elected officials and city managers spend much of their time searching for new sources of revenue. Local government finance changes frequently as new state laws, court decisions, and initiatives alter their revenue sources. Generally speaking, local governments are low on the food chain of government revenues. As problems occur at other levels of government, sources of money are taken away from local governments. As a result, city officials are adept at finding new sources.

Proposition 13 of 1978 severely limited the property tax, which is the major source of revenue for local governments (see Chapter 12). It limits the property tax to a maximum of 1 percent of assessed value of property and caps the rate of increase in the future. Following its passage, local government property tax revenues were cut by half and cities and counties had to raise user fees and local taxes, as well as lobby the state to divert significant state funds to local governments to make up much of the property tax loss. As a result, local governments have relied more heavily on the state general fund and have seen a shift of power from local jurisdictions to the state. As the state economy went into a pronounced recession and schools were required by the courts and voters to increase educational funding, local governments lost significant amounts of state revenue and had to look for other revenue tools to finance local services. For example, in the mid-1990s taxes on utilities were popular in California cities. Most cities also used the authority granted under the state constitution to impose other local taxes like hotel and business licenses as well as a variety of fees like those for sewer connections, building permits, and development impact. In response to the perceived abuses in the use of local taxes and fees, California voters passed an initiative in 1996 to prohibit new utility taxes and other special assessments and fees without the support of two-thirds of voters.

One tool frequently used by California cities to raise revenue and provide new public services is *redevelopment*. Cities can create redevelopment districts, a form of special district within the boundaries of a city. Under California law, a redevelopment district is a blighted area within the city designated for changes in the use of land. The designation of a redevelopment district is a completely public process and the presence of the blight must be clearly established. Once the district is created, the redevelopment agency can borrow money to pay for improvements in public facilities like street construction and parking, and the cost of buying some of the land and property from the existing owners through the use of eminent domain. Once the improvements are made, property values presumably will increase, and the district sells the land to new owners who are expected to build structures for new stores or other uses, which will increase the tax revenue of the city. The increased taxes paid by the new owners are used to pay for the improvements that were made and other public services in maintaining the operation of the redevelopment district. Redevelopment agencies are also required to spend parts of their increased tax revenue on low- and moderate-income housing.

In this manner, cities attempt to add wealthier taxpayers to the community and attract new facilities for the residents. Many cities have used redevelopment to breathe new life into deteriorated areas by creating new shopping centers and recreation facilities, and attracting new industries. Taxes from these new sources can make up for some of the lost revenue from businesses that previously occupied the land. While many cities have been aided by redevelopment, some cities have found it difficult to attract the new land use. When that happens, land remains vacant and ultimately city residents must pay for the cost of improvements. Some critics also wonder about the limited effect of redevelopment agencies when many cities in the same region are competing for industries and businesses with tax money. Some redevelopment agencies have limited power of eminent domain, which causes concerns about land and property being wrongly designated as blighted and homeowners not receiving fair market value for their property. Therefore, the use of redevelopment in California continues to be controversial among local governments.

Local Governments and Voting

We praise local governments as the place in our political system where citizens have the most influence. However, voter turnout in city elections is usually quite low. Less than 30 percent of the registered voters participate in the average city election in California. In contrast, over half of those registered to vote typically cast ballots in presidential elections.

Why are most local elections ignored by their residents? Several reasons are frequently given. Media attention is sporadic, given the large number of elections and the fact that most cities represent a small portion of the media's circulation. Therefore, voter knowledge about local elections is quite limited. Also, little effort is made in our society to interest the average citizen in local government. Schoolchildren, for example, seem to learn a great deal about the national government but very little about local government. Beyond this, several unique characteristics of local elections tend to encourage low voter turnout.

Local elections in California are carried out on *nonpartisan ballots*. Candidates may be members of a political party, but party designations will not be put on the ballot. For most people, "political party" is an important clue to the nature of the candidate. It provides the voter with a general idea of how the candidate feels about certain important issues and how the candidate relates to other elected officials. A nonpartisan ballot thus deprives the voter of important clues to the candidate's positions. Lacking such knowledge, the citizen may prefer not to vote. (For a further discussion of California's weak party tradition, see Chapter 5.)

At-large elections, where several city council members are chosen over the entire city, make it more difficult for the candidates to know the voters personally. In smaller districts, often the candidates can campaign door to door, and they know many of the voters personally. At-large elections, however, distance elected officials from their local constituencies and discourage personal candidate-voter contact, and therefore voters' interest in the election is likely to decline.

Studies also show that cities providing more services in-house by their own employees, as opposed to those contracting out their services, are likely to have a higher voter turnout in local elections because city governments "have more direct control over some of the basic issues that affect residents' quality of life," and therefore generate more interest in voters when local officials are up for election (e.g., Hajnal and Lewis 2003, 658). Based on this argument, as cities and counties continue to contract out public services, voter turnout in local elections is unlikely to improve.

Beliefs of Local Government Decision Makers

Holders of power have the ability to make public policy. To what end this policy is made depends on the values, beliefs, and feelings of those with power. Usually people who wield power have a general set of values in mind when decisions are made. We call this series of interrelated values an *ideology*. An ideology organizes one's attitudes and helps one make sense of the world of politics. It also shapes one's view of the appropriate scope of government.

Currently, most attitudes toward politics at the national, state, and local levels are related to two dominant ideologies: the *conservative* view generally associated with the Republican Party, and the *liberal*, related to the Democratic Party.

Conservatives generally believe that government is at best a necessary evil. Society operates well when government does only those things that are absolutely necessary, and the private sector is permitted to operate without too much governmental interference. Conservatives are pessimistic about the ability of government to accomplish significant changes in people or ways of life. They tend to rely on private institutions like businesses, churches, and private charities rather than government to assist needy individuals. To conservatives, government should be limited and play a secondary role to private institutions. For example, conservatives favor fewer governmental regulations and a greater reliance on the market to provide jobs and health care. However, conservatives do not always oppose governmental intervention, such as using governmental power to restrict abortion.

Liberals, on the other hand, believe that government should be a positive force in society. Liberals argue that government should be used to improve social conditions and redistribute wealth through taxation. They also feel that the private sector must be controlled and steered by government to best promote the general welfare. Consequently, liberals favor a larger government and one that is geared toward advancing the interests of the lower and middle classes. Liberals do not always favor governmental actions, such as those allowing prayers in public schools.

The ideologies of local officials, however, seem to tell us less about the practice of government. Often local governments that maintain very extensive services are located in areas where the citizens support conservative officials in state and national elections. Anaheim, for instance, elects mostly conservative state legislators and congressional representatives. Yet the city is involved in major expenditures and projects that seem to be associated with a greater governmental role in the local economy. The city owns a major league baseball stadium, an indoor events center that hosts major league hockey, a convention center, and two golf courses. The city also operates the only municipal electric system in Orange County and owns part of the San Onofre nuclear power plant. City officials were instrumental in luring Disneyland to the city and are paying some of the costs of a major addition to the park.

This expansive view of the role of government, common in an otherwise conservative environment, suggests a third ideology that may more accurately be described as *community conservationist* (Agger et al. 1964). Supporters of this position see government as a partner with the private sector in helping the development of the community. Government expenditures that attract business or enhance the desirability of industrial or commercial interests are supported. Therefore baseball stadiums and transportation systems are built for the purpose of increasing trade and commerce in the cities. Proponents of this position view officials like city managers as a source of innovation leading to enhanced business opportunities and commercial activities. Such enhancement may include some measures usually defined as social interventions in nature, such as low-cost housing and public transportation. These policies are supported by local constituents, however, only if they enhance the economic health of the community.

Regional Government

All urban areas contain a *council of governments*, a voluntary body that is responsible for coordinating transportation and land use plans for the region and has significant input into the actions of other area wide districts. The Southern California Association of Governments, for example, is the largest council of government in the United States. The association prepares plans for air quality, growth management, transportation, and waste management in the region encompassing six counties: Los Angeles, Orange, San Bernardino, Riverside, Ventura, and Imperial.

Urban counties also contain transportation agencies, which are responsible for developing major transportation networks for automobiles and mass transit. The Orange County Transportation Authority, for example, provides countywide bus, paratransit, and Metrolink commuter-rail services to county residents. Recent initiatives have required many of these agencies to prepare congestion management plans that require cities to control traffic congestion when they decide on future growth and development. For example, Orange County voters approved Measure M in 1990, a 20-year initiative funded by a half-cent sales tax to improve the county transportation infrastructure. In 2006, the county voters approved the renewal of this initiative for another thirty years.

The California coast is governed in part by the statewide *Coastal Commission*, which was first established by Proposition 20 in 1972 and later made permanent by the California Coastal Act of 1976. Working with coastal cities and counties, the commission plans and regulates the use of land and water in the coastal zone. Land use changes that potentially affect access to beaches and the coastal environment must be approved by this commission or the local government.

Last, an *air quality management district* regulates all major urban areas. These governments can enforce regulations that affect air quality. The South Coast Air Quality Management District, for example, is the air pollution control agency for all of Orange County and parts of Los Angeles, Riverside, and San Bernardino counties—one of the most populated and smoggiest urban areas in the United States. The authority of these agencies includes controlling and regulating moving sources of pollution (primarily cars), in addition to the traditional stationary sources, such as factories and commercial areas that emit pollutants. The emphasis on mobile sources has led to a concern for car travel in the greater Los Angeles area. Therefore, the local air quality management district has encouraged carpooling, bicycling, and land use patterns that better coordinate jobs and residences.

All of these regional governments generate conflict with cities and counties as they attempt to assume authorities and powers traditionally thought to be those of the city and county. Land use decisions, for example, what each resident can do with his or her own property, now must meet the approval of several regional agencies. City officials often do not take direction from regional governments willingly. Therefore, conflict between the regional agencies and cities and counties has increased in recent years and will most likely become more significant in the years ahead.

Conclusion

California local governments operate within a conflicting environment. As weak actors, politically and legally speaking, they must constantly react to court rulings and the decisions of other governments. The Jeffersonian tradition of strong local government may clash with the need to promote livable regions where traffic flows freely, air is clean, natural resources are preserved, and all citizens have equal access to public services. The interest in having more centralized authority reflects the Madisonian tradition of larger governments capable of solving the problems that small governments have difficulty coping with and agreeing on with one another. Just as Madison feared the factional nature of small government, regional governments frequently find local officials insensitive to the problems of society that span city boundaries.

Some fear that the cost of regional governments in regulations and fees will ruin the economy. Others believe that failure to handle the problems of traffic congestion and environmental degradation will lead to economic decline in the region. They argue that strong regional government is needed to plan, coordinate, and work out compromises between different cities with competing goals. On the other hand, other people see stronger governments in local communities and neighborhoods where citizens could be partners with public administrators seeking better ways of attacking the problems that directly affect the public. To proponents of this perspective, regional governments distance citizens from local governments and encourage conflict between public administrators and citizens. Therefore the conflict represented in the ideas of Hamilton, Madison, and Jefferson is still with us, as local governments face the problems and prospects of an increasingly populated urban society.

Chapter 12
COMPARING CALIFORNIA AND FEDERAL POLICIES
Sarah Hill and Paul Peretz

The United States is organized on federal principles. States have constitutions of their own and can pass policies which cannot be simply vetoed by the Federal government. Those who support federalism argue that it has a number of benefits not available to countries where the central government can decide all policies. It is argued that federalism encourages government to be more responsive to local needs, it disperses power, thereby preventing tyranny and it allows people to move to areas that have chosen policy mixes that they favor.

These arguments have implications for the types of policies that one would expect to see at the federal, state and local levels. One would expect to see the national level handle policies where it is important that the entire country has the same policy, where a single large policy is more efficient than many smaller policies and where there is little difference in preferred policy amongst citizens. One would expect state and local governments to handle policies where there are strong local preferences, where different citizens have very different tastes and preferences and where small scale is as efficient as large scale. As we shall see the original division of policies closely mirrored these implications. Developments since have made the policy division less closely mirror the arguments, but on the whole there is still considerable logic to the division of responsibilities.

History

In the U.S. Constitution formed in 1789 the Federal Government was explicitly given responsibility for defense, foreign policy, monetary policy and interstate trade regulation. Most other types of government policy were seen as the province of states and local governments. States and localities handled such things as roads, sewage, maintaining law and order, building prisons and hospitals and stopping fires. When California became a state in 1850 this division of responsibilities was still in place.

In 1850 government at all levels was very small by today's standards. Over the next hundred and sixty years there was a large increase in the amount spent on existing functions of government such as defense and transportation and a vast expansion in government programs aimed at dealing with societal problems that had arisen as the country transformed from a sparsely populated agricultural country to a densely populated industrial power. Education, regulation of industry, parks, welfare, old age pensions and medical care were all basically private responsibilities in 1850. By 2011 these had become large government programs.

In 1902, the first year for which we have reliable data, government spent $1.6 billion which was about 7 percent of everything spent in the country. Local government spent 58 percent of this money, state governments spent 12 percent and the federal government spent the remaining 30 percent. Over the next century government expenditures increased to 32 percent of all spending, and the Federal share of government spending rose to 57 percent. Changes in the Federal Constitution and in some state constitutions which allowed sales and income taxes, together with transportation and communication changes which brought the country closer together, led to the role of local government becoming less important and the role of state government and federal government becoming more important.

As the three levels of government grew, what they did became more intermixed. While there are still policies that are primarily federal, primarily state or primarily local there are also a lot of policy areas where more than one level of government takes an active part.

Federal Policies

Figure 12.1 shows spending by the Federal government and by the California government. We have multiplied the Federal figures by California's share of the population of the United States to give a rough idea of how much the Federal

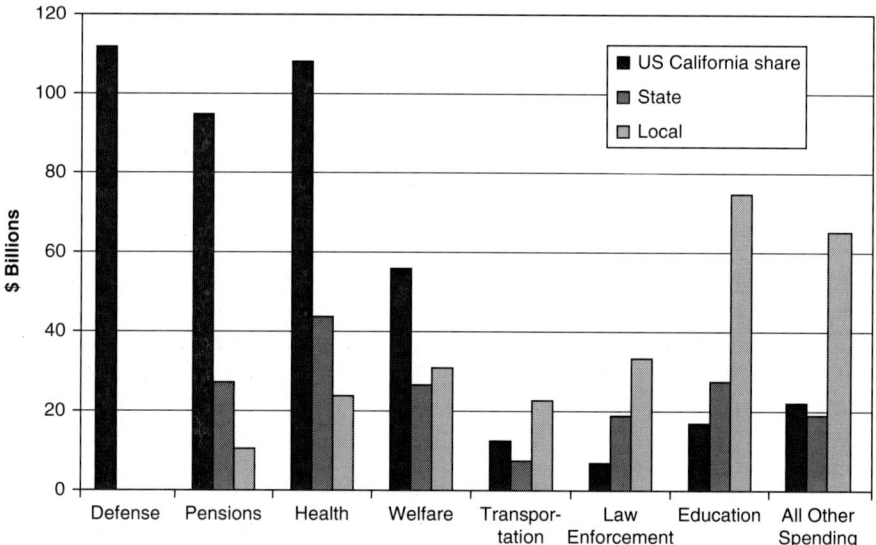

Figure 12.1 Federal, State and Local Spending for California
Source: The Data For this chart was compiled by *www.usgovernmentspending.com* from government sources. I have multiplied the Federal spending by California's share of the U.S. population to approximate the amount spent on California.

government spends for California in each of the spending areas compared to how much the California State Government spends. The figures show that Federal spending is generally more important to California and that there is considerable variance from area to area. Some policy areas are pursued almost exclusively at the Federal level. In this section we will look at the largely federal programs. We will then turn to the policies that California spends money on, in almost all of which the Federal government plays a large part.

Defense and Foreign Policy

Virtually all spending on foreign affairs and defense takes place at the federal level. This is one of the areas where spending has expanded considerably. In 1789 when the Constitution was signed there were 718 members of the armed forces. By 1850, when California became a state, the number had risen to 20,824. Today there are approximately 1.9 million members of the armed services, about 91 times as many as in 1850. There are also an additional 1.1 million members of the ready reserve. The United States has become the world's dominant power and spends as much on defense as the next eight nations put together.

Nonetheless we currently spend less of our budget on defense than we used to in the recent past. During the cold war with the Soviet Union we had a nuclear arms race, spent heavily on conventional weapons, dispensed foreign aid to bolster American influence abroad and fought two major wars to halt the spread of Communism in Asia. Since the disintegration of the Soviet Union in the 1990s, and the abolition of Communism in Russia and Eastern Europe, we no longer have a serious rival for military and economic supremacy. As a result we spend much less of our Gross National Product on defense. As recently as 1986 we were spending 6.2 percent of our GNP on defense. Today we spend only about 4.3 percent, despite ongoing conflicts in Iraq and Afghanistan.

However other countries are reducing their spending at about the same rate. Most noticeable is that Russia, formerly our chief enemy, and the only other country with a large nuclear arsenal, has reduced its armed forces from 3.9 million men in 1986 plus reserves to around 1.2 million today plus a 750,000 ready reserve. The margin of technological superiority has also widened, and the entities that we consider hostile are now small countries like Iran and North Korea, and small terrorist groups, rather than major nations like Russia and China. As a result, despite the post 9/11 political rhetoric, the United States is generally safer today than at any time in the last sixty years.

Security for the Elderly

The federal level also takes primary responsibility for the elderly. Social Security provides the elderly with pensions, Medicare provides them with medical care and Supplementary Security Income and Medicaid give income and medical care to the elderly who are not covered by Social Security or Medicare. Compared to defense, these are all relatively new programs. Social Security began in 1935.

Medicare and Medicaid started in 1965. Supplemental Security Income began in 1972, though the patchwork of state programs it replaced was begun much earlier. Despite their relative newness, programs for the elderly are now the largest programs in the Federal Budget. Social Security and Medicare alone account for around 32 percent of all federal spending.

These programs have made a huge difference in the lives of elderly Americans. The biggest change has been in the income levels of the elderly. In 1950, when Social Security was still a relatively small program and the elderly were spending much of their meager income on medical care, the elderly were three times as likely as the rest of the population to fall below the poverty level. Today, while the elderly still have incomes that are on average below those of the population as a whole, they are no more likely than the rest of the population to fall below the poverty level. There is also an improvement in the health of the elderly, with whites living about three years longer than they did when Medicare was introduced in 1965, and blacks living about five years longer. While some of this is due to general improvements in medicine, the fact that the increase is greatest amongst poorer Americans supports the idea that Medicare and Social Security are partly responsible.

Economic Policy

The Federal government also is primarily responsible for the monetary and fiscal policies that influence the state of the economy. Even though the Constitution gave the right to coin money to the Federal Government, the use of monetary and fiscal policy to control the economy is a relatively recent activity. Until the office of the Comptroller of the Currency was founded in 1863, paper money was largely issued by state chartered banks. Serious regulation by the Federal government began with the creation of the Federal Reserve in 1913, but it was not until 1962 that the Federal Government seriously tried to co-ordinate monetary and fiscal policy to control the economy. In recent years fiscal policy (the manipulation of government spending and taxing to control the economy) has come to take a back seat to monetary policy, which changes interest rates to speed up or slow down the economy.

This too is an area where federal intervention has generally improved the welfare of Americans. The nineteenth century was marked by huge booms and equally huge busts, with the busts resulting in large numbers of unemployed people. This boom-and-bust cycle culminated in the Great Depression. In the ten years after 1929 the unemployment rate fluctuated between 14.3 percent and 24.9 percent. In 1933 one in every four workers was unemployed. In the fifty-year period since 1962 the unemployment rate has averaged 6 percent and has never exceeded 10.6 percent.

At first sight the events of the last few years seem to undermine this rosy view. But in fact the events of the last few years have underscored the change. A decade of weak State and Federal financial regulation led to a financial crisis similar to that in the early days of the Great Depression. But monetary stimulus by the Federal Reserve and fiscal stimulus from both the Bush and Obama Administrations prevented this from happening. Instead we got an unusually severe Recession which lasted 18 months rather than a Great Depression lasting ten years, with unemployment peaking in early 2010 at 10.6 percent nationally and 13.2 percent in California rather than the 20–25 percent rates of the Great Depression. Congress also passed a massive Financial Reform Act to address the regulatory weaknesses. While not perfect, it is better than what emerged from the Great Depression.

State and Local Government

State and local governments have virtually no policy areas where they still have complete responsibility for policy. To a greater or lesser degree state and local governments share policy responsibility with the federal government. In some cases, like primary education, the state and local governments bear the vast bulk of the costs and make most of the decisions. In other areas like welfare policy the Federal government both bears the major financial burden and sets many of the rules which states and counties must follow.

In the policy areas where there is sharing between the Federal government and the states, it can take place in three major ways. In some cases the state and Federal governments both spend money in a policy area but on different things. The Federal government for example builds and maintains the interstate highway system, while intrastate roads are constructed and maintained by the state or localities. In other cases the federal government supplies part of the money and the state supplies part, with decisions being shared. An example would be the CalWORKS welfare program which is operated by the state of California within guidelines set by the Federal government. Lastly there is an elaborate system of Federal grants which give money to the state or to localities on the condition that they do something that the Federal government wants them to do. Examples would be grants for gang abatement and for slum clearance.

There are a vast number of policy areas. Here we will look only at the most important policies in terms of the effect they have on the lives of Californians. We will start with the infrastructure programs which enable California to function and grow, go on to look at the California criminal justice system and California's three primary social programs, health, education and welfare. We will conclude with a brief examination of the California Budget system which allocates funding between the competing programs.

Infrastructure Policies

The three major infrastructure policy areas are water, utility regulation and transportation. The most interesting in California is water. Much of central and Southern California is a semi-arid area with little surface water except in the mountain regions. This has been transformed into a fertile and heavily populated area primarily through five massive water projects, the Owens River and Colorado River projects which supply water to the Los Angeles Basin, the Tuolumne River project which supplies San Francisco with water, the Central Valley project which takes water from the San Joaquin and Sacramento rivers to the rest of the central valley, and the Feather River project which moves water up to 700 miles south to provide water primarily to urban areas. These projects, some of which are exclusively California projects and others of which involve Federal government cooperation or subsidies, make possible most of the agriculture of the central valley and southern California and also provide water to the inhabitants of Los Angeles, San Diego, San Francisco and the multitude of cities that surround them. In recent years this water grab has been tempered by attempts to preserve wetlands and lakes and by the lack of obvious new sources of water. Disputes between farmers, urban users, environmentalists and governments in other States have threatened the supply of water to the growing population. One of the achievements of the Schwarzenegger Administration was to get these different entities to agree to a new bond proposal that would solve some of the looming problems. It is expected to be put before voters in 2012.

Gas, electricity and telephone are primarily provided by the private sector although some California cities have their own gas or electricity generation systems. Government gets involved in all three because they need right of ways over public land, because they are natural monopolies that would overcharge if left to themselves and because they are so essential to the functioning of households and businesses. For most of the last 70 years the Federal and the California State governments were primarily regulators of large private local monopolies such as AT&T and California Edison, which produced and delivered the utilities. Both the federal and local government had as their primary concern avoiding price gouging by the monopoly supplier.

In the last twenty years there has been a strong push towards introducing competition, sparked by a body of work in economics that seemed to show that it would be more efficient than regulated monopoly and would deliver the utilities at a lower price. This has worked fairly well in the telephone area, which now has more choice and somewhat lower prices. Enthused by the seeming success of telephone deregulation, a number of states introduced competition into the electricity and gas industries. No state was more enthusiastic than California. Pushed by a governor (Pete Wilson) with presidential ambitions, the state legislature introduced the most extreme form of electricity competition in the late 1990s. The results were disastrous. The local companies no longer felt responsible for producing sufficient power and the out-of-state companies that had bought the existing power plants proceeded to charge prices up to fifty times what had been charged before. There were brownouts and blackouts as out of state companies withheld supplies of natural gas and electricity. This 2000 crisis was badly handled by Governor Davis, who subsequently became the first Governor to be recalled in California history, in large part as the result of how he mishandled this problem. The crisis led to a retreat from electricity deregulation, though some elements remain. But the issue has not gone away. Recent projections show the peak summer demand for electricity should exceed the supply in the next few years.

Transportation is the third major kind of infrastructure policy at the state level. Like the others there is federal, state and local influence. In California about twenty percent of the money spent on transportation comes from the federal government, about thirty percent from local governments and about fifty percent from the State of California. In California most transportation is by car. Only about four percent of commuters in Southern California use public transit, and with the exception of San Francisco, where a federally subsidized light rail system has pushed the number of commuters using transit to eleven percent, the story is not notably different in Northern California. Yet, despite this reliance on the car, and contrary to the myth that California has a car culture, Californians are about average in car ownership and actually drive less than other Americans.

During the 1950s and 1960s successive growth oriented governors and legislatures invested heavily in road building, especially freeway construction. This building slowed during the 1970s and 1980s as Californians fought freeways in their neighborhoods and environmental laws slowed road building. Road building slowed even further during the 1990s when California's long recession led state politicians to continually delay road building in order to satisfy more vocal constituencies fighting for the limited funds available. Between 1990 and 2007 the number of miles driven in California increased 30 percent while the number of freeway miles added was only 3 percent. The result was increasing gridlock on California's roads. The number of hours Californians spent delayed on freeways more than doubled between 1992 and 2007. This is unlikely to get better in the next few years as reduced tax revenues will constrain transportation spending.

Overall the story in infrastructure is one of delayed expenditures leading to current shortages. California's long recession and poor political leadership led to severe under investment in roads, gas and electric transmission lines and power plants while its population increased remorselessly. As a result we can expect problems in all these areas in the next decade.

Public Safety

The criminal justice system is a series of side-by-side systems both between the Federal government and the state, and the state and the localities. The Federal government has its own independent court system and a number of police forces of which the FBI is the largest. Although the Federal system only deals with about 2% of all court cases, the cases tend to be more important and the United States Supreme Court can review decisions by the California Supreme Court for compatibility with the protections in the U.S. Constitution.

Within California the responsibility for public safety is shared between the state, the counties and the cities. The court system is run by the state which is also the home base of the California Highway Patrol and most of California's prisons. Policing is primarily done at the county and city level and about a third of all prisoners are in county and municipal jails (see Chapter 9 for a discussion of the state court system). Here we will look chiefly at the broad policy dimensions.

Contrary to what most people believe, the overall crime rate has been falling in California and other states. Property crime peaked in California in 1980 and violent crime in 1992. Between 1992 and 2007 the violent crime rate halved from 1,104 per 100,000 people to 507 per 100,000 people. In the same period, property crime fell from 3,208 per 100,000 people to 1,803 per 100,000 people. The major factors appear to be a decline in the percent of the population in the crime prone teenage and early adult years, a slow fall in the popularity of drugs, good economic conditions from 1992 to 2007 and an increase in the number of criminals in prisons.

One might expect that faced with the decline in violent crime the people of California might reduce the priority given to public safety and spend more on other policy areas. But exactly the reverse has happened. California passed more and more laws that raised criminal penalties, especially for drug possession, culminating in the so-called three-strikes law of 1994 which gives lifetime imprisonment for a third crime if one of the crimes was violent. The result has been a huge increase in incarceration rates. In 1987 there were 67,000 adults in State prisons. By 1992, when crime peaked, there were 109,000. By 2007 there were 171,000 adult prisoners. Given that it costs the state approximately $48,000 a year to keep adults in our overcrowded prisons (as opposed to around $11,600 to educate them at a California State University), this is a huge investment in a largely unproven crime reduction method. Other crime enforcement expenditures have also risen in the face of the declining crime rate. In 1992 around 149,000 people were employed in state law enforcement. By 2009 the number had risen to 228,000, a 53 percent increase. Real spending (in 2007/8 dollars) on law enforcement rose from around 20 billion dollars in 1992/3 to 28 billion dollars in 2007/8, a 66 percent increase. Overall then, the law enforcement area shows an odd pattern whereby falling crime rates have not sunk into the public consciousness. Faced by public fear, politicians have provided more and more law enforcement at a time when it one could argue that the money would have been better spent on infrastructure or education.

Education

Primary and secondary education, the largest single responsibility of the states, has relatively little input from the federal government. The Federal government has special responsibility for Native Americans and for the children of servicemen and gives a variety of grants to improve education. But most of the money comes from state and local sources as do most of the decisions. An educated population is key to the continued growth of any state, so this is an area that deserves particular government attention.

California spends about $9000 (2007-2008) per student educating about 6.4 million children in the kindergarten through 12th grades (K-12). This is less than the $9,500 average for the United States with California ranking 31st among the states in per pupil spending. Until 1971 education in California was primarily a local responsibility paid for largely through property taxes. But financing education at the local level led to very uneven education in California, with rich school districts spending far more than poor ones. In *Serrano v. Priest* (1971) the California Supreme Court held that funding schools with local property taxes was unconstitutional because it led to unequal funding for rich and poor school districts. Additionally in 1978 Proposition 13 cut the overall size of property taxes by more than half.

In response to *Serrano* and Proposition 13 the state has taken on a much larger role in K-12 education, making itself largely responsible for financing primary and secondary education and mandating to some degree how the money would be spent. This has led to some equalization of funding but has greatly weakened local control of the schools. While 42 percent of education spending comes from local government in the United States as a whole, in California only 28 percent comes from local sources.

How successful is education policy in California? In the 1950s and early 1960s education was a largely local responsibility and California had a generally good, though somewhat unequal, K-12 system. Spending per pupil was amongst the top ten states in the 1960s. But in recent years as responsibility has moved to the state level, property taxes have fallen and school enrollment has become more minority-dominated, California has done a poorer job. Not only is spending lower than the national average, but in recent years California has ranked 49th among the states in the number of students per teacher, with 21 students per teacher compared to the U.S. average of 15.

The conventional wisdom is that the lower spending in primary and secondary education leads California schoolchildren to score lower than those in most other states on standardized tests, but because such tests are not always comparable this folk wisdom should be taken cautiously. When one compares SATs across states California has slightly more than the average number of students taking the SATs (and hence college bound), and their scores are very close to the U.S. average despite the quarter of California students for whom English is a second language. Controlling for this, Californians actually do better than the U.S. average.

The pattern is however less favorable at the lower grades. Consider an examination from 2009 that allows comparison with other states. On the mathematics portion California 8th graders ranked 48th of 50. On the reading portion California 8th graders came out 49th of the 50 states. In considering these numbers it is important to realize the difficult task that California faces with its public education. About one in two students comes from a low income family, and about one in four is an English language learner (ELL). These demographics explain in part California's low performance in on standardized exams. But even controlling for ethnicity, whites, blacks and Hispanics all did worse than children in these groups in other states.

Nor do things get better in high school. Overall about 83 percent of current high school students graduate and about 81 percent of all Californians are high school graduates. This is below the average for the United States. Forty-three of the fifty states have higher high school graduation rates than California. This result too is partly the result of the large number of foreign-born students in the state. But, even allowing for this, clearly a case can be made for smaller classes and more educational spending in California.

Higher education is primarily a state level function, although the University of California gets a substantial amount of its income from Federal research grants. In contrast to its K-12 system, California has a first class higher education system. The Master Plan for Higher Education was passed by the state legislature in 1960 and specifies the roles of the three higher education systems. At the top is the research oriented University of California system which takes the top 12 percent of California students. Five of the 20 most highly ranked public universities in the country belong to this system. Below this, taking the next 20 percent or so of students, are the teaching oriented California State Universities. The third tier is made up of the Community College system, which both teaches people trade and technical skills, and funnel students into the California State and University of California systems.

While fees for all three systems have increased during the current fiscal crisis, they are well below the national average for comparable institutions. For instance, in 2009 a Cal State undergrad would have paid about $4,000 in fees, while the average at comparable public universities would have been $6,500. Fees for the Community Colleges are the lowest in the country and are only 27 percent of the national average. Having such low fees means that higher education is more accessible to low income students, however, it also means that the state carries a higher than average burden for supporting public higher education. In 2009 the 213,000 full-time equivalent students in the University of California System each cost the state $20,600 per year. The 341,000 students in the California State system each cost the state $11,600 per year and the 1,300,000 in the Community College system each cost $5,400 per year.

The outcomes for higher education also look better than those for lower education. In 2007 29.5 percent of Californians had a BA or better degree, slightly above the national average of 27.5. However it is fair to point out that many of these degrees were obtained out of state.

While the figures on California education are not as grim as sometimes portrayed, the trends are disturbing in a state where many industries rely on well-educated people. At every level the percentage educated has improved but generally less than the rest of the nation. It is believed that the state's economy is going to demand an increasingly educated workforce. California will need to improve its education system to meet these future needs.

Health

Healthcare policy has recently been undergoing significant changes in the United States. For some time the country's healthcare system has been a hybrid system of private insurance (usually provided through employers) and public programs to provide healthcare to those who are poor or elderly. The major government programs are Medicare, Medicaid, and the Veterans Healthcare System. Medicare is administered by the federal government and provides benefits to those who are 65 and older as well as to those with permanent disabilities. The Veterans Healthcare program is also administered by the federal government and serves U.S. veterans.

Medicaid is designed to provide healthcare to those who are low income, and it operates as a joint program between the federal and state governments. Medi-Cal is California's Medicaid program, with 6.9 million beneficiaries in 2009, or about 1 in 6 Californians. Since the goal of Medi-Cal is to help those in poverty, its beneficiaries are primarily children (48 percent), people with disabilities (14 percent), and seniors (13 percent), with only 25 percent of beneficiaries being adults. The average cost to the state per beneficiary was about $4,500 in 2009, but in terms of where the money is spent, 63 percent of the Medi-Cal spending in 2009 was for seniors and people with disabilities. There has been an increase in the number of recipients in recent years due to changes in federal and state law that expanded eligibility to working families and near poor children. In addition, the current recession has also increased the number of Medi-Cal recipients. In sum this results in about 14 percent of the state's general fund being spent on Medi-Cal.

The difficulty is that even with these programs, almost 25 percent of the California population under 65 was uninsured, meaning that California ranked 6th in the nation for the percentage of the state's population that is uninsured. Research shows that not having health insurance leads to a lower quality of life and shorter life expectancy, as well as having potentially devastating financial effects in the case that a serious illness arises.

In order to address ongoing concerns about the uninsured in the United States, in March 2010 Congress and President Obama approved the Affordable Care Act (ACA). The goal of the act is to ensure that a much higher percentage of the population is covered by a health plan, and it is hoped that this will be achieved through a mixture of policy initiatives. The changes included in the ACA are expansions to public programs (such as Medicaid), mandates for employers to provide health insurance to their employees, barring insurance companies from denying coverage for pre-existing health conditions, and perhaps most controversially, a mandate that individuals must have health insurance or pay a tax penalty. The law will be gradually implemented through 2014, at which point it is estimated that 94 percent of Californians will be insured.

In order to make it feasible for individuals to purchase health insurance, the ACA requires states to create insurance exchanges, or marketplaces, where those who are uninsured can purchase insurance by comparing prices and plans, giving them the purchasing power that large companies have when purchasing health insurance for their employees. The federal government will also provide subsidies to low- and middle-income citizens in order to help them make these insurance purchases.

The full implications of the ACA for California are not yet completely known, as several parts will not even be implemented for a few years. However, California is already a leader among the states in implementing the ACA. In the fall of 2010

Governor Schwarzenegger and the California legislature approved legislation creating the first healthcare exchange in the United States, with it being set to begin in 2014. Many will be watching carefully to see the outcome of this program and the implementation of the other parts of the ACA in California, particularly to determine whether they achieve the desired outcome of greatly increasing the percent of the population that has healthcare coverage.

Welfare

Unlike education, which is primarily a state and local function, welfare in the United States is a shared function of the Federal government, the California government and California counties. With the exception of the Earned Income Tax Credit, an exclusively Federal welfare program, the Federal and California State governments each pay about half of the costs of welfare and the delivery system is at the county level. Decisions about the size of welfare and the conditions under which it will be paid are shared between the Federal government and the state. The five major delivery systems in California are Medi-Cal (discussed above), which provides health care to the poor and to near poor children and nursing home care to the poor, SSI/SSP, which provides assistance to the disabled and elderly poor, In Home Support Services (IHSS) which provides services to the disabled and elderly poor who stay at home rather than going to a nursing home, CalWORKS, which provides cash aid primarily to poor female headed families and Food Stamps to poor families, called SNAP in California. Table 1 shows the number or recipients for each program, the average amount spent on each family and the overall expenditure on the programs.

SSI/SSP and IHSS

Supplemental Security Income/State Supplementary Payments, the second largest (after Medicaid) of the joint Federal/State welfare programs gives money to the

Table 12.1 Main California Welfare Programs

	Annual Spending in millions	Recipients	Average monthly payment
SSI	$9.13	1,262,282	603
aged		361,017	506
blind		19,450	650
disabled		881,815	642
IHSS	$4.69	425,086	920
SNAP	$6.26	3,501,623	148
CalWORKS	$3.52	1,435,058	507
General Relief	$0.38	148,206	215

blind, the disabled and poor elderly people not eligible for Social Security, or who receive only minimal Social Security payments. In Home Support Services provides home help with such things as cleaning, shopping and simple medical procedures to essentially the same population. These are both relatively uncontroversial programs as most of the population thinks that it is fair to help support the disabled, the blind and poor retired people. About two-thirds of the recipients are disabled and about a third are poor elderly people. The number of people receiving SSI/SSP benefits has increased from around 950,000 in 1992/3 to around 1.3 million today. The number receiving IHSS has doubled since 2000 and is likely to increase further.

Because the home help program partly substitutes for much more expensive nursing home care successive Administrations have viewed the IHSS program as cost saving, and have supported its rapid expansion. But the program has had some growing pains. Because there is considerable public support for the people who receive SSI, there has been little change in policy over the years. But the number receiving home help has increased very rapidly in the last decade in an effort to reduce the amount that Medi-Cal spends on nursing home care. About 95 percent of helpers are hired by the person being helped. This eases the problem of helpers being undesired by the person being helped but has increased the amount of fraud in the program. Also any rapidly growing program gets more scrutiny in bad budget times. It is clear the Brown Administration is looking seriously at reducing the growth and costs of this program.

If policy in SSI/SSP has been relatively stable, the same cannot be said about California's third largest program, Temporary Aid to needy Families (TANF) (called CalWORKS in California.) This program gives money and in kind benefits to poor families with children. About 90 percent of these families are headed by females.

TANF and Food Stamps

In the years since 1935 a hodge-podge of different programs have been assembled to help mothers with dependent children. At the heart of this collection of programs is TANF, a cash support program primarily for female-headed families. Surrounding it is a Food Stamps program (SNAP in California), two types of housing programs, a program for pregnant mothers (WIC), a childcare program and a negative income tax called the Earned Income Tax Credit (EITC). It was these programs, rather than the larger welfare programs discussed above that the average person considered welfare. All except the EITC are jointly funded by the State and the Federal Government and are administered in California primarily by the counties.

In 1996 the length of time that adults (but not their children) could remain on TANF was cut to no more than two years at a time and no more than five years in a lifetime, with some exceptions for difficult cases. The various programs were also increasingly administered as one coherent program rather than as many disparate programs, and there was a stronger emphasis on finding employment for female heads. It was argued that these changes would push poor women into the job market and, in the long run, pull more of them out of poverty.

The combination of the new law, a reduction of birth rates among young women and the 9-year economic expansion of the 1990s led to a big reduction in welfare rolls, with the new law probably accounting for around a third of the reduction. Between 1995 and 2008 the California rolls fell by almost 48 percent. Several studies have shown that most of those who left the rolls were successful in finding employment. However California had a lower reduction in rolls and less employment growth than most other states, primarily because it made CalWORKS less draconian than equivalent programs in other states. Despite this, of the 5.3 million Californians below the poverty level in 2009 only 1.3 million were enrolled in CalWORKS.

The reform measures were clearly successful in reducing welfare rolls, but it is important to ask whether they have reduced the poverty rate. In the United States as a whole, poverty barely shifted between 1997 and 2007, despite 10 years of economic growth. In California, however, the rate did fall from 16.6 percent to 12.7 percent. But the rate has since rebounded to 15.3 percent in 2009 and will probably be higher still in 2010 and 2011. The major effect of the Act appears to be moving female heads of household from being poverty level welfare recipients, to being poverty level workers.

Defeating poverty is a tough task. The reality is that poverty in America is caused by basic factors such as poor education, poor language skills, addiction, mental and physical illness and criminality which require much more intervention than the country wants to pay for.

The California Budget System

It is universally acknowledged that California has had one of the most dysfunctional budget systems in the United States. As a result California in recent years has lurched from one budgetary problem to another. At the heart of the problem is California's easily amended Constitution. One amendment required a two-thirds majority to pass a budget bill. Others require the same majority for tax bills. This gives the minority party in the legislature veto power over the budget. This was intended to promote compromise, but because legislators have gerrymandered their constituencies to give themselves fat majorities, and because another initiative ensured that they would have short terms in office, there is little reason for the minority party to compromise. The result has been budgetary gridlock. In addition the experiment with direct democracy (see Chapter 4) has led to initiatives increasing spending and reducing taxes. Although Proposition 13, reducing property taxes is the best known, there have been scores of amendments to increase spending or reduce taxes. This complicates an already difficult task for lawmakers. Although it was officially balanced, the California Budget has been out of balance for most of the last decade. This has led to excessive borrowing by California and has given us the lowest credit rating of any state. We currently face a deficit of $25 billion, around 12 percent of total California State spending and around 30 percent of the state's General Fund spending.

The fiscal pain of the last two years has however had an effect on voters. A Proposition was passed in 2009 which gave the authority over state level reapportionment to a citizen commission rather than the legislature. This may produce constituencies more evenly balanced between the parties. A 2010 Proposition removed the requirement of a two-thirds majority to pass the budget. This weakens the ability of the minority party to sabotage the budget process. The election of Jerry Brown, a Democrat, means both the Governorship and both houses of the legislature are held by Democrats, reducing the conflict between the two branches that characterized the Schwarzenegger era. But the tax limitations remain and it is difficult to see how a balanced budget can be constructed without tax increases.

As this goes to press in April 2011, Jerry Brown is proposing to put a Proposition before voters to extend temporary tax increases passed last year and make substantial cuts in higher education, redevelopment and welfare. If the Proposition fails, or never makes the ballot, we can expect further cuts in these areas, combined with major cuts in K-12 education and criminal justice spending and probably another real budget deficit covered up with accounting tricks and borrowing.

Conclusion

In the last two hundred years we have moved from being a country where government was small and most functions were undertaken by the family, the church and business, to one where government is an indispensable part of the average American's life. Within government we have moved from doing a majority of things at the local level to relying most heavily on the Federal level. The tasks which states and localities thought were reserved for themselves are now generally undertaken by states, the Federal government and the localities working together. This does not however mean that the states are powerless to affect their own destiny. California has had to choose between various alternative ways of spending its money and the choices clearly have consequences. In the 1950s and 1960s California chose to emphasize infrastructure, transportation and education spending and built amazing water delivery and road systems, good public schools and an excellent higher education system, while somewhat neglecting its poorer citizens. In the 1990s and 2000s California has emphasized spending on criminal justice, health and welfare, creating an unusually generous safety net for the poor and reduced crime. But even before the recent fiscal crisis this had come at some cost. The infrastructure was strained, the roads were overcrowded, K-12 education was less good than in other states, and higher education was slowly deteriorating. How to deal with these problems in a time of acute fiscal scarcity without harming our poorer citizens will be a challenging task for our political leaders.

REFERENCES

Abney, Glen and Thomas P. Lauth (1986). *The Politics of State and City Administration.* Albany, NY: SUNY Albany Press.

Administrative Office of the United States Courts, *Annual Report* 2008 http://www.supremecourts.gov/publicinfo/year-end/2008year-endreport.pdf

Agger, Robert, Daniel Goldrich, and Bert Swanson (1964). *The Rulers and the Ruled.* New York: John Wiley & Sons.

Baer, Denise and David A. Bostis (1988). *Elite Cadres and Party Coalitions.* New York: Greenwood Press.

Baldasarre, Mark (2008, January). *California's Post-Partisan Future.* San Francisco, CA: Public Policy Institute of California, Greenwood Press.

Bann, Carolyn and Norma Riccucci (1995). "Personnel Systems in Labor Relations: Steps Toward a Quiet Revolution" in Thompson, Frank J., *Revitalizing State and Local Public Service Performance: Strengthening Performance, Accountability and Citizen Confidence.* San Francisco: Jossey-Bass.

Behn, Robert (2001). Rethinking Democratic Accountability. Washington, D.C.: Brookings.

Berg, Charlene (1980). The Orange County Republican Central Committee. Public address.

Bernstein, Dan (1997). "'98 Campaign Frenzy Begins; Reform Law Has Groups Chasing 'Independent' Cash." *Sacramento Bee,* January 18, 1.

Briscoe, Jerry B. and Charles G. Bell (1986). "The New Sacramento Lobbying Corps."

Broder, David. 2002. *Washington Post* Weekly Edition.

Bureau of Census (2006). *Statistical Abstract of the United States: 2006.* Washington, DC: U.S. Department of Commerce.

Burke, Robert E. (1953). *Olson's New Deal for California.* Berkeley: University of California Press.

Cain, Bruce E. and Roger Noll, eds. (1995). *Constitutional Reform in California: Making State Government More Efficient and Responsive.* Berkeley: Institute of Governmental Studies Press.

California Commission on the Fair Administration of Justice (2008) http://www.courtinfo.ca.gov/

California Data Brief, Vol. 9, No. 1 (Fall), 3. 2004. Berkeley, CA.: Institute of Governmental Studies, University of California.

California Department of Finance (2007). *California Statistical Abstract.* Released in January 2007; January 13, 2009 http://ww/dof.ca.gov/HTML/FS_DATA/STAT-ABS/Statistical_Abstract.php

California State Personnel Board (2007). *Annual Census of Employees in the State Civil Service, 2006–2007 Fiscal Year.* Released in November 2007; January 13, 2009 http://www.spb.ca.gov/WorkArea/showcontent.aspx?id=3962

Caress, Stanley M. (1966). "The Impact of Term Limits on Legislative Behavior: An Examination of a Transitional Legislature." *PS: Political Science & Politics* XXIX (4), December.
City of Garden Grove v. *Superior Court (Kha)*, 2007 S.O.S. 6933.
Commission on the Future of the California Courts (1993). *Justice in the Balance: Report of the Commission on the Future of the California Courts*. San Francisco: The Judicial Council of California, Administrative Office of the California Courts.
Council of State Governments (1997). *Book of the States, 1996–97*. Lexington, KY: Council of State Governments.
Craft, Cynthia H. (2000). "Proposition 34: Campaign Finance Reform." *California Journal*, September, 34–35.
Crouch, Winston C. (1978). *Organized Civil Servants: Public Employer–Employee Relations*. Berkeley: University of California Press.
Dalton, Russell J. (1996). *Citizen Politics: Public Opinion and Political Parties in Advanced Industrial Democracies*. New York: Chatham House.
DeLaet, Debra L. (2000). *U.S. Immigration Policy in an Age of Rights*. Westport, CT: Greenwood.
Donovan, Todd, Shaun Bowler, David McCuan, and Ken Fernandez (1998). "Contending Players and Strategies: Opposition Advantages in Initiative Campaigns" in *Citizens as Legislators: Direct Democracy in the United States*, edited by Shaun Bowler, Todd Donovan, and Caroline Tolbert. Columbus: Ohio State University Press.
Downs, Anthony (1967). *Inside Bureaucracy*. Boston. Little, Brown.
Edsall, Thomas B. (1986). "Republican America." *The New York Review*, April 24.
Elazar, Daniel J. (1972). *American Federalism: A View from the States*. New York: Crowell.
Elling, Richard C. (1992). *Public Management in the States: A Comparative Study of Administrative Performance*. Westport, CT: Praeger.
Fairlie, Henry (1978). "Direct vs. Representative Democracy." *The Los Angeles Times* (August 2), Part IV, p. 2.
Federal Elections Commission (1996). *http://www.fec.gov/paclon18.htm*
Federal Judicial Center Annual report 2008 *http://www.fjc.gov/public/pdf.nsf/lookup/AnnRep08.pdf/$file/AnnRep08.pdf*
Fiorina, Morris P. (1996). *Divided Government*. New York: Allyn & Bacon.
Fiorina, Morris with Samuel J. Abrams and Jeremy C. Pope (2005). *Culture War? The Myth of a Polarized America*, 2nd ed. New York: Pearson/Longman.
FPPC (1986). Bulletin, Vol. 12, No. 4 (April 1), 2.
_____. 1996. California Campaign Finance: State Law as Changed by Proposition 208. Sacramento, CA.
Followthemoney.org http://www.followthemoney.org/database/StateGlance/state_ballot_measures.phtml?s=CA&y=2010 retrieved on April 22, 2011.
Gamson, William A. (1968). *Power and Discontent*. Homewood, IL: Dorsey Press.

Green, Veron, Sally Coleman Selden, and Gene Brewer (2000). "Measuring Power and Presence: Bureaucratic Representation in the America States," *Journal of Public Adminstration Research and Theory*, Vol. 11, No. 3, pp. 379–402.

Griggs v. Duke Power Company (1971). 401 U.S. 424.

Gonzales v. Raich (2005), 545 U.S. 1.

Gordon, Stacy B. and Cynthia L. Unmack (2003). "The Effect of Term Limits on Corporate PAC Allocation Patterns: The More Things Change. . . ." *State and Local Government Review*, 35(1), 26–37.

Hager, Phillip (1988). "Prosecutors Win Edict in Use of Confessions." *Los Angeles Times* (Feb. 2), part 1, p. 14.

Hajnal, Zoltan and Paul Lewis (2003). "Municipal Institutions and Voter Turnout in Local Elections," *Urban Affairs Review*, Vol. 38, No. 5, pp. 645–668.

Jefferson, Thomas (1999). *Jefferson: Political Writings (Cambridge Texts in the History of Political Thought)*, edited by Joyce Appleby and Terence Ball. New York: Cambridge University Press.

2007 Judicial Facts and Figures http://wwwcourtinfo.ca.gov/

Judicial Council of California, *Annual Report* 2008 http://www.courtinfo.ca.gov/jc

Katz, Jeffrey L. (1991). "The Slow Death of Political Patronage." *Governing*, 58–62.

Key, V. O., Jr. (1967). *Politics, Parties and Pressure Groups*. New York: Crowell.

Kernell, Samuel. 1997. *Going Public: New Strategies of Presidential Leadership, Third Edition*. Washington, DC: Congressional Quarterly Press.

Legislative Analyst's Office (2004). *An Initial Assessment of the California Performance Review*. Released on August 24, 2004; January 13, 2009 http://www.lao.ca.gov/2004/cpr/082704_cpr_review.pdf

Lipset, Seymour Martin. (1996). *American Exceptionalism: A Double-Edged Sword*. New York: Norton.

Little Hoover Commission (1995). *Too Many Agencies, Too Many Rules: Reforming California's Civil Service*. Released in April 1995; January 13, 2009 http://www.lhc.ca.gov/lhcdir/133rp.html

Madison, James (1787). *The Same Subject Continued: The Union as a Safeguard Against Domestic Faction and Insurrection, Federalist No. 10*.

Maisel, L. Sandy (1990). *The Parties Respond* (1990). Boulder: Westview Press.

Mayhew, David R. (1986). *Placing Parties in American Politics: Organization, Electoral Settings, and Government Activity in the Twentieth Century*. Princeton: Princeton University Press.

McConnell, Grant (1966). *Private Power and American Democracy*. New York: Knopf.

McConnell, Grant (1970). *Private Power and American Democracy*. New York: Vintage Books.

McCuan, David and Stephen J. Stambough, eds. (2005). *Initiative-Centered Politics: The New Politics of Direct Democracy*. Durham, NC: Carolina Academic Press.

Moncrief, Gary and Joel A. Thompson (2001). "On the Outside Looking in: Lobbyists' Perspectives on the Effects of State Legislative Term Limits." *State Politics and Policy Quarterly*, 1(4), 394–411.
Naff, Katherine (2006). "Prospects for Civil Service Reform in California: A Triumph of Technique Over Purpose?" in *Civil Service Reform in the States: Personnel Policies and Politics at the Subnational Level,* edited by J. Edward Kellough and Lloyd G. Nigro. Albany, NY: SUNY Albany Press.
Nigro, Lloyd, Felix Nigro, and J. Edward Kellough (2007). *The New Public Personnel Adminstration,* 6th ed. Belmont, CA: Thomson/Wadsworth.
Niskanen, William (1971). *Bureaucracy and Representative Government.* Hawthorne, NY: Aldine de Gruyter.
Olson, Mancur, Jr. (1965). *The Logic of Collective Action.* New York: Schocken Books.
Pew Center on the States (2005). *Grading the State 2005: A Look Inside.* Released in February 2005; January 13, 2009 *http://www.pewcenteronthestates.org/uploadedFiles/wwwpewtrustorg/Reports/Government_Performance/GPP_Report_2005.pdf*
Pew Center on the States (2008). *The State Management Report Card for 2008.* Released in March 2008; January 13, 2009 *http://www.pewcenteronthestates.org/uploadedFiles/Grading-the-States-2008.pdf*
Popkin, Samuel L. (1994). *The Reasoning Voter: Communication and Persuasion in Presidential Campaigns.* Chicago: University of Chicago Press.
Price, Charles M. and Charles G. Bell (1996), *California Government Today.* Belmont, CA: Wadsworth.
Reinhold, Robert (1988). "No Tilt as Yet from New California High Court."*New York Times* (National Ed., Jan. 1), p. 18.
Rogin, Michael and John Shover (1970). *Political Change in California: Critical Elections and Social Movements, 1890–1966.* Westport, CT: Greenwood.
Rozell, Mark J. and Clyde Wilcox (1999). *Interest Groups in American Campaigns: The New Face of Electioneering.* Washington, D.C.: CQ Press.
Samish, Arthur H. and Bob Thomas (1959). *The Secret Boss of California.* New York: Crown.
Samish, Arthur H. and Bob Thomas (1971). *The Secret Boss of California.* New York: Crown.
Schwarzenegger, Arnold (2005). Letter to the Little Hoover Commission accompanying his reorganization plan, *A Government for the People for a Change.* Released in January 2005; January 13, 2009 *http://cpr.ca.gov/CPR_Report/pdf/lhc_letter.pdf*
Shafritz, Jay M., J. Steven Ott, and Yong Suk Jang (2005). *Classics of Organization Theory,* 6th ed. Belmont, CA: Thompson and Wadsworth.
Starr, Kevin (1973). *Americans and the California Dream: 1850–1915.* Oxford.: Oxford University Press.
Starr, Kevin (1990). *Material Dreams: Southern California Through the 1920s.* Oxford: Oxford University Press.
Stone, Barbara S. (1991). Interview.

Strother, Dane (1997). "Campaign Finance 'Reforms' Don't Work." *New York Times*, February 1 (Op-Ed page).
Tocqueville, Alexis de (1956). *Democracy in America*, edited by Richard D. Heffner. New York: New American Library.
Tullock, Gordon (1965). *The Politics of Bureaucracy*. Washington, D.C.: Public Affairs.
U.S. Bureau of the Census (1980). Statistical Abstract of the United States. Washington, D.C.: U.S. Government Printing Office.
Vaca, Jeffrey A., ed. (1997). *Legislative Report*. Sacramento: Office of Governmental Affairs, The California State University, July 3.
Velie, Lester (1949a). "The Secret Boss of California." Colliers, Vol. 124 (August 13), 11–13, 71–73.
_____ (1949b). "The Secret Boss of California." Colliers, Vol. 124 (August 20), 12–1,; 60, 62–63.
Verba, Sidney, Kay Lehman Schlozman, and Henry Brady. (1996). *Voice and Equality: Civic Voluntarism and American Politics*. Cambridge Harvard University Press.
Wattenberg, Martin P. (1996). *The Decline of American Political Parties, 1965–1994*. Cambridge: Harvard University Press.
Weber, Max. (1949). *The Methodology of the Social Sciences*. New York: Free Press.
West, William (2005). "Administrative Rulemaking: An Old and Emerging Literature," *Public Administration Review*, Vol. 65, No. 6, pp. 655–668.
Wildavsky, Aaron. 1969. "The Two Presidencies," pp. 230–243 in *The Presidency*, ed. Aaron Wildavsky. Boston: Little Brown.
Wilson, James Q. (1966). "A Guide to Reagan Country." *Commentary* 43 (May).
Wilson, Pete (1996). "Competitive Government." Office of the Governor, http://www.osp.ca.gov/complete.htm.
Wilson, Woodrow (1887). "The Study of Public Administration," *Political Science Quarterly*, Vol. 2, June, pp. 197–222.
Wold, John T. and John H. Culver (1987). "The Defeat of the California Justices: The Campaign, the Electorate, and the Issue of Judicial Accountability." *Judicature* 70 (No. 6, April–May), 348–355.
Wolfinger, Raymond and Fred Greenstein (1969). "Comparing Political Regions: The Case of California." *American Political Science Review*, March.
Zaller, John R. (1992). *The Nature and Origins of Mass Opinion*. New York: Cambridge University Press.

INDEX

A

abortion rights, 27
absentee ballots, 25, 31, 32
ACA (Affordable Care Act), 167–168
accountability, 125
    Administrative Procedure Act and, 130
    of interest groups, 54, 60
    of private and nonprofit
        organizations, 119
    public employees and, 125, 131
Administrative Procedure Act, 130
administrators, public, 118–122
affirmative action, 22, 113, 134–135
Affordable Care Act (ACA), 167–168
African Americans, 17, 18
air quality management districts, 153
Allen, Doris, 38
Alpine County, 146
amendments, constitutional, 36, 42, 113
American Federation of Labor–Congress
    of Industrial Organizations
    Committee on Political Education
    (COPE), 63
Anderson, John, 27
anti-immigrant activity, 14
appellate courts, 103, 104, 107–108
appointments
    judicial, 109–110
    political, 76–77, 97, 118–119, 133
Arsneault, Shelly, 35
Articles of Confederation, 142
Asia, immigration from, 18
Assembly, California, 67, 87, 90–91,
    94–95. *See also* legislature, state
assembly members, 90–91
at-large elections, 152
Attorney General, 73, 109, 126, 126

B

ballot measures. *See* propositions, ballot
ballots, 25, 31, 32, 151
Bankruptcy Court, U.S., 105
Barber, James, 82
bargaining advantages, gubernatorial, 79
Bass, Karen, 18
beliefs, political, 11–12, 152–153
"Big Five" group, 95
Bill of Rights, California, 2
Bird, Rose, 109, 115
blanket primary elections, 8, 29, 46, 92–93
Board of Equalization, 72, 73
Board of Supervisors, 145–146
boards, independent, 126
Boyum, Keith, 68
Brown, Edmund G. "Jerry," 19, 132
    against financial crisis, 81, 82
    governing experience, 83
    role in budget process, 2011, 75–76
Brown, Pat, 78
Brown, Willie, 18, 38, 61
Brown v. Board of Education (1954),
    111–112
Buckley v. Valeo (1976), 63
budget process, 74–78, 84, 93, 96–97,
    130–131, 170–171
bureaucracy, 7, 121–122, 125, 137
Bush, George H. W., 144
Bush, George W., 16, 26
Bustamante, Cruz, 80
butterfly ballots, 32
Buzan, Bert C., 45, 57

C

California Coastal Act (1976), 154
California Coastal Commission, 126,
    153–154
California Commission on the Fair
    Administration of Justice, 107–108
California Constitution, 3–9
    amendments to, 36, 42, 113
    Article VI, 103
    Bill of Rights in, 2
    comparison to U.S. Constitution, 10
    initiatives and, 36
California Constitutional Convention
    (1879), 142

Index

California Democratic Council (CDC), 53
California Performance Review (CPR), 118, 124, 136–137
California Public Interest Research Group, 64
California Republican Assembly (CRA), 52
California Republican League (CRL), 52
California Superior Court, 105
California Supreme Court. *See* Supreme Court, California
California Youth Authority (CYA), 106
CalWORKS, 161, 168, 169, 170
campaign contributions, 60–61, 62, 65, 66–67, 95–96
campaign finance reform, 63–67
campaign management firms, 47, 53, 68
capital punishment, 107–108, 115
careers, political, 88, 91
Carter, Jimmy, 26
CDC (California Democratic Council), 53
Central Valley project, 162
centrism, 47, 49
chads, 32
character and leadership, 82–83
charters, 124, 143, 145
checks and balances, 71–72
Chinese, 14
circulation title statement, 36
cities, 4, 147–148
    charter, 143
    elections in, 151–152
Citizens United v. *Federal Election Commission*, 64
City of Garden Grove v. *Superior Court (Kha)* 2007, 145
civil laws, 102
Civil Service Act (1913), 131
civil service system, 47, 119, 124, 125, 133–134
Clinton, Bill, 26, 74
Coastal Commission, 126, 154
cohesion, ideological, of legislators, 49–51
Commission on Judicial Appointments, 109
Commission on Judicial Performance, 110
commissioners
    attorneys as, 109
    insurance, 74
commissions, independent, 126

Common Cause, 64
communities, immigrant, 13–14
community conservationist, 153
Congress, U.S., 90–91, 98–99
conservatism, 16, 46, 52, 152
    in primary elections, 28
    in Southern California, 17
constituent function, 90
Constitution, California. *See* California Constitution
Constitution, U.S., 1–2, 103
    comparison to California Constitution, 10
    court system and, 101
    Full Faith and Credit clause, 112
    state initiatives and, 36
Constitution, U.S. (1789), 142, 157
constitutional courts, 103
constitutional initiatives, 36, 44
Constitutional Revision Commission, 8–9
constitutions, state, 1, 2, 9
controller, 73
conventions, state party, 51
COPE (American Federation of Labor–Congress of Industrial Organizations Committee on Political Education), 62–64
council-manager government, 14, 148
councils of governments, 153
County Central Committee, 52
county governments, 4, 141, 145–147
    elections and, 31
courts, 101–108, 111–112
courts of appeal. *See* appellate courts
CPR (California Performance Review), 118, 124, 129, 136–137
CRA (California Republican Assembly), 52
crime, 111, 164
criminal laws, 102
crises and executive leadership, 82
CRL (California Republican League), 52
CYA (California Youth Authority), 106

D

Davis, Gray, 5, 38, 80, 82, 83, 162
de Tocqueville, Alexis, 141
death penalty cases. *See* capital punishment
defense spending, 159

Index **181**

delegates, 51, 88–89
democracy, 88–89
   direct. *See* direct democracy
   grassroots, 139
   representative, 35, 40–43
Democratic party, 15, 19, 49
   extra-party groups of, 52
   history in California, 22–23
   on national level, 54
   party coalition in, 27
   progressivism and, 46
   redistricting and, 91
   use of Internet by, 54
Democratic Volunteers Committee (DVC), 53
demographics, 11, 24–25, 49
Department of Personnel Administration (DPA), 132
deregulation, 162
Deukmejian, George, 6, 114
direct democracy, 5, 14, 35, 40–44, 72, 170
   interest groups and, 68
   progressivism and, 59
discrimination, 112, 134
districts
   legislative, 91–92
   school, 141, 143, 149
   special, 141, 149–154
divorce laws, 111–112
DNA testing, 115
Dole, Bob, 22
domestic rights, 113
Dornan, Bob, 11
Downs, Anthony, 122
DPA (Department of Personnel Administration), 132
DVC (Democratic Volunteers Committee), 53

E
Earned Income Tax Credit (EITC), 169
economy, state of the, 160
education, 143–144, 161, 164–165
EITC (Earned Income Tax Credit), 169
elderly, funding for, 159–160
elections
   at-large, 152
   blanket primary, 8, 46, 92–93
   general, 28
   high stimulus, 28
   of judges, 109
   nonpartisan, 7, 151
   primary, 28–30
   retention, 7, 115
Electoral College, 84
electoral process, 62
electoral votes, 26
electorates, 22–23, 28–31, 46. *See also* voters
   demographics of California, 24–25
   table of comparisons, California and national, 33
Elementary and Secondary Education Act (1965), 144
employee associations, 132, 133
employees, public, 118–119, 125, 131–135, 137
endorsements, party, 47
Environmental Impact Statement, 130
Epstein, Leon, 48
Eu v. *SF Demo. Comm* (1988), 47
executive branch
   crises and leadership by, 81–82
   leadership, 69–71, 76–77
   plural elected, 6, 71–73
expertise, use of, by public employees, 121
extra-party groups, 47, 52–53

F
Fair Political Practices Commission (FPPC), 64
Fairlie, Henry, 43
Feather River project, 162
FEC (Federal Election Commission), 62
Federal Controlled Substances Act, 145
Federal Election Campaign Act, 62–64
Federal Election Commission (FEC), 62
federal government. *See* government, federal
federal grants, 161
Federal Reserve, 160
Feingold, Russell, 63
Fiber-Ostrow, Pamela, 101
Finance, Department of, 130
financial obligations, state, 43
Fiorina, Morris, 49
fiscal constraints, 8

fiscal policy, 160
527 organizations, 63
Florida, 31
focus and interest group, 58, 62
Food Stamp Program, 169
foreign policy, 159
Fourteenth Amendment, 101
FPPC (Fair Political Practices Commission), 64
freedom of speech, 96
Full Faith and Credit clause, 112

G
Garamendi, John, 6
Garfield, James, 26
gay marriage. *See* same-sex marriage
general elections, 28, 29–30
general law
    cities, 143
    counties, 145
Gianos, Phillip L., 1
GNP (Gross National Product), 159
gold, discovery of, 12
Goldwater, Barry, 16
Gonzales v. *Raich* (2005), 144
Gore, Al, 26
"Governator," 81
government, federal, 122, 143–144, 157–158
government, local, 7–8, 124, 139–155
    cities, 147–149
    count of, 141
    county governments, 145–147
    elections, 151–152
    relationship to state government, 142–143
    revenue sources, 150–151
    special districts, 149–150
government, regional, 153–154
government, state
    California, 123–124
    elections and, 31
    federal government, 123
    PACs (political action committees) and growth of, 62
    policy issues and, 161
    relationship to local government, 142–143

Government Performance Project (GPP), 136–137
governor, 6, 71–79, 74, 85, 96–97
GPP (Government Performance Project), 136–137
granted powers, 2
grass roots movements, Internet-based, 54
Great Depression, 160–161
Green Party, 27
Griggs v. *Duke Power Company* (1971), 134
Grodin, Joseph, 109, 115
Gross National Product (GNP), 159

H
Hamilton, Alexander, 142
Hawaii and same-sex marriage ruling, 112
head of state status, symbolic, 77–78
head of the state status, 77–78
Health and Human Services, Department of, 127
health program, 166–168
high stimulus elections, 28
higher education, 166
Higher Education Act (1965), 144
Hill, Sarah, 157
Hispanics, 17, 18, 19
Holder, Eric, 42
home-rule provision, 143, 147
homosexuals, tolerance of, 14
Horcher, Paul, 38
housing prices, 20

I
ideology, political, 152–153
IHSS (In Home Support Services), 168, 169
immigrants and immigration, 12–19, 22, 113
Immigration Act (1951), 18
impeachment, 110
incorporation
    as a city, 147
    selective, 101
industries, signature, 14
infrastructure, 161–163
In Home Support Services (IHSS), 168, 169
initiatives, 3, 4, 5, 35, 38–43
    constitutional, 36, 44
    interest groups and, 38, 68

party affiliation and, 29
progressivism and, 59
statutory, 36, 44
voting on, 30
insurance commissioner, 74
interest groups, 4–5, 47, 57–68, 123
    campaign management firms and, 53
    initiatives and, 38, 68
    Speaker of the Assembly and, 95
Internet, impact of, on grass roots movements, 54
Issa, Darrell, 38, 39
item veto. *See* line-item budget veto

J

Japanese Americans, 15
Jarvis, Matthew G., 11, 87
Jefferson, Thomas, 140–141
Johnson, Hiram, 36, 45, 60, 72, 78, 82
judges, 7, 108–110, 112–113
judicial branch, 112–113
Judicial Council of California, 106
judiciary
    appellate courts, 103, 104, 107–108
    caseload, 105
    limited jurisdiction courts, 108
    nonpartisan, 6–7
    superior court subdivisions, 106
    Supreme Court, 103
    table of organization, 104–105
    trial courts, 103–106
Justice Courts, 108
justices, appellate court, 107

K

Kennedy, John Fitzgerald, 26
Key, V. O., 50

L

labor unions, 62–63
land use, 153–154
Latin America, immigration from, 18
Latinos, 18, 19, 24
laws
    criminal and civil, 102
    private, 102–103, 106, 112
    public, 102–103, 106, 112–113

leadership
    character and, 82–83
    executive, 69–71, 76–77, 82
    gubernatorial, 74–77
    media image and, 80
    in state legislature, 94–95
legislative courts, 103
legislators, 49–51
    professional, 87–88
    weakened role of, 79
legislature, state, 7, 87, 90–91
    ballot propositions and strength of, 43
    committee structure, 92–93
    election to, 90–91
    functions of, 89–90
    interest groups and, 60–61
    power of the governor and, 72, 74–77
    professional model for, 87–88
liberalism, 16, 28, 152
lieutenant governor, 73
limited jurisdiction courts, 108
line-item budget veto, 6, 74, 76, 84
Little Hoover Commission (2005), 133, 135–136
lobbyists, 5, 58, 60–62
Lockyer v. City and County of San Francisco, 113
Los Angeles, 8, 17
Los Angeles County, 146, 147
Los Angeles Massacre (1871), 14
loyalty, party, 22
Lucas, Malcolm M., 115

M

Madison, James, 58, 142
majority rule, 40, 48
majority-minority state, 19
marginal voters, 28
marijuana, 144–145
marijuana, legalization of, 42–43
marriage
    laws, 112
    same-sex, 16, 22, 39, 41, 111–114
Master Plan for Higher Education, 166
mayor-council government, 148–149
McCain, John, 63
McConnell v. FEC (2003), 63

Measure M (1990), 154
media
coverage of elections by, 96, 151
image and leadership, 80
Medicaid, 167
Medi-Cal, 167, 168–169
Medicare program, 167
merit system, 119, 125, 133, 133–134
Metropolitan Water District, 149
Mexican Americans, 14–15
Mexico, immigration from, 18
middle class and progressivism, 59
migration patterns, 12, 13, 17–18
military defense, 159
minority rights, 41
mobilization, 24
monetary policy, 160
motor voter registration, 25
Municipal Courts, 108
municipal government, 141

N
Nader, Ralph, 27
National Defense Education Act, 144
National Rifle Association (NRA), 57
negotiations, in court cases, 110–111
Neustadt, Richard, 79
New Deal, 22
Niskanen, William, 122
Nixon, Richard, 26
No Child Left Behind Act (2001), 144
"no" votes, 41
nominees, party, 46
nonpartisan elections, 7, 151
nonprofit organizations, 119
nonvoters, 24
nonvoting vote, 93
Northrop, Alana, 35
NRA (National Rifle Association), 57

O
Obama, Barack, 54
obstructionism, 48
Office of Administrative Law, 130
Olson, Mancur, 54
Orange County, 11, 16, 146–147
Orange County Transportation
Authority, 153
organization theory, 122

outsourced jobs, 119
oversight function, 89
Owens River and Colorado River
projects, 162

P
PACs (political action committees),
62–63, 64
participation in party politics, 51
partisanship, 23, 47, 92–93
party affiliation and initiatives, 30
"party in government," 50
party system. *See* political party system
Patriot Act (2001), 144
patronage, 47
Peretz, Paul, 11, 157
Perez, John, 19
Perot, Ross, 26–27
Personnel Administration, Department of
(DPA), 132
personnel management, 132–133
persuasion, power of, 79, 81
picket fence federalism, 123
plea bargaining, 110, 111
plural elected executives, 6, 71–73
polarization, 49–51
policy issues, 27, 33, 58, 158–161
political action committees (PACs),
62–63, 64
political appointments, 76–77, 96,
118–119, 133
political culture, 11–12, 15–16, 19–20
political party system, 4, 19–20, 45,
48–49, 51–54
coalitions in, 27
cohesiveness of, 49–51
interest groups and, 59
primary elections and, 92–93
weakness of, 5–6, 51
politics
initiative-centered, 68
private law issues and, 111–112
Poole, Keith, 50
population growth, 12–13
post-partisanship, 47–48
powers
delegated, 2, 121–122
executive, 69–79
preambles, 2

president pro tempore (Senate), 94–95, 98
presidential elections, 26
   public financing of, 63
Presidential Power and the Modern Presidents (Neustadt), 79
presidential powers, 71, 74–77
primary education, 165
primary elections, 28–30, 46, 92–93. *See also* blanket primary elections
Pringle, Curt, 61
private laws, 102–103, 106, 111
private sector, 119
professionalism, 87–89, 125, 126, 131
Progressive movement, 35–36, 45–46, 72, 125
progressivism, 3, 35–36, 59
property taxes, 8, 150, 164–165, 170
Proposition 8 (2008), 16, 39, 41, 113
Proposition 9 (1974), 64
Proposition 11 (2008), 92
Proposition 13 (1978), 8, 150, 165, 170
Proposition 14 (2010), 30, 46, 92
Proposition 19 (2010), 42
Proposition 20 (1972), 154
Proposition 20 (2010), 9
Proposition 22 (2000), 41, 112, 113–114
Proposition 22 (2010), 8
Proposition 25 (2010), 8, 9
Proposition 26 (2010), 8
Proposition 34 (2000), 64, 66, 96
Proposition 60 (2004), 30
Proposition 62 (2004), 30
Proposition 68 (1988), 64
Proposition 73 (1988), 64
Proposition 103 (1988), 73
Proposition 140 (1990), 7, 67, 79, 87–89
Proposition 187 (1994), 16, 18, 22, 113
Proposition 198 (1996), 29, 46
Proposition 208 (1996), 64, 66, 96
Proposition 209 (1996), 22, 113, 134–135, 135
Proposition 212 (1996), 64
propositions, ballot. *See also* initiatives; recall elections; referendums
   as checks on elected officials, 71
   judges and, 113, 115
   progressivism and, 35–36
   state legislature and, 42
   types of, comparative table, 44

public administrators, 118–122
public control
   rulemaking and, 130, 130
   value of, 124
public laws, 102–103, 106, 112–114
Public Policy Institute of California, 47, 49
public programs for poor, 143–144
public relations firms, use of, 53
public safety, 163
public services, 147

R
railroads, power of the, 3, 60
Ralph C. Dills Act, 133
Reagan, Ronald, 78, 80, 144
recall elections, 3, 5, 35, 37–38
   cost of, 39, 41
   of judges, 110
   progressivism and, 35–36, 59
red tape as public control, 130
redevelopment districts, 150–151
redistricting, 91–92
reelection loss, 110
referendums, 3, 5, 35–37, 43, 59
reforms
   California, 64–65
   campaign finance, 63–67
   federal, 62–64
regionalism, 3, 15–16, 153
regulations, 130–131
religion and California regionalism, 17
Renne v. *Geary* (1991), 47
repetition, in organization theory, 122
representation function, 89–90
representative democracy, 35, 40–43
Republican party, 16, 22, 49
   extra-party groups of, 52
   history in California, 23
   on national level, 54
   party coalition in, 27
   redistricting, 91
   use of Internet by, 54
retention elections, 7, 115
retirement benefits, 87
reunification, family, 18
Reynoso, Cruz, 109, 115
Rockefeller, Nelson, 16
roll-off voting, 30–31

Roosevelt, Franklin D., 71
Roybal, Ed, 18
Rozell, Mark J., 57
rulemaking, 120, 130
Rules Committee, 94
rural courts, 108

S

same-sex marriage, 16, 22, 39, 41, 111–114
Samish, Arthur, 60
San Bernardino County, 146
San Francisco, 17
San Joaquin Valley, 15, 16
Sanchez, Loretta, 11
school districts, 141, 143, 149
Schwarzenegger, Arnold, 5, 6, 8, 9, 38, 83
   2009 role in budget process, 75
   achievements of, 162
   California Performance Review (CPR) executive order, 118
   centrist approach to government, 47–48
   letter to Little Hoover Commission (2005), 135–136
   use of media image by, 80–81
secondary education, 164–165
Secretary of State, 73
selective incorporation, 101
self-interest, 11
Senate House, 87, 94–95, 98
senators, state, 90–91
separation of powers doctrine, 2, 72, 142
Serrano v. *Priest* (1971), 165
settlements, in court cases, 110, 111
signature requirements
   initiatives, 36
   recall elections, 37–38
   referendums, 37
Simon, Bill, 38
Simpson, O. J., 102
Skowronek, Steven, 81
SNAP, 168, 169
social security, 159–160
social services and county government, 146–147
"soft money" loophole, 66
South Coast Air Quality Management District, 154

Southern California, 15, 16, 17
Southern California Association of Governments, 153
Southern Pacific Railroad, 3, 14, 36, 45, 142
SPB (State Personnel Board), 125, 132–133
Speaker of the Assembly, 94–95, 98
special district government, 141, 149
specialization, in organization theory, 122
spending, 10
   campaign. *See* campaign finance reform
   crime enforcement, 164
   education, 164–166
   elderly, funding for, 159–160
   federal government, 157–159
   initiative measures campaign, 30
   on initiatives, 39
Spitzer, Scott, 69
SSI/SSP (Supplemental Security Income/State Supplementary Payments), 168–169
staffing, legislative, 87–88
Stambough, Stephen J., 45, 57
State Central Committee, 52
state constitutions, 1, 2, 9
State Election Code, 52
state employees. *See* employees, public
State Employer-Employee Relations Act, 133
state governments. *See* government, state
State Personnel Board (SPB), 125, 132–133
statutory initiatives, 36, 44
stem-cell research issue, 22
superagencies, 124, 127–129
Superintendent of Public Instruction, 73
Superior Court, California, 105
Superior Courts, 103, 105, 106, 108
Supplemental Security Income/State Supplementary Payments (SSI/SSP), 168–169
Supreme Court, California, 64, 107–108, 112
   Proposition 22 (2000), 113
   Serrano v. *Priest* (1971), 165
Supreme Court, U.S., 46, 47, 108
   Eu v. *SF Demo. Comm* (1988), 47
   Federal Election Campaign Act and, 63
   Griggs v. *Duke Power Company* (1971), 134
   McConnell v. *FEC* (2003), 63

Renne v. *Geary* (1991), 47
ruling on marijuana, 144–145
supreme courts, 107, 108

T

TANF (Temporary Aid to Needy Families), 169
taxing, 10
Temporary Aid to Needy Families (TANF), 169
term limits, 7, 79, 87, 91
    impact on leadership in state legislature, 95
    interest groups and, 67
    redistricting and, 91–92
third party presidential candidates, 26–27
three strikes rules, 111, 164
Thurmond, Strom, 27
Ting, Yuan, 1, 117, 139
Townsend, David, 66
townships, 141
transportation, 153, 161–163
treasurer, 73
trial courts, 103–106
tribunals, 103
Truman, Harry, 26
trustees, 89
Tullock, Gordon, 122
Tuolumne River project, 162
turnout, 24–26, 27, 28, 151–152

U

unions, 132
United Republicans of California (UROC), 52
United States Congress, 90–91, 98–99
United States Constitution. *See* Constitution, U.S.
United States Supreme Court. *See* Supreme Court, U.S.
Unruh, Jess, 53, 60–61
urban areas, 153–154
UROC (United Republicans of California), 52
utility regulation, 161–162

V

Veterans Healthcare program, 167
veto power. *See* line-item budget veto
visibility, power of, 79
voter registration, 46
voters, 24–26, 28, 41, 48, 89, 96. *See also* electorates
voting
    absentee, 25
    crossover, 29
    local elections and, 151–152
    roll-off, 30–31
voting patterns, 15–16, 25–26

W

Walker, Scott, 132
Wallace, George, 27
Warren, Earl, 23, 46, 60, 78, 82
water supply, 161–162
welfare programs, 168–170
Whitaker and Baxter (firm), 53
Whitman, Meg, 19
WIC program, 169
Wilcox, Clyde, 57
Wilson, Pete, 15, 17–18, 22, 162

Z

Ziegler, Richard, 62